James Redpath

Talks about Ireland

James Redpath

Talks about Ireland

ISBN/EAN: 9783741133688

Manufactured in Europe, USA, Canada, Australia, Japa

Cover: Foto ©Thomas Meinert / pixelio.de

Manufactured and distributed by brebook publishing software (www.brebook.com)

James Redpath

Talks about Ireland

TALKS ABOUT IRELAND.

BY

JAMES REDPATH.

"What does mercy to Ireland require? Is it mercy to let the landlords go on, drain, drain, drain forever? Is it mercy to let them go on squeezing the helpless peasant down to the skin of the potato?"—LONDON TIMES, March 12, 1847.

NEW-YORK:
P. J. KENEDY, PUBLISHER,
5 BARCLAY STREET.
1881.

MICHAEL DAVITT,
Founder of the Irish National Land League.

DEDICATION.

—✦—

TO

THE ILLUSTRIOUS IRISH STATESMAN WHO FOUNDED THE IRISH NATIONAL LAND LEAGUE;

TO

THE CLEAR-EYED IRISH PATRIOT WHO FIRST SHOWED HOW IRELAND MAY BE SOCIALLY EMANCIPATED;

TO

THE PURE-HEARTED IRISH HERO WHOM THE HEATHEN POWER THAT ARRAYS VICTORIA IN PURPLE ATTIRES IN A CONVICT'S GARB;

TO

MICHAEL DAVITT,

NOW IN A BRITISH DUNGEON, WITH AFFECTIONATE ADMIRATION, I DEDICATE THIS BOOK.

JAMES REDPATH.

NEW-YORK, MAY 10, 1881.

CONTENTS.

I. FAMINE AND THE LANDLORDS. 9
  [Revised from the *Irish World's* Report.]

II. FAMINE AND THE PRIESTS. 32
  [Report of the *Irish-American*]

III. A WELCOME TO AN IRISH STATESMAN. 34
  [Revised from the New-York *Sunday Democrat's* Report]

IV. A SOUPER-JEW'S IRISH POLICY. 37
  [Reported by an Irish Stenographer.]

V. CONFISCATION AND EXCOMMUNICATION. 39
  [Revised from the Dublin *Nation's* Report.]

VI. "A MOST TREASONABLE SPEECH." 44
  [Revised from the Castlebar *Telegraph's* Report]

VII. HARVESTING FOR THE LAND LEAGUE. 50
  [Report of the Dublin *Freeman's Journal.*]

VIII. "BETWEEN TWO LORDS SLAIN." 52
  [Revised from the Castlebar *Telegraph's* Report.]

IX. ST. BRIDGET AND BRIDGET. 61
  [From the Boston *Pilot.*]

X. "PARNELL AND HIS ASSOCIATES." 65
  [From the Brooklyn *Eagle.*]

XI. WILLIAM BENCE JONES, MARTYR. 76
  [From the Boston *Globe.*]

XII. IRISH CRIMES AND OUTRAGES. 71
  [From the Chicago *Tribune.*]

XIII. "AN EXILE OF ERIN." 75
  [From the Chicago *Inter-Ocean.*]

XIV. LANDLORDS AND LAND LEAGUERS. 90
  [From the Omaha *Herald*, Nebraska.]

XV. THE TRUE REMEDY. 94
  [From the Kerry *Sentinel.*]

PUBLISHER'S CARD.

The following letter from Mr. Redpath must suffice as a Preface:

595 *Lexington Avenue, New-York, May 15, 1881.*

Dear Sir: I send herewith, carefully corrected, my lecture, delivered last winter, on " Famine and the Landlords," and such other of my public utterances, in Ireland and the United States, on Irish topics, as I have had the leisure to revise. My brother, Mr. John V. Redpath, will supply such explanatory notes as may be needed.

As I shall leave for Ireland in a few days, I can make no further contributions to the literature of the Land War until I come back to America.

I went to Ireland in February, 1880, as special correspondent of the New-York Tribune, to depict the Famine that then brooded over the western counties of that cruelly oppressed Island. On my return to this city, I was asked to deliver a lecture for the benefit of the Land League by Mr. John Devoy (ex-convict), Mr. John Dillon (son of a refugee of 1848, and now himself in jail), Mr. John Boyle O'Reilly (ex-convict), and Hon. Patrick A. Collins (now President of the Irish National Land League of America), and by other Irish-Americans, most of whom had been convicted in Ireland of the fact of loving liberty and therefore hating the House of Brunswick, or whose fathers had suffered for these virtues during the last thirty years.

I delivered this Lecture for the Land Leagues of New-York, Boston, and Rochester a year ago, and then returned to Ireland. I publish it now to show the true character of the Irish landlords, of whom Mr. Gladstone, John Bright, and Secretary Forster are the hireling lackeys. It is the only general account of the Famine of 1880 thus far published on either side of the Atlantic.

The other Talks were made at different times and places. They abound in facts that are disgraceful to the English character as well as to the English Government; and I trust they will serve again, thus gathered together, as they have served when published separately, to vindicate the Irish people and their leaders, and to arouse American sympathies for that wronged but unconquerable race.

It is probable that you may find repetitions of facts in some of these different Talks; but that is a defect, if it shall be discovered, that I cannot now remedy.

Yours truly,

JAMES REDPATH.

To Mr. P. J. Kenedy, New-York.

TALKS ABOUT IRELAND.

I.

FAMINE AND THE LANDLORDS.

Mr. Chairman, Ladies, and Gentlemen:
ONE day, about three months ago, I was riding in an Irish jaunting-car in the parish of Islaneady, in the County Mayo. My companion was the Rev. Thomas O'Malley. He had been the parish priest of Islaneady for more than twenty years. It was one of my first rides in the country and everything was new to me. As we drove out, we met large numbers of the country women—comely maidens, sturdy matrons, wrinkled grandmothers—trudging along with bare feet in the cold mud on their way to the market, at Westport. Nine women out of every ten go barefooted in the rural districts of the West of Ireland. Here and there, on both sides of the road, I saw, as you see everywhere in the County Mayo, the ruins of little cabins that had once been the homes of a hardy and hardworking and hospitable peasantry.
I turned to Father O'Malley and asked him:
"Have there been many evictions in your parish?"
"Yes!" said the old man; "when I was a young priest, there were 1,800 families in this parish, but ——" his face grew sad and his voice quivered with emotion as he added, "there are only six hundred families now."
"Well," I said, "what has become of the missing twelve hundred families?"

"They were driven out," he answered, "by famine and the landlords."
"Famine and the landlords!"
Now, if this answer had been made by one of the Irish Land Reformers—by Mr. Parnell [applause] for example, or Michael Davitt [renewed applause], I should have regarded the phrase as an excellent "bit" of rhetorical art—as a skillful coupling of two evils not necessarily mates—and I should have smiled at the forced marriage, and then thought no more about it.
But the words impressed me profoundly when they came from the lips of an old priest, a cadet of an ancient Irish family, a man of the most conservative temperament, whose training and whose office might have been expected to intensify his natural bias in favor of existing institutions and established authority. For the Catholic Church, as you know, is the most potent conservative force in our modern society. It teaches its adherents to render unto Cæsar the things that are Cæsar's, and it rarely arrays itself against the civil authority.
Yet I found that in Ireland wherever there was famine, there the Catholic priests did not hesitate to declare, both in private and in print, that the primary causes of Irish destitution were the exactions of the landlords.
So I shall take for the text of my talk to you to-night the words of the

old priest—"Famine and the Landlords"—the twin curses of Ireland.

Everybody knows that there is a famine in Ireland. But the extent of it, and its severity, have been so persistently understated, and the statistics that I shall give you so greatly exceed the estimates that have been published, that before I begin to tell you what I know about the famine—and especially what I know about it not from personal observation but from evidence—I feel that I owe it as a duty to the sufferers from the famine, for whom I shall plead to-night, to present the credentials, so to speak, that entitle me to represent the distressful districts of Ireland.

During my recent visit to Ireland I gave both my days and nights to the study of the famine. I interviewed the representative managers of the Duchess of Marlboro's fund, the Mansion House fund, the Philadelphia fund, the Herald fund, and the National Irish Land League fund. I interviewed Catholic priests and Protestant clergymen, British officials and American Consuls, Irish journalists and Irish drummers, Irish lords and Irish peasants—everybody I met, everywhere, who knew anything about the famine from personal observation. I never had to tell where I came from, because I asked so many questions that nobody ever doubted for a single moment that I was what Father O'Farrell called me the other day—"A pure, unadulterated Yankee." [Laughter.]

I read all the published reports and records and correspondence of the three great relief committees of Dublin. I read every letter that appeared in the leading Irish and London journals about the famine for more than six weeks. I read every letter that the Land League received for a week—more than five hundred letters from more than five hundred different districts of Ireland. I received over eighty long letters from prominent Catholic priests, each one of them describing the present condition of his own parish. I received also, from nine of the Catholic bishops in the distressed districts, letters in which their lordships described more briefly than their priests, but more comprehensively, the existing destitution in their dioceses.

I succeeded in obtaining abstracts from the latest reports of the local committees of the Mansion House. There are six hundred and ninety local committees. Each committee represents a different district of destitution. Now listen to the composition of these local committees. There are on them one thousand three hundred and thirty-one Catholic curates and priests; five hundred and sixty-eight Protestant clergymen; seven hundred and twenty-two justices of the peace; five hundred and thirty-one medical officers; eight hundred and twenty-four poor-law guardians, and more than six thousand other lay members; in all, over ten thousand of the most respectable persons, both as to personal character and social standing, and all of them living in the distressful districts.

Now, whenever I do not quote from the letters of my own correspondents, or whenever I do not state the results of my own observation, I shall report the words and statistics of the Mansion House committees, because every one will see that the controlling members of these committees—all of their laymen loyal subjects of the queen, and friends or lackeys of the landlords—have the strongest political reasons for underestimating the numbers of persons in distress in their respective districts, and not a single motive, except the motive of humanity, for stating the exact number of the sufferers in their neighborhood.

In order to impeach or to discredit the statistics derived from the reports of the Mansion House committees, it will be essential, as you see, to show first that it is possible, and then that it is credible, that more than 10,000 gentlemen of Ireland, of both creeds and of every calling, should have conspired to deceive the world about the Irish distress. I shall not call witnesses from the committees of the Land League, because *they* might be suspected of exaggerating the distress in order to demonstrate the evils of a government by landlords. I shall show the imperative need of the Irish Land League by the evidence of its enemies and the friends of the landlords.

From six hundred and ninety districts six hundred and ninety reports made to the Mansion House demonstrate the appalling fact that there are:

In the Province of Leinster ... 28,000
In the Province of Ulster 180,000
In the Province of Munster ... 233,000
In the Province of Connaught . 422,000

In all Ireland 863,000

persons at this very hour whose strongest hope of seeing the next harvest moon rise as they stand at their own cabin doors, rests, and almost solely rests, on the bounty of the stranger and of the exiles of Erin. I have not a shadow of a shade of doubt that there are to-day in Ireland one million of people hungry and in rags—and by and by I may show you why—but I can point out province by province, county by county, and parish by parish, where eight hundred and sixty-three thousand of them are praying, and begging, and clamoring for a chance to live in the land of their birth. Eight hundred and sixty-three thousand! Do you grasp this number? If you were to sit twelve hours a day to see this gaunt army of hunger pass in review before you, in single file, and one person was to pass every minute, do you know how long it would be before you saw the last man pass? Three years and four months! [Sensation.]

Remember and note well that these statistics are not *estimates*. They are the *returns*, carefully verified, of the actual numbers on the relief rolls, *or* of the numbers reported by the local committees as in real distress.

You all know that statements and tabulated statistics have little influence on public opinion. So, to show to you how great the famine is, and to help you to gauge it, I shall ask you to go with me rapidly from province to province, and from county to county, to locate and distribute the destitution. I shall not try to entertain you. I should despise any audience that expected to be entertained in listening to the story of a famine. I shall be satisfied if I succeed in stimulating you to continue to act the part of the Good Samaritan to this poor people, that lie wounded and bleeding—having fallen among thieves; while the part of the priest and the Levite in the parable is played by the British Government and the Irish landlords—from the miserly Queen on the throne down to the crafty Earl of Dunraven—[hisses]—who not only have passed by on the other side, but who have justified and eulogized, and who uphold the thieves. [Hisses.]

Mr. Redpath here stepped forward and asked:

"Whom are you hissing? Are you hissing me?"

VOICES.—"No!" "No!" "The Queen!" "Not you!" "The Queen!" "The Queen!"

MR. REDPATH.—Oh! Thank you! You do well to *hiss* her. She deserves to be hissed in America. Do you know that Queen Victoria even after she knew from the Duchess of Marlboro, that there was universal and terrible distress in the West of Ireland, contributed only one day's wages to relieve it? Why, a poor working girl of Boston, a seamstress, after she listened to my lecture here last Sunday, gave fifty dollars for the relief of the distress I had so inadequately described. She would not tell her name. She said: "God knows my name—that's enough." That fifty dollars represented her savings for six months. Yet *she* gave it freely and without hope of the reward even of thanks or reputation in this world! In the Roll of the Hereafter, when the list of the "Royal Personages" of this earth is called, surely the name of that poor seamstress will stand high above the name of the queen of England. [Applause.]

But I ought to say that I was not satisfied with the vast volume of documentary and vicarious evidence that I had accumulated. I personally visited several of the districts blighted by the famine, and saw with my own eyes the destitution of the peasantry, and with my own ears heard the sighs of their unhappy wives and children. They were the saddest days I ever passed on earth, for never before had I seen human misery so hopeless and undeserved and so profound. I went to Ireland because a crowd of calamities had overtaken me that made my own life a burden too heavy to be borne. But in the ghastly cabins of the Irish peasantry, without fuel, without blankets, and without food—among half-naked and blue-lipped children, shivering from cold, and crying from hunger—among women who were weeping because their little ones were starving—among men of a race to whom a fight is better than a feast, but whose faces now bore the famine's fearful stamp of terror—in the West of Ireland, I soon forgot every trouble of my own life in the dread presence of the great tidal wave of sorrow that had overwhelmed an unhappy and unfortunate and innocent people.

I must call witnesses less sensitive than I am to Irish sorrow to describe it to you—no, not to describe it, but to give you a faint and far-away outline of it. Or, rather, I shall call witnesses who feel, as keenly as I feel, the misery they depict, but who write of it, as they wept over it, alone and unseen.

But before I summon them, let us make a rapid review of the immediate or physical causes of the famine. You will see when I come to distribute the destitution by counties that the further we go west the denser becomes the misery.

The famine line follows neither the division lines of creeds nor the boundary lines of provinces. It runs from north to south—from a little east of the city of Cork in the south, to Londonderry in the north—and it divides Ireland into two nearly equal parts. The nearer the Western coast the hungrier the people.

The western half of Ireland—from Donegal to Cork—is mountainous and beautiful. But its climate is inclement. It is scourged by the Atlantic storms. It is wet in summer and bleak in winter. The larger part of the soil is either barren and spewy bogs or stony and sterile hills.

The best lands, in nearly every county, have been leased to Scotch and English graziers. For, after the terrible famine of '47, when the Irish people staggered and fainted with hunger and fever into their graves—by tens of thousands, and by hundreds of thousands; when the poor tenants, too far gone to have the strength to shout for food, faintly whispered for the dear Lord's sake for a little bread,—the landlords of the West answered these piteous moans by sending processes of ejectment to turn them out into the road-side or the poor-house to die, and by hiring crow-bar brigades to pull down the roof that still sheltered the gasping people. [Hisses.] As fast as the homeless peasants died or were driven into exile, their little farms were rented out to British graziers. [Hisses.] The people who could not escape were forced to take the wettest bogs and driest hill-slopes. These swamps and slopes were absolutely worthless. They could not raise enough to feed a snipe. By the patient toil of the people they were redeemed. Seaweed was brought on the backs of the farmers for miles to reclaim these lands.

The landlord did not spend one shilling to help the tenant. He did not build the cabin. He did not fence the holding. He did not drain the bog. In the West of Ireland the landlord does nothing but take rent. I beg the landlord's pardon; I want to be perfectly just. The landlord *does* two things beside taking the rent. He makes the tenant pay the larger part of the taxes, and as fast as the farmer improves the land the landlord raises the rent. And whenever, from any cause, the tenant fails to pay the rent, the landlord turns him out and coniscates his improvements. [Hisses.]

The writers who combat communism say that communism means taking the property of other people without paying for it. From this point of view Ireland is a shocking example of the evils of communism, for the Irish landlords of the West are communists and the lineal descendants of a line of communists. [Cheers.]

The landlords charge so high a rent for these lands that even in the best of seasons the tenants can save nothing. To hide their own exactions from the execration of the human race, the landlords and their parasites have added insult to injury by charging the woes of Ireland to the improvidence of the people. Stretched on the rack of the landlord's avarice, one bad season brings serious distress to the tenant; a second bad season takes away the helping hand of credit at the merchant's; and the third bad season beckons famine and fever to the cabin door.

Now the summer of 1879 was the third successive bad season. When it opened, it found the people deeply in debt. Credit was stopped. But for the confidence of the shop-keepers in the honesty of the peasant, the distress would have come a year ago. It was stayed by the kind heart of the humble merchant. *Therefore*, the landlords have charged the distress to the system of credit!

There was a heavy fall of rain all last summer. The turf was ruined. Two-thirds of the potato crop was lost, on an average, of the crop of all Ireland; but, in many large districts of the West, not a single sound potato was dug. One-half of the turnip crop perished. The cereal crop suffered, although not to so great an extent. There was a rot in sheep in some places, and in other places an epidemic among the pigs. The fisheries failed. The iron mines in the South were closed. Everything in Ireland seemed to have conspired to invite a famine.

But the British and American farmers were also the innocent causes of intensifying Irish distress.

In Donegal, Mayo, Galway, and the Western Islands, the small holders for generations have never been able to raise enough from their little farms to pay their big rents. They go over every spring, by tens of thousands, to England and Scotland, and hire out to the farmers for wages. They stay there till the crops are harvested. But the great American competition is lowering the prices of farm produce in Great Britain and the prices of farm stock; and, therefore, the English and Scotch farmers, for two or three years past, have not been able to pay the old wages to these Irish laborers. Last summer, instead of sending back wages to pay the rent, hosts of Irish farmhands had to send for money to get back again.

These complex combinations of misfortune resulted in universal distress. Everywhere, in the strictly agricultural regions of the West, the farmers, and especially the small holders, suffered first, and then the distress spread out its ghoul-like wings until they overshadowed the shop-keepers, the artisans, the fishermen, the miners, and more than all, the laborers who had no land but who had worked for the more comfortable class of farmers.

These malignant influences blighted every county in the West of Ireland, and these mournful facts are true of almost every parish in all that region.

Looking at the physical causes of the distress, every honest and intelligent spectator will say that they are cowards and libelers who assert that the victims of the famine are in any way responsible for it. [Cheers.]

Looking at the exactions of the landlords, none but a blasphemer will pretend that the distress is an act of Providence. [Applause.]

I shall not attempt to point out the locality and density of distress in the different districts of the counties of Ireland. I could talk for two hours on each province, and never repeat a single figure or fact. I must content myself by summoning to my aid the stern and passionless eloquence of statistics, and, by showing you the numbers of the distressed in each county, enable you to judge, each of you for yourself, how wide-spread is the misery and how deep.

THE PROVINCE OF LEINSTER.

Let us run rapidly over Ireland. We will begin with the least distressful province—the beautiful province of Leinster. Leinster is the garden of Ireland. There is no finer country in the temperate zone. There is no natural reason why poverty should ever throw its blighting shadows athwart the green and fertile fields of Leinster.

There are resident landlords in the rural districts of Leinster; and wherever in Ireland the owners of the soil live on their own estates, the peasantry, as a rule, are more justly dealt with than when they are left to the tiger-mercy of the agent of the absentee. But it is not the fertile soil only, nor the presence of resident proprietors only, nor the proximity of markets only—nor is it these three causes jointly—that account for the absence of such a long procession of distress as the other provinces present.

In some of the fairest counties of Leinster, eviction has done its perfect work. Instead of toiling peasants you find fat bullocks; instead of bright-eyed girls you find bleating sheep. After the famine of 1847, the men were turned out and the beasts were turned in. The British Government cheered this infamy, for Irishmen are rebels—sometimes; but heifers are loyal—always. There is less distress in the rural districts of Leinster because there are fewer people there.

In the 12 counties of Leinster, there are 38,000 persons in distress—in Dublin, 250; in Wexford, 870; in King's County, 1,047; in Meath and in Westmeath, 1,550 each; in Kildare, 1,567; in Kilkenny, 1,979; in Carlow, 2,000; in Louth, 3,050; in Queen's County 4,743; in Wicklow, 5,450; in Longford, 9,557.

In Carlow, in Westmeath, in Louth, and in one district of the Queen's County, the distress is expected to increase. In Kildare and in King's County, it is not expected to increase.

You see by this list how moderate the returns are—how strictly they are confined to famine or exceptional distress, as distinguished from chronic or ordinary poverty; because there are thousands of very poor persons in the city of Dublin, and yet there are only two hundred and fifty reported as in distress in the entire county. They belong to the rural district of Glencullen.

Longford leads the list of distressed counties in Leinster. There are no resident proprietors in Longford. Up to the 1st of March not one of them had given a single shilling for the relief of the destitute on their estates. [Hisses.] The same report comes from Kilkenny. [Hisses.]

The distress in Leinster is among the fishermen and small farmers and laborers. In Wicklow the fishers are kept poor because the Government refuses to build harbors for their protection. In Westmeath "the laboring class and the small farmers are in great distress." That is the report of the local committee, and I can confirm it by my personal observation.

The province of Leinster contains one-fourth of the population of Ireland, but it does not contain more than one-thirtieth part of the prevailing distress. So I shall take you to one parish only—to Stradbally in the Queen's County. It is not included in the reports of the Mansion House Committee.

Dr. John Magee, P. P., of Stradbally, wrote to me quite recently:

"In this parish, one of the most favorably circumstanced in Leinster, such has been their misery that for the last three months I have been doling out charities to one hundred and twenty families. Some of them I found in a state of utter starvation,—an entire day, sometimes, without a morsel of food in the cabin.

"But most miserable of all, and what makes the case so affecting, very many of our small farmers (whose pride would hide their poverty) are now reduced to the same plight,—the rack-rent (or excessive rent) having robbed them of every available salable chattel they possessed.

"I had missed for some time one of our farmers, holding about thirty-five acres. On inquiry, I found that he was confined to his house for want of clothing, and that he had eaten his last potatoes and the only fowl left on the place. To add to his misery, the rack-warner had waited on him the day before to come in with his rent.

"In the past week, I gave stealthily to one of our farmers—holding over sixty acres of land, and who used to have a stock of eighteen or twenty milch-cows—a bag of Indian meal, to save his family from starvation. The man, with tears in his eyes, told me that 'his children had not eaten a morsel for the last twenty-four hours,' and I believed him.

"Of the two hundred and forty families in my parish, one-fifth of them are in the same miserable condition,— without food, without stock, without seed for the land, without credit, and without any possible hope from the justice or the sympathy of the English Government."

Father Magee is not only a good Irish priest but a profound student of Irish history. Will you let me read to you what he wrote to me about the causes of Irish famines?

"If I were asked," he wrote, "why is it that Ireland is so poor, with abundance of foreign grain and food in our ports, whence this famine that alarms even the stranger, my answer would be"—

Now listen:

"Speak as we may of short and scanty harvests, the real cause is landlords' exactions, which drain the land of money, and which leave nothing to buy corn.

"Landlord absolutism and unrestrained rack-rents have always been, and are at present, the bane and the curse of Ireland. If the harvest be good, landlordism luxuriates and abstracts all; if scanty or bad, landlordism seizes on the rood or cattle for the rack-rent."

This is the learned priest's accusation. Now let us listen to his speculations:

"I have in my own parish," he says, "five or six landlords—not the worst type of their class—two of them of Cromwellian descent, a third an Elizabethan, all enjoying the confiscated estates of the O'Moores, O'Lalors, and O'Kellys, whose sons are now the miserable tenants of these estates— tenants who are paying, or trying to pay, forty, eighty, and, in some cases, one hundred and twenty per cent. over the Government valuation of the land. Tenants who are treated as slaves and starved as beggars. If these tenants dare gainsay the will of the lord"—

Father Magee doesn't mean the will of Heaven, but the caprice of the landlord. [Laughter.]

"If they gainsay the will of the landlord, or even complain, they are victimized on the spot.

"This land system pays over, from the sweat and toil of our inhabitants, ninety million dollars yearly to six or seven thousand landlords, who do nothing but hunt a fox or hunt the tenantry." [Cries of "Shame!" and hisses.]

These good landlords, you know, have a "wicked partner"; and I want you to hear what Father Magee knows about the "wicked partner."

"The [British] Government, that upholds this cruel system, abstracts thirty-five millions more from the land in imperial taxation, while there is left for the food, clothing, and subsistence of five millions of people not more than fifty million dollars, or about ten dollars per head yearly." [Sensation.] Isn't that just damnable? [Applause.]

"This is the system," says Father Magee, "that produces our periodical famines; which shames and degrades us before Europe; which presents us, periodically, before the world as mendicants and beggars before the nations. * * * And will any one blame us, cost what it may, if we are resolved to get rid of a system that has so long enslaved our people?"

Blame you! Blame you! Faith, no matter what you do to get rid of such a system, devil a bit will I blame you, Father Magee! [Laughter and applause.]

It was in this province that I gained my first personal knowledge of the fierce celerity with which the Irish landlords, in years of distress, rally to the assistance—*not* of their tenants but the famine. I went down from Dublin to attend an indignation meeting over an eviction in the parish of Ballybrophy, near Knockaroo, in the Queen's County.

As we drove from the railway station I noticed that three men jumped into a jaunting-car and followed us. I asked my companion if he knew who they were? "Oh, yes," he said, "it is a magistrate and two short-hand writers paid by the Government; they follow us wherever we go to get evidence of seditious language to try and convict us; they have constabulary with loaded muskets at all our meetings; they think they can overawe me but they only exasperate me." It was Michael Davitt. [Cheers.]

Sure enough, when we got to the meeting, there was a platoon of armed constabulary at it. No one pretended that there was any risk of a riot at Ballybrophy, for everybody there belonged to the same party. Next week a party of Orangemen threatened—in advance—to break up a meeting of the Land League in a county in Ulster. Not a constable was sent there, and the Orange rioters were allowed to disperse the audience and shed the blood of peaceful citizens. [Hisses.]

Why was this meeting called at Ballybrophy? Malachi Kelly, a decent old man, with a wife and five children, had been turned out of his house into the road by his landlord—a person of the name of Erasmus Dickson Barrows. Mr. Kelly had paid his rent, without failing once, for thirty consecutive years. All his life long he had borne the reputation of an honest and temperate and industrious man.

His rent at first was five hundred and thirty-five dollars a year. He made improvements at his own cost. The rent was instantly raised to six hundred and forty dollars. The landlord solemnly promised not to raise the rent again, and to make some improvements that were needed. Relying on this pledge, Mr. Kelly spent fifteen hundred dollars in erecting permanent buildings in 1873. The landlord instantly raised the rent again—this time to seven hundred and seventy-five dollars. In other words he fined Mr. Kelly one hundred and ten dollars a year for the folly of believing a landlord's pledge and for the offense of increasing the value of his landlord's estate. Last season Mr. Kelly's crop was a total failure, and the old man could not pay the rent for the first time in his life. So he was turned out in his old age, homeless and penniless; and the buildings that he had erected at his own cost became the property of his landlord. ["Shame!"]

Michael Davitt made a speech on this eviction, and I did not notice that the loaded muskets of the constabulary overawed him. [Applause.] All the time he was talking I kept wondering to myself: How is it that Mr. Davitt knows what I wanted to say? He uttered my opinions, for he denounced the landlord. [Applause.]

THE PROVINCE OF ULSTER.

English writers and their American echoers have so persistently asserted that Ulster is always prosperous—and they have so unanimously attributed this prosperity to the superior fertilizing qualities of the Presbyterian faith [laughter]—that some of you will be surprised, perhaps, when I assert, as my belief, that there are probably two hundred thousand persons in distress at the present moment in this "prosperous" province.

Thrusting aside for a moment the Presbyterian political pretenses, it is of vital importance, on entering this province, to emphasize the fact that the system of land-tenure in Ulster, or rather in the Protestant counties of Ulster, was and still is as different from the system of land-tenure in the Catholic provinces as the American freedom of to-day is different from the Southern slavery of the past. I weigh my words. And it should be stated, with an equal emphasis, that the tenant-at-will system that blights the Catholic counties of Ireland to-day is one of the sad legacies of that long reign of terror known in Irish history as the era of "Protestant Ascendency."

Ever since the days when the old Irish were driven by English conquest—to use a famous phrase—into "Hell or Connaught," the tillers of the soil in the Ulster Plantation have been protected—by an unwritten law called the "Ulster Custom"—in the rights that they earned by their labor on their farms.

The English and Scotch emigrants brought over with them their English and Scotch theories and usages. It was not usual for the landlords to give formal leases, but the Ulster Custom gave the tenant not only a legal right to the value of his improvements, not only substantial perpetuity of tenure, but also the good-will of his farm—that is to say, a prior right to his tenancy from which he could not be arbitrarily evicted without compensation. This tenant-right was justly regarded as a valuable property. It was marketable. The good-will of a farm was often more valuable than the tenant's improvements on it.

In the Catholic provinces of Connaught and Munster there was no such custom as the Ulster custom. There was no such stability of tenure. There was no such right to the good-will of the farm. There was no such recognition of the tenant's rights of property in improvements that had been made by his own labor and capital. The tenants in the Catholic provinces have always been tenants-at-will—and a tenant-at-will is merely a serf of the soil. But it is not everywhere in Ulster that tenants' rights are respected. It is only in the strictly Protestant parts of Ulster, and even there the small farmers are beginning to see and to feel that they have no *adequate* protection against the pitiless exactions of the landlords as exhibited in an excessive increase of rent.

Pharaoh is hardening his heart up in Ulster; and Aaron and Moses—or, in modern language, Parnell and Davitt—will soon "sound the timbrel o'er Egypt's dark seas." [Applause.]

And now allow me to expose the hypocritical pretext that it is owing to Protestantism that Ulster is prosperous.

The face of oppression is so hideous even to its own eyes that it always wears the mask of some power that the human race respects. Legree posed as Moses. The auction-block of the slave-trader was built behind the altar of the Christian church. In Ireland the pitiless persecutions of the Catholics have been palliated by the pretext that they were needed to maintain Protestant ascendency, which was identified with Christian civilization.

With the doctrine of the right of private judgment in its mouth, political

Protestantism in Ireland has persecuted the Catholics for conscience' sake for nearly three centuries.

The American Protestant youth are taught that the Roman Catholic Church has been the only religious persecutor in modern times. When I was a little boy I was taught that the Church of Rome and the Church of England were the only religious persecutors—for my father was a Scotch Presbyterian, and he never forgot to inculcate the lesson taught by the history of the Lowland Covenanters. Yankee boys, and Scotch boys, and English boys are never told the sad and blood-red story of the persecutions of the Catholics of Ireland.

The history of the persecutions of the Irish Catholics by the Protestant political power in Ireland, is one of the saddest chapters in the annals of modern Europe. It is a history of penal laws framed in Hell and executed by fiends in the name of Jesus Christ. [Applause.] It swept the entire gamut of crime. Its seven notes were proscriptions, perjuries, confiscations, priest-huntings, hangings, massacres, and calumnies.

Landlordism and Protestantism play the part in Irish history that the two chained giants whom John Bunyan called Popery and Paganism play in that famous Puritan story—"Pilgrim's Progress." They curse and howl at the victims whom they can no longer torture. For, when the progress of civilization rendered it imperative for England to extract the fangs of Protestant hate in Ireland, it began that career of calumniation that has not yet closed.

One reason why the Protestant province of Ulster is more prosperous in parts than the Catholic provinces of Ireland is, because Protestant estates were never confiscated there—for Protestants were the receivers of the stolen estates of Catholics; because *their* clergymen (unlike the Catholic priests) were never hunted and hanged or banished; because it was never a capital offense to teach *their* children to read—as it *was* a death penalty to teach the Catholic youth; because the Protestants of the North were protected by the English Government, while the Catholics of the South were persecuted by it. [Applause.]

It is true that these crimes belong to the past, but it is also true that the *results* of these crimes remain.

It was Macaulay who gave the widest circulation to the theory that it was Protestantism that had fertilized Ulster, and Catholicism that had blighted Connaught. Well, although "what I know about farming" does not exhaust the science of agriculture, it does seem to me that one ton of guano is better for a crop—especially a crop of potatoes in Connaught—than all the thirty-nine articles of the Church of England, with the five points of Calvinism thrown in.— [Laughter.]

And, ladies and gentlemen, one ray of common sense by any common man is vastly more valuable to the intellect than the most dazzling calcium-light brilliancy even of a Macaulay.

If it was the Catholic religion that blighted the Catholic provinces of Ireland, why was it that the French Catholic peasants *were* as wretched before *they* owned their lands as the Irish Catholic peasants *are* to-day?

It is not a question of spiritual theses, but of temporal leases; it is not what faith we hold about our home in the next world, but what hold we have on our home in this world. [Applause.]

Macaulay knew these facts. Macaulay professed to believe in the mysteries of the Christian religion. Macaulay was familiar with the history of Protestant rule in Ireland. Do you know that I have sometimes wondered, when Macaulay sat down to write this indictment of Irish Catholicism, that a terrible vision of the Day of Judgment, on a background of hell-flames, did not rise up before him and paralyze his hand? [Loud and prolonged applause.]

I am not a Catholic, and I do not recall these crimes to condemn Protestantism, nor to seek Catholic applause. I am a Protestant of Protestantism. I conciliate nobody, and I ask favors of no man; but I hate with a hatred inextinguishable every form of oppression, and I shall strike at it in the future as I have done in the past, without waiting to inquire its name, or to look at its flag. Protestantism in Irish history has only been another name for the spirit of caste. [Applause.]

In the province of Ulster, on the first day of March last, the local committees of the Mansion House, 131 in number, reported that there were in distress, in eight counties, 160,880 persons—in Antrim, 220; in Down, 800; in Armagh, 10,455; in Monaghan, 7,447; in Cavan, 34,709; in Fermanagh, 12,768; in Tyrone, 7,447; in Donegal, 87,034. Fourteen of the Ulster committees report that the distress is likely or certain to increase. The most moderate estimate, therefore, of the army of hunger in the province of Ulster—including the county of Londonderry—would put the figures at 180,000. It is more probably 200,000.

Yet this vast aggregation of human misery exists in a province in which the Belfast manufactories employ large numbers of boys and girls, and so to a considerable extent relieve the agricultural classes, both by sending back wages to the cabins in the country, and by affording a home market for their produce. And, in justice to the Catholic provinces, let it be remembered that the reason why there are no manufactories in Connaught and Munster, is because the English Parliament for several generations, by positive legislation, prevented their establishment, and because, since these infamous laws were repealed, their disastrous results have been conserved by combinations among the English manufacturers.

In Antrim, in Down, in Armagh, in Monaghan, in Cavan, in Tyrone, and in Donegal, the committees report that the distress is increasing, or certain to increase.

The Catholic Bishop of Clogher wrote to me about the distress in his great diocese. Nearly all of his diocese is in Ulster. It comprises the County of Monaghan, most of the County Fermanagh, a large tract of Tyrone, with portions of Donegal and Louth. It has a population of 235,000 souls. The diocese is divided into forty parishes. He writes that in ten of these parishes there is considerable distress, going much beyond the state of things in ordinary years, but nothing to excite grave alarm. But in the remaining thirty parishes there exists *grievous distress*, varying in amount and extending over 100 to 200 families in some parishes, 300 to 500 in others. Ten per cent. of these families have no food at all—*not a mouthful*—except what they receive from charity, and all the rest are suffering more or less severely from want of food and clothing and seeds. The laborers everywhere, who have no farms, were suffering more than in ordinary times, because the farmers can no longer afford to pay them. His Lordship added that it is hard to see why our destitution in food and clothing must not continue, and even go on increasing, until the arrival of the next harvest.

Now, let us rapidly glance at the different counties of Ulster as they are described by the local committees of the Mansion House:

In the County Antrim, the Mansion House committees report that "the people are impoverished to an extent unknown since '47, and the clergy and gentry are besieged by the people for aid."

There is only one report from the County Down—from Kilcoo, where there are eight hundred persons in distress, whose numbers it is stated, "must increase," and where "the distress is decidedly grave."

In the County Armagh, in five districts, the first local estimate of the number of persons in distress was ten thousand. Later reports show that the numbers are increasing. At Creggan, in this county, the poverty is so general that the county court judges expressed their astonishment at the vast number of civil decrees, and in many cases stayed execution.

In these three counties there are two Catholic dioceses, and I received letters from the bishops of both of them.

Bishop Dorrian, of Down and Connor, wrote that in his diocese:

"We have much distress in many parts, but hunger and want in some three or four parishes, in the mountainous and glen districts. . . . I fear many small holders cannot labor or seed their lands but shall have to give up their farms and become homeless."

The Bishop adds:

"If remunerative employment had been started at first, all might have gone on well; for the wages of one would have, in a sense, supported the entire family, and upheld self-respect without idleness and degradation supervening. It is now too late, I fear. It is a dark page on which we read of distress, and yet nothing but the degrading sympathy of process-servers, or sending round the hat for alms, as if we were unwilling or unable to earn our bread—resources of industrious work by land and sea on every side around us."

The diocese of Dromore includes part of the County Down, the County Armagh, and a small portion of Antrim.

Bishop Leahy wrote to me:

"In four or five parishes of this diocese there prevails a fearful amount of distress, and unless relieved it will probably become more terrible before the ripening of the potatoes. . . . The poor who hitherto were able, though with difficulty, to support their families from the produce of their scanty holdings, are ashamed to solicit alms and go, under cover of night, to the parish priest to make known their wants."

From the County Monaghan there are reports from twelve districts, in which there are seven thousand four hundred and forty-seven persons in distress. Four districts report that the distress will increase. At Emyvale the people are "without food and fuel"—one thousand of them. At Killeevin, there is "no corn, no seed potatoes, no credit; they are living on half the necessary amount of food." From Trydavnet they write: "Every shilling from every source exhausted; thirty families to-day, with not even meal to help them." At Castleblayney the people are "in dire distress; suffering every hardship that poverty and destitution can inflict." At Drum, "fever of a violent type has broken out from sheer want."

In County Cavan there are reports from thirty-six districts. The first local estimates reported over twenty-six thousand (26,185), the latest returns thirty-five thousand, with six predictions of the probability or certainty of an increase. I have not the time to quote even a single sentence from each of these thirty-six reports. I can only select a sentence or two from half a dozen of them. In Arva "very many have not wherewith to purchase a day's provisions. They are so deeply sunk in debt, their credit gone, they are now reluctantly obliged to seek the bread of charity. Farmers who were accustomed to employing laborers are now themselves pressing for relief." In Ballinagh there are over one thousand four hundred persons in distress, the "distress in many cases amounting to absolute destitution." In Ballymachugh and Drumlummon eight hundred and eleven persons are "in need of the first necessaries of life." From Bailieborough (where there are eight hundred and fifty destitute persons) comes the sad report: "Last week a man who held six acres died of want; if no relief, many struggling farmers will be driven to the work-house." From Glengevlin comes the cry: "Very

PATRICK EGAN,
Treasurer of the Irish National Land League.

many are actually starving; others on the brink of starvation. For God's sake, send something at once." In Killeshandra the "poor farmers are now eating their seed potatoes and last store of meal; will have nothing to maintain themselves till next crop." From Templeport comes the report: "Distress has been borne in silence till they reached the very point of starvation."

These are not isolated instances; it is everywhere the same sad story of want heroically borne by a peasantry who would never beg if they could get work to do.

From the County Fermanagh, I have reports from eighteen districts. The reports show that there were nearly thirteen thousand in Enniskillen. The distress is characterized as "deep" and "universal"; in Ballaghameehan, as "deepest"; in Tallaghy, as "great"; in Blackbog, as "extreme"; in Clenish, as "terrible." In Derrygonnelly, the people are "in great want; no food; no fuel; starvation facing them." At Maguiresbridge, nearly four hundred are in a starving condition. From Tempo, the report is one six words long: "No food, no fuel, no work." At Mulleek, six hundred and thirty-four persons are in distress—mostly small farmers, who get a meager living by turf-making. The committee write from Mulleek:

"It is sad to see hundreds crowded at the committee-door, waiting from twelve o'clock, noon, till eight at night, under a drenching rain. Several poor men and women came to the priest's house and fainted with hunger and exhaustion. The appearance of the poor is appalling."

From the County Tyrone there are returns from eleven districts. They report eleven thousand four hundred and ninety persons in distress, and that the distress is increasing in three districts. In Dromore, "The distress is very general: no potatoes, no seed, or such as, if planted, will produce famine next year." In Fintona, "Unless prompt and generous assistance arrives, numbers will die of hunger." In Egorten, "Great distress: no fuel, no potatoes." In Kildren, "Many small farmers in sore distress, without even the necessaries of life." In Pomeroy, "No money, no credit, scarcity of food and fuel." And so on!

Donegal is the north-western county of Ireland. I have a large number of letters and forty-eight official reports from Donegal.

In every part of this county the destitution is appalling,—not a parish escapes,—and the distress is everywhere increasing. The whole county is a-hungered and in tatters. Entire parishes of families have absolutely no means of subsistence. The population of the county is two hundred and thirty-seven thousand. The number of persons on the Relief lists is eighty-seven thousand—more than one-third of the population of Donegal.

Major Gaskill is one of the inspectors of the Duchess of Marlboro's Committee. I found that he invariably underestimated the distress; yet he admitted that he was astounded by the scenes of misery that he witnessed in Donegal, even after he had visited Galway and Mayo.

The aggregate of eighty-seven thousand persons in distress includes those unfortunate people only who depend almost solely on charity for their support. It does not count those to whom every purse in America would open if Donegal were an American State, instead of an Irish county.

In the parish of Donegal, for example, "two hundred families are really in need who are left unattended to from want of funds." In Culdaff "four hundred and twenty-five families are in great destitution." In Fannet "very many people are in actual starvation." From Kilcor, the committee writes: "If we fail one week in relieving, the consequences would be fearful." In Lower Templecrone and Arranmore Island, "the poverty of the people is such that if immediate steps be not taken to relieve the distress, deaths from hunger must be the immediate result." From Killaghter comes the report: "The whole of the population of St. John's Point are on the very verge of starvation, depending upon a chance fish for support." At Glencolumbkill, the Mansion House Committee report: "*Some are eating the black sea-weed.*"

Father Logree, of Kilcor, wrote to me:

"I can safely declare that along the sea-coast there are over one hundred families who have no bedclothes."

He means in his own parish only.

Father James Stephens, of Killybegs, describes one family in his parish:

"Thomas Gallagher, of Correan: eleven of a family; five of them with bass-mats tied around them for clothing. No fire; no bed, but straw."

Father J. Maguire, of Cloumany, wrote to me:

"I was called to attend a man who the doctor declared was dying from a disease brought on from want of nourishment. The man was rolled up in what once had been a shawl. This and an old sheet were the only covering he had on him. The house was destitute of every kind of furniture. The children were literally naked and gathered around a few smoldering sods."

The seas that lash the stormy coast of Donegal are full of fish, and yet the dwellers by the sea-shore are famishing for food. Why? The English organs of the Irish landlords say because the people are improvident and lazy. It is a lie. [Loud applause.] Deep-sea fishing requires strong boats. These people have been plundered by their absentee landlords so mercilessly and long that very few of the fishermen can afford to build strong boats. But deep-sea fishing along this coast cannot be carried on at all until piers and sheltered landing-places are built by the Government to protect the fishermen. The Government refuses to build them unless the people of the district contribute one-fourth of the amount. The starving tenants cannot contribute that proportion; and the landed gentry who *could* afford it refuse to contribute a single shilling. [Hisses.]

Do you ask me as Americans have often asked me—Are the landlords doing nothing amidst all this distress? Certainly, they are doing something in the province of Ulster. Listen to a report of how one landlord, "a noble lord," helped the distress on his own estates in the County Cavan.

It is the Rev. Father Joseph Flood who speaks:

"In the midst of cries of distress around me, while Protestants and Catholics, here as elsewhere, are struggling to keep together the bodies and souls of this year's visitation, I was hurried off to witness the heartless eviction of five whole families—thirty souls in all—of ages varying from eighty years to two years. [Cries of "Shame!"]

"At twelve o'clock to-day—in the midst of a drenching rain—when every man's lips are busy discussing how relief can be carried to this home and that, an imposing spectacle presented itself through a quiet part of the parish of King's Court.

"A carriage containing Mr. Hussey, jr., son of the agent of Lord Gormanston; behind and before it, about a dozen outside cars—with a resident magistrate, an inspector of police, about forty of her majesty's force, the sheriff, and some dozens of as rapacious-looking drivers and grippers as I ever laid my eyes upon.

"There is a dead silence at the halt before the first doomed door. That silence was broken by myself, craving to let the poor people in again after the vindication of the law.

"The sheriff formally asks—'Have you the rent?'

"The trembling answer is:

"'My God! how could I have the whole rent—and such a rent—on such a soil—in such a year as this?'

"'Get out!' is the word, and right heartily the grippers set to work. ["Shame!" and hisses.] On the dungheap is flung the scanty furniture, bed and bedding. The door is nailed. The imposing army marches on to the next holding, till every house has been visited and every soul turned out.

"At this moment there is a downpour of rain on that poor bed and bedding, and on that miserable furniture; and an old man, whose generations have passed their simple lives in that house, is sitting on a stone outside with his head buried in his hands, thinking of the eighty-three years gone by. [Sobs.] And are these tenants to blame? No! It is on the records of this parish that they were the most simple-minded, hard-working, honest and virtuous people in it." [Sensation.]

This is the sort of contribution that the landlords have made to the distress in the province of Ulster. [Hisses.]

THE WEST OF IRELAND.

Let us now, in spirit, take the shoes from off our feet as we draw nigh the holy ground of Connaught and Munster. There is nothing on this earth more sacred than human sorrow. Christianity itself has been called the Worship of Sorrow. If this definition be a true one, then the Holy Land of our day is the West of Ireland. Every sod there has been wet with human tears. The murmurs of every rippling brook there, from time out of mind, have been accompanied by an invisible chorus of sighs from breaking human hearts. Every breeze that has swept across her barren moors has carried with it to the summits of her bleak mountain slopes (and I trust far beyond them) the groans and the prayers of a brave, but a despairing, people. The sun has never set on her sorrows, excepting to give place to the pitying stars that have looked down on human woes that excel in numbers their own constellated hosts. [Applause.]

I have heard so much and I have seen so much of the sorrows of the West, that when the memory of them rises up before me, I stand appalled at the vision. Again and again, since I came back from Ireland, I have tried to paint a picture of Western misery; but again and again, and as often as I have tried,—even in the solitude of my own chamber, where no human eye could see me,—I have broken down, and I have wept like a woman. If I could put the picture into words, I could not utter the words. For I cannot look on human sorrow with the cold and æsthetic eye of an artist. To me a once stalwart peasant—shivering in rags, and gaunt, and hollow-voiced, and staggering with hunger— to me he is not a mere picture of Irish life; to me he is a brother to be helped; to me he is a Christian prisoner to be rescued from the pitiless power of those infidel Saracens of the nineteenth century—the Irish landlords and the British Government. [Prolonged applause.]

I know not where to begin nor what county to select in either of these unhappy provinces.

Let us first glance at

THE PROVINCE OF MUNSTER.

There are six counties in the province of Munster. The Mansion House has two hundred and fifty local committees there. Their reports show that there are in distress two hundred and thirty-two thousand seven hundred and fifty-nine persons in this province—in

Waterford (in round numbers)				..8,100
Tipperary	"	"	"	..17,000
Limerick	"	"	"	..17,000
Clare	"	"	"	..43,000
Cork	"	"	"	..70,000
Kerry	"	"	"	..75,000

In Waterford, in Limerick, and in Tipperary—with their aggregate of forty-two thousand persons on the relief lists—the distress is quite severe in some districts, but it is neither so general nor so extreme as on the coast. The miners, the mechanics, the laborers, the turf-makers, the fishermen, the cottiers, and the small farmers with "long families," are the chief sufferers in these counties.

In the County Cork there are less than one-eighth of the population in distress. Eastern Cork is a fertile county. It contains the great city and port of the South of Ireland. There is no unusual poverty in the east of it; but in South-western Cork, and in Kerry, the same scenes that I called local eye-witnesses to describe in Donegal, and that I shall summon other eye-witnesses to describe in Connaught, are common in every barony and in every parish. I met several Catholic priests from South-western Cork in Dublin, and I received more than a dozen letters from as many different districts of it. Their stories were all alike,—only the scene differed, —always the same cries of distress. I could talk an hour about the suffering in these counties alone.

County Clare is not so destitute as Kerry or South-western Cork, for the famine broods everywhere along the coast, and in some places it has called on fever to assist her—and the landlords—to crush the spirit or to exterminate the Irish race. But even from Clare we hear of "little children and infants crying in vain for food"; of whole districts—I quote the words of the committee—"actually starving, or threatened in the near future with starvation"; and at one parish—Coolmeen—of "a crowd of a hundred people ready to fall from hunger." More than one-fourth of the people of the County Clare depend for their daily food on foreign benevolence. What need of words in presence of this one fact?

Out of every hundred persons in County Kerry, thirty-eight depend on charity to keep them from death by starvation. From every part of the county comes the same sad message: "No work, no food, no fuel, no clothing." In Valencia Island, last winter, there were families of children literally naked,—with not a rag to shield their little bodies from the cold Atlantic winds. Father Lawler wrote that, out of one hundred and twenty families he visited, one hundred were without a blanket of any shape or description.

Hunger haunted the coast. Father Maurice O'Flaherty wrote: "No amount of word-painting at my command will be able to convey to you the impoverished and wretched state in which these poor creatures, living along the sea-coast, are steeped. I know, as a fact, that many—very many—among them have been living on turnips once, and sometimes twice a day for the last three weeks. I am aware that several, especially heads of families, have gone to bed fasting, in order to spare something for their starving children, who were crying for food. Some of these poor creatures have to do with one meal of "stirabout" for twenty-four hours. ("Stirabout" is Indian meal boiled with water and a little salt.) In all, or nearly all, the cases we visited, two hundred in number, not one had a cow, or pig, or sheep, or seed potatoes, or credit, or anything else, except the few stones of meal they have got from our Relief Committee."

I will just give one short extract from one report out of fifty reports to the Mansion House. It occurred in a letter from Ferreter Dingle:

"The word 'distress' very inadequately describes the situation and suffering of many and many a family here. They are suffering from that most brutalizing of feelings to which humanity is subject—the gnawing of hunger. Fancy fathers and mothers going to bed supperless that their children may have something left to stay the pangs of hunger, and, after all this self-sacrifice, these children without any food for twenty-four hours!"

I said that in the three inland counties of Munster—Waterford, Limerick, and Tipperary—the distress is not so extreme as in the coast counties. Yet you will err if you think that the poverty there is of the same type as we find in our American cities. What we call distress in America, the Irish peasants would thank God for as comfort.

Dean Quirke, of Tipperary, for example, wrote to me that, although in his vicinity nobody had actually died from hunger, yet he personally knew men in his own parish whose lives had been shortened by the famine. And the committee at Clogher wrote to the Mansion House that "farmers holding twenty to thirty acres of mountain land, come down to the Chairman, under cover of night, to get a little Indian meal to keep their families from starvation."

But now I must do my duty to the landlords, and tell you what they are doing in this year of distress in the Province of Munster.

When I wrote to Dean Quirke, of Tipperary, and asked him the cause of the distress, he promptly answered: "Rack-rents, bad land laws, insecurity of tenure." After he described the poverty in his own neighborhood, he added: "The farmers throughout the whole county of Tipperary, seeing they had no means of paying their rents and their debts, held public meetings—generally attended by the clergy—at which they showed the impossibility of paying the amount of rent that they had paid in prosperous years. I presided at one of these meetings. Not one disrespectful word was said of any landlord."

I hope you understand that it is Dean Quirke who is speaking, and who was chairman. If I had been chairman, I think there would have been disrespectful remarks made of the landlords. [Laughter and applause.]

"The farmers," continued Dean Quirke, "requested an abatement of rent for the present year of distress, on account of the failure of the crops and the low price of produce. . . . Only some six or seven paid any attention to this reasonable appeal, . . . while the bulk of the landlords treated the whole proceeding as *Communism !*" [Hisses.]

They seem to have the same breed of landlords in County Clare. Father Kenney, the parish priest of Scarife, wrote to me:

"There are two hundred and ten families now in want in my parish. When I have appealed to the landlords to take into account the depression of the times, that answer has been that political agitators have raised the cry for their own political purposes."

Of course, it is always the lamb that dirties the water away down the stream when the wolf is drinking at its source! [Applause.]

When I was in Dublin, I had a long talk with Lord Randolph Churchill, the son of the Duchess of Marlboro. [Hisses.]

Oh! don't hiss him. He's a pretty good fellow—*for a lord*. [Laughter.] We can't all be born in the upper ranks, you know—it was n't his blame that he was not born an American citizen. [Laughter.]

Well, I am going to tell you what Lord Churchill said, in illustration of the folly of the reforms that are advocated by the Land League. I am violating no confidence in repeating his conversation, because he knew that I would report it. I wrote down his remarks in stenographic notes, and submitted the manuscript for his correction before I printed it.

In talking about Cork, Lord Churchill said that there were six thousand cases of " absolute want "—those were his words—out of a population of thirty-one thousand persons at Skibbereen. The Committee of the Mansion House, at Skibbereen, at a later date, report that:

"The poor people are coming to us, starvation depicted in their looks, with the bitterest tales of woe. We are hearing hourly enough to melt the hardest hearts."

Father Davis, the parish priest of Skibbereen, wrote to me:

"*Four-fifths* of the entire population are at this moment destitute and begging for aid."

This is a very much larger estimate, you see, than Lord Churchill's. The lord said one-fifth; the priest said four-fifths.

"In Castletown," said Lord Churchill, "out of a population of 14,000 there are 1,600 cases of distress."

The Mansion House reports show that there are now 2,232 persons in distress in Castletown; "in the most abject state of destitution," they say, "without food, without clothing, without seed."

"In Castletown," continued Lord Churchill, "there are 600 occupiers of land rated under £4, and there are 700 more who rate at under £10. Here we have a Union, with 1,300 persons, the annual value of whose holdings does not exceed £10. This raises an interesting question of peasant proprietorship. There are politicians who want to convert these tenants into owners. These unfortunate people have not got—at the present moment—any available means of subsistence, any capital with which to cultivate the land, any stock, or any credit; and yet it is proposed to make them owners of the soil. When they are in such distress, *even when they have landlords to rely on in some degree to alleviate it*—for, of course, it is for the interest of the landlord to stand by his tenants—what would be their condition if they had no one to fall back on?"

Well, let us see how the landlords stand by their tenants in this very district that Lord Churchill selected, when he made this challenge for them.

At Drumbogue, where there are 1,300 persons in distress, there is "not a single resident landlord in the district, and only one of them is giving work."

At Goleen, the Mansion House Committee say that exorbitant rents are the cause of the distress there.

At Kilcaskin, the distress is attributed to bad land laws.

At King William's Town, high rents are linked with bad crops as the causes of the poverty of the farmers.

At Cloyne, "excessive rents" are named as the cause of the distress—and it is added, "the landlords of the farmers in distress are absentees."

Bear in mind that the Mansion House has no sympathy with the Land League, and that this is the evidence of their local committees.

Now let me quote from my own correspondents:

Good old Canon Brosnan, in writing from his parish in Kerry, near by, after describing the homes of his people, adds:

"These miserable holdings are let at double and treble the Government valuation—frequent instances not being wanted in which such crushing amounts are exceeded."

Father Davis, the parish priest of Skibbereen, writes to me:

"This entire district is held under two landlords—Sir Henry Beecher, Baronet, and the trustees of Lord Cranberry. These two proprietors have exacted the rents without the reduction of one cent—*and*, they have not contributed one penny to the meagre funds of our committee." [Cries of "Shame!" and hisses.]

This is the way, my Lord Randolph Churchill, in which the tenants can rely on their landlords. [Applause.]

THE PROVINCE OF CONNAUGHT.

And now let us enter Connaught—the land of human desolation.

Connaught has a population of nine hundred and eleven thousand three hundred and thirty-nine souls. Out of this vast multitude of people, nearly one-half—or, to be statistically exact, four hundred and twenty-one thousand seven hundred and fifty persons—are reported to be in extreme distress by the local committees of the Mansion House. From every county come *official* announcements that the destitution is increasing.

A geographical allocation of the distress gives to the County

Leitrim	(in round numbers)		47,000
Roscommon	"	"	46,000
Sligo	"	"	58,000
Galway	"	"	124,000
Mayo	"	"	143,000

These round numbers are thirty-seven hundred and fifty under the exact figures. What need of verbal evidence to sustain figures so appalling?

From each of these counties on the western coast, and from every parish of them, the reports of the committees give out the same dirge-like notes: "No food," "no clothing," "bed-clothing pawned," "children half-naked," "women clad in unwomanly rags," "no fuel," "destitution appalling," "privation beyond description," "many are suffering from hunger," "seed potatoes and oats are being consumed by the people," "their famine-stricken appearance would make the stoniest heart feel for them," "some families are actually starving, and even should works be started the people are too weak now to work." [Sensation.] These saddening phrases are not a bunch of rhetorical expressions: each one of them is a literal quotation from the business-like reports of the local committees of the Mansion House! ["Shame!"]

In the province of Connaught, the destitution is so general and profound that I could not tell you what I myself saw there, within the limits of a lecture. I shall select one of the least distressful counties—the County Sligo—and call again eye-witnesses of its misery.

And my first witness shall be a distinguished bishop, at that time unfriendly to Mr. Parnell—Bishop McCormack.

The Bishop wrote to me that in each of the twenty-two parishes of his diocese there prevails " real and undoubted distress"; and that, from the returns made to him by his priests, he finds that the number on the parochial relief lists is from seventy to seventy-five per cent. of the whole population of the diocese. His Lordship adds that this state of destitution must last till August.

Good words are like good coins—they lose their value if they are uttered too freely. I have used the word distress so often that I fear it may pall on you. Let us test it in the fire of the sorrow of Sligo.

Dr. Canon Finn, of Ballymote, wrote to me that the priests in his parish tell him that the little children often come to school without having had a mouthful of breakfast to eat, and that vomiting and stomach sickness is common among them.

Why?

"I know whole families," writes the Canon, "that have to supplement what our committee gives by eating rotten potatoes which they dig out, day by day." [Sobs.]

Father John O'Keene, of Dramore West, wrote to me that "there are four hundred families in his parish dependent on the relief committees, and one hundred almost entirely in want of clothing, and the children in a state of semi-nudity." ["Shame!"]

Four hundred families! Let us look at the mother of just one of these four hundred families.

Listen to Father O'Keene:

"On Sunday last, as I was about going to church, a poor young woman, prematurely aged by poverty, came up and spoke to me. Being in a hurry, I said: 'I have no time to speak to you, Mrs. Calpin. Are you not on the relief list?' 'No, Father,' she said, 'and we are starving.' Her appearance caused me to stop. She had no shoes, and her wretched clothing made her a picture of misery.

"I asked her why her husband had not come to speak to me.

"She said: 'He has not had a coat for the last two years, and as this is Sunday, he did not wish to trouble Thomas Feeney for the loan of one, as he sometimes lends one to him.'

"'Have you any other clothes besides what I see on you?'

"'Father, I am ashamed,' was the reply; 'I have not even a stitch of underclothing.'

"'How many children have you?'

"'Four, Father.'

"'What are their ages?'

"'The oldest, a boy, eight years; a girl, seven; another, four, and a little one on the breast.'

"'Have they any clothes?'

"'No, Father. You may remember that, when you were passing last September, you called into the house, and I had to put the children aside for their nakedness.'

"'Have you any bed-clothes?'

"'A couple of guano-bags.'

"'How could you live for the past week?'

"'I went to my brother, Martin MacGee, of Farrelinfarrel, and he gave me a couple of porringers of Indian meal each day, from which I made Indian gruel. I gave my husband the biggest part, as he is working in the fields.'

"'Had you anything for the children?'

"'Oh, Father,' she said, 'the first question they put me in the morning is: "Mother! Have we any meal this day?" [Sobs and groans.] If I say I have, they are happy; if not, they are sad, and begin to cry.'

"At these words she showed great emotion, and I could not remain unmoved.

"This," adds Father O'Keene, "is one of the many cases I could adduce in proof of the misery of my people."

Are the landlords doing nothing for these people? Certainly. There are nine hundred families in the parish of Bruninadden, in the county of Cork. Canon McDermott is the priest there. Hear what he wrote to me:

"The lands are in part good; but the good lands are chiefly in the hands of landlords and graziers. You can travel miles over rich lands and meet only the herds or laborers of some absentee landlord. Thirty landlords own this parish; twenty-seven of them are absentees. The three resident proprietors are poor and needy themselves. You can judge of the condition of the tenant-farmers and of their relations with their landlords by a statement of facts.

"There are in my parish two iron huts,—one to protect the bailiff of an absentee landlord, the other to protect a resident landlord.

"Again, in a district containing one hundred and sixty families, eighty-nine processes of ejectment were ordered to be served by the landlords; but, in some cases, the process-servers declined to act; and, in others, the processes were forcibly taken from them."

It is not always a pastime to serve processes of ejectment on a starving and desperate peasantry. [Applause.]

The good Canon continues: "Allow me to state the condition of some of those on whom processes were to have been served:

"Pat Grady, of Lugmore, has fourteen children, thirteen of them living with him in a small hut. He holds about five acres of unreclaimed land, for which he pays at the rate of £1 12s. ($8) an acre. He owns neither a cow nor a calf. He has not a morsel to feed his children except the twenty-five pounds of Indian meal I dole out to him each week. To-day I saw his ticket from a pawnbroker for his very bedclothes. His children sleep on straw, or on the bare floor."

But the landlord wanted his rent for all that. [Hisses.]

"Pat Gormanly," writes the Canon, "with five in a family, is precisely in the same destitute condition. He is threatened with an ejectment for non-payment of rent, while his family are starving for want of the commonest food. [Hisses.] "I could adduce," he concludes, "hundreds of cases quite as bad. Matthew Dasey came three times for his meal. His mother had been two days without food. He himself staggered and fell twice from hunger, on his way home." [Groans and sobs.] These starving and staggering peasants, when they ask for food, receive from their landlords processes of ejectment. [Hisses and sobs.]

Ladies and Gentlemen:—I shall call no more witnesses, although I could summon hundreds, of character unimpeached and unimpeachable, who would tell you tales of wretchedness quite as harrowing, from every barony and parish of the West of Ireland. I have chosen to quote local testimony rather than to give my own evidence, because some hearers might have thought, if I had described only what I saw myself, that the truth of my reports of Irish destitution had been warped in the fires of my indignation against oppression; and because, as I have always, I trust, preferred to fight on the side of the falling man, that the wrongs I saw had been unduly magnified by the lenses of my sympathy for their victims. At another time I may tell what I saw in Ireland. To-night I must sum up my evidence in the fewest words.

I have seen sights as sad as most of my witnesses have described.

I have seen hundreds of barefooted and bareheaded mothers standing for an hour in the rain and the chilly wind, patiently and anxiously waiting to get an order for Indian meal to feed their famishing children at home.

I have seen a family of five boys dressed like girls, in garments rudely fashioned from potato-bags, because their parents were too poor to buy boys' clothing.

I have visited a dozen populous parishes where four-fifths of the entire population depended for their daily bread on foreign charity.

I have been in several villages where every man, woman, and child in them would have died from hunger within one month, or perhaps one week, from the hour in which the relief that they now solely rely on should be refused, because the men have neither a mouthful of food nor any chance of earning a shilling, nor any other way of getting provisions for their families until the ripening of the crops in autumn.

I have entered hundreds of Irish cabins in districts where the relief is distributed. These cabins are more wretched than the cabins of the negroes were in the darkest days of slavery. The Irish peasant can neither dress as well, nor is he fed as well, as the Southern slave was fed, and dressed, and lodged. Donkeys, and cows, and pigs, and hens live in the same wretched room with the family. Many of these cabins had not a single article of bedclothing, except guano-sacks or potato-bags, and when the old folks had a blanket it was tattered and filthy.

I saw only one woman in all these cabins whose face did not look sad and care-racked, and she was dumb and idiotic. [Sensation.]

The Irish have been described by novelists and travelers as a light-hearted and rollicking people—full of fun and quick in repartee—equally ready to dance or to fight. I did not find them so. I found them in the West of Ireland a sad and despondent people; care-worn, broken-hearted, and shrouded in gloom. Never once in the hundreds of cabins that I entered —never once, even—did I catch the thrill of a merry voice nor the light of a joyous eye. Old men and boys, old women and girls, young men and maidens—all of them, without a solitary exception—were grave or haggard, and every household looked as if the plague of the first-born had smitten them that hour. Rachael, weeping for her children, would have passed unnoticed among these warm-hearted peasants; or, if she had been noticed, they would only have said: "She is one of us." [Sobs.] A home without a child is cheerless enough—but here is a whole land without a child's laugh in it. Cabins full of children and no boisterous glee! No need to tell these youngsters to be quiet. The famine has tamed their restless spirits, and they crouch around the bit of peat-fire without uttering a word. Often they do not look a second time at the stranger who comes into their desolate cabin.

My personal investigations proved that the misery that my witnesses have outlined is not exceptional but representative; that the Irish peasant is neither indolent nor improvident, but that he is the victim of laws without mercy, that without mercy are enforced; and my studies, furthermore, forced me to believe that the poverty I saw, and the sorrow, and the wretchedness, are the predetermined results of the premeditated policy of the British Government in Ireland, to drive her people into exile. [Hisses.]

This, also, I believe and say—that Ireland does not suffer because of over-population, but because of over-spoliation; because she has too many landlords and not enough land-owners. [Applause.]

Irish landlordism is in the dock to-day charged with the high crime and misdemeanor of starving a great people. I am one of the jury that has sat and taken evidence. "Guilty or not guilty?" My verdict is—guilty. [Tremendous applause.] The Irish people will never be prosperous until Irish landlordism is abolished. [Long continued applause.]

Let me say a few words to my auditors of American birth.

Americans believe that it is England that rules Ireland; and that the Irish in Ireland enjoy the same rights that the English enjoy in England. The belief is an error. England delegates the most important of all legislative powers—the power of taxation—to the absentee landlord; and he assigns the odious task of impoverishing the people to his irresponsible agents. Every Irish landlord is a little local Plantagenet with no salutary fear of a veto by strangulation; and the British Government is only his vassal and his executioner.

The Irish landlord has no more pity for his tenant than the shark has for the children of the sailor who falls between his jaws. [Applause.] If American landlords, even in law-abiding New England, were to act as the Irish landlords act, they would perish by the eager hands of vigilance committees. [Applause.] If Shakespeare had known them, he would have made Shylock an Irish landlord. [Applause.] If Dante had seen the misery that these miscreants have wrought, as my own eyes have seen it in the West of Ireland, he would have gone there to paint more lurid pictures of human wretchedness than he conceived in his *Inferno*. [Applause.]

From 1847 to 1851, one million and a half of the Irish people perished from famine and the fevers that it spawned. [Sensation.] This appalling crime has been demonstrated by a man whose love of Ireland no man questioned, and whose knowledge of her history no man doubted—John Mitchell. [Applause.] These victims of landlord greed and British power were as deliberately put to death as if each one of them had been forced to mount the steps of a scaffold. And why? To save a worse than feudal system of land-tenure—for it is the feudal system stripped of every duty that feudalism recognized [applause] — the corpse that breeds pestilence after the spirit that gave protection has fled—a feudal system that every Christian nation, excepting England only, has been compelled to abolish in the interests of civilization. [Applause.]

Now, what are the duties of the friends of Ireland? Our first duty is to feed the people who are starving. If I have opened your hearts, I beg of you that you will not say, "God help them!" Just help them yourself.

They don't need more prayers. They need more meal. [Applause.]

I trust that I have shown you to-night, by the testimony of more than ten thousand witnesses, that the accounts of the Irish famine have not been exaggerated in America. I know that not one-tenth of the sad truths have been told about it. It is true, I hope, that not more than a score or more of peasants have died from hunger. The organs of the landlords say so; and it is almost the only truth that they have told. No thanks to the landlords for this mercy! If the peasants had depended on the landlords for help in this their time of need, one hundred thousand of them would lie moldering in the graves from which the charity of Australia, and Canada, and America has rescued them.

My statistics were brought down to the 1st of March. But the latest dispatches from Ireland by cable show that the distress is not decreasing, but increasing. The bishops and the priests whom I met or who wrote to me before I left Ireland, and the Lord Mayor of Dublin, within a week, agree in sanctioning the declaration of the Mansion House Committee that, "if the experience of former famines be a guide, the greatest distress will be found in the months of June, July, and August," and that "it is to be apprehended that, whilst the crops are ripening, the people will perish."

A few days ago, the London *Times* said either that the "distress was diminishing," or that it "was likely to decrease now." Don't believe it! The London *Times* rejoiced when the famine of '47 swept the Irish peasantry by thousands into their graves. [Hisses.] It has had no change of heart. The landlords would like to see the Irish expelled, even by famine or by death. It is no longer the old cry of—"To Hell or Connaught!" The landlords have got Connaught now, and by and by I believe that they will get ——. [Roars of laughter.] You seem to misunderstand me. [Laughter.] What I meant to say was that, whereas, once the British Government drove the Irish into Connaught, now it wants to drive them out of it. [Laughter.]

What is the next duty of the friends of Ireland? After you have fed the hungry peasant, how can you help to improve his condition, permanently, without acting in violation of your duty as citizens of the United States?

I answer without hesitation, and with the emphasis that profound conviction alone can justify, you can help him by holding up the hands of the Irish National Land League in the irrepressible conflict now begun between the people and the aristocracy for peasant proprietorship. [Prolonged applause.]

The English themselves established the precedent of giving international aid to foreign agitation for the abolition of social wrongs in other lands. They gave money to our antislavery societies. Let us pay it back with compound interest. [Applause.]

They cast their bread on the American waters, and now I hope it will return to them before many days. [Renewed applause.]

There are honest Americans, true friends of the Irish race, who sincerely believe that your duty should begin and end with alms-giving. I do not agree with them. I honor the good Samaritan for binding up the wounds of the traveler, but I also believe that the thieves who waylaid him should have been brought to the scaffold. [Applause.] As long as the landlords have the power to rob, the peasant will be his victim. His power must be broken. [Applause.]

And now, with all my heart, I congratulate the Irish people that they have thrown out a banner, beneath whose folds beneficent every man of every creed of the Irish race can do battle—the Banner of Peasant Proprietorship. [Applause.] A banner that the Home Ruler may carry without abjuring his just aspirations for legislative independence. [Applause.] A banner that the Separatist may adopt without abandoning the other, and I hope the coming flag of a Republican Nationality. [Loud applause.]

It is a banner of peace and of progress. For what was statesmanship in Germany and France cannot be Communism in Connaught and Munster. [Applause.]

Archimedes said that if he could find, outside of this planet, a fulcrum for his lever, he could overturn the world. The fulcrum that is needed to overthrow British tyranny in Ireland is the homestead of the peasant. [Applause.] The man who owns his farm is a social rock; the tenant-at-will is a thistle-down.

Plant a race of peasant proprietors, and by and by a crop of armed men will spring up [applause]—a race of men who will not beg for justice, but demand it; a race of men who will not agitate for independence, but declare it. [Applause.]

The flag that will yet lead to Irish nationality was first unfurled by the son of an evicted tenant—Michael Davitt [applause]; and it is now upheld by that rarest of all rare men in Ireland, a decent landlord—Charles Stewart Parnell. [Applause.]

II.

FAMINE AND THE PRIESTS.

[At a farewell banquet given in Boston, Massachusetts, to the Rev. Father Fulton, S. J., Mr. Redpath made a speech on the "Irish Famine and the Irish Priests." The subjoined passage of it, published originally in the New York *Irish-American*, has been translated into nearly every language of Europe:]

I DISCOVERED a new character in Ireland—not new to Ireland, for he has been a thousand years there—but new to me; for, although I had heard enough and had read enough about him, I found that I had never known him. It was the Irish Priest.

My father was a Scotch Presbyterian, and I was reared in the strictest traditions of that faith. No undue influence was ever brought to bear on my youthful mind to prejudice me in favor of the Catholic Church. [Laughter.] I can recall that I once heard read, with a somewhat tempered approval, certain kind and conciliatory remarks about the devil—written by a famous Scotchman of the name of Robert Burns; but I cannot remember a single generous or brotherly expression of regard for the Roman Catholics or for their faith. They were never called Catholics. They were "Papists" always. The Catholic Church was commonly referred to in my boyhood under the symbolic figure of a famous lady—and not an estimable lady—who had a peculiar fancy for scarlet garments, and who lived and sinned in the ancient city of Babylon. [Laughter.]

I believed that I had put away these uncomely prejudices of my early education—but the roots of them, I found, must still have remained in my mind; for how else could I explain the surprise I felt—even the gratified surprise—that these Irish priests were generous and hospitable, and warm-hearted and cultivated gentlemen? For so I found them always; and I met them often and everywhere. I believe that I have no more cordial friends anywhere in Ireland than among the Irish priests; and I am sure that in America there is no man—the words of whose creed do not keep time to the solemn music of the centuries-coronated anthems of the Ancient Church—who has for them a more fraternal feeling or a sincerer admiration. [Applause.]

The Irish priest is the tongue of the dumb Samson of Ireland. But for the Irish priest thousands of Irish peasants would have been dead to-day, even after ample stores of food had been sent from America to save them. Many a lonely village, hidden among the bleak mountains of the West, would have been decimated by famine if the priest had not been there to tell of the distress and to plead for the peasant.

The Irish priest justifies his title of Father by his fatherly care of his people. He toils for them from dawn till midnight.

It is a vulgar and a cruel slander to represent the Irish priests as living in idle luxury when Irish peasants are famishing around them. I have entered too many of their lowly homes— as a stranger unexpected—but, as a stranger from America, never unwelcomed—I have seen too often and too near their humble surroundings to listen with indifference or without indignation to aspersions so unworthy and untrue. I can hardly conceive of a severer test to which sincerity and self-sacrifice can be put than these Irish priests endure without seeming to be conscious that they are exhibiting uncommon courage or proving that they have renounced the world and its ambitions; for—educated men with cultivated tastes—they live in an intellectual isolation among illiterate peasants, in poverty and obscurity; and they neither repine at their fate nor indulge in the subtile pride of self-conscious self-consecration. [Applause.]

For one—and, albeit, one of *this* world only—I profoundly honor self-sacrifice and self-renunciation—whatever banner they carry, whatever emblem they cherish, or whatever tongue they speak. [Applause.]

I saw one scene in Ireland that lingers lovingly in my memory. It was at a meeting, in the West, of a local committee of the Duchess of Marlborough's Fund. An Irish "lord" was the chairman, not a bad man, either— for a lord; but *every* lord has the spirit of an upstart, and this lord, at times, was insolent to his betters—the toilers—and a little arrogant to his equals—the tradesmen of the district.

There was a deputation in the room of dejected peasants from one of the islands in the bay near by.

It had been reported to this committee that, at a sub-committee meeting, where the orders for Indian meal were distributed, the tattered and hungry crowd had been somewhat disorderly; that is to say, they were starving, and had clamored impatiently for food, instead of waiting with patience for their petty allocations. "My lord" rebuked their ragged representatives, harshly, and in a domineering tone; and, without asking leave of his associates on the committee, he told them that if such a scene should occur again their supply of food would be stopped. I was astonished that he should presume to talk in such tones before any American citizen—he, who ought, I thought, to have his hand on his mouth and his mouth in the dust, in presence of the damnatory facts that he lived on an estate from which peasants, now exiles in America, had been evicted by hundreds, and that neither he, nor his brother, a marquis, whom he represented, had given a shilling for the relief of the wretched tenants on his wide domains, nor reduced his Shylock rental, although thousands of these tenants, at that very hour, were living on provisions bought by the bounty of citizens of the United States and of other foreign lands.

One of the ragged committee pressed the claims of his famishing constituency with an eloquence that was poor in words, but rich in pathos. "My lord" said that he would try to do something for them; but he added, and again in a dictatorial tone, "that although her Grace, the Duchess of Marlborough, might consent to relieve them, they had no right to expect it; that the funds were hers not theirs;

that the noble lady was under no obligations to relieve them."

The poor man, hat in hand, was going away, sorrowful.

I sat, a heretic, beside a priest, a republican beside a lord; and I thought, with no little inward indignation, that I was the only person in the room, and I a stranger, whose heart throbbed with pity for the stricken man. For my hands were gnawing with hunger—just famishing—for a taste of his lordship's throat. [Laughter.]

But, as I looked around the room, I saw a sudden flash in the priest's eye that told of a power before which the pride of ancestral rank is but as grass before a prairie fire.

"I beg your lordship's pardon!" said the priest, with a sublime haughtiness; "I do not agree with you. The money does *not* belong to 'Her Grace.' She holds the money in trust only. We *have* a right to it. It belongs to the poor!" [Applause.]

The lord was cowed; the peasant won. [Applause.]

No man but a priest, at that table, would have dared to talk in that style to a lord.

More than eighteen centuries have passed since a Roman judge said to a Missionary of the Cross: "Almost, thou persuadest me to become a Christian." I do not believe that there has lived a man since then who felt more profoundly than I did at that moment the spirit that prompted that immortal declaration. As long as that priest was in that room, I think I was a loyal son of the Church. [Applause.]

I started as if I had been in a dream. Was this the nineteenth century or the fifteenth? For, again, I saw the arm of the lordling raised to smite the poor man; again I saw rise between them the august form of the Mother Church; and again I saw the weapon of the oppressor broken into fragments against the bosses of her invincible shield. [Applause.] And, as I looked at these fragments, I saw, among them, the shattered relics of the pharisaical conceit that I had been the solitary sympathizer with the poor man. I did not pick them up. I shall have no use for them in this world again. I had thrown down an invisible gage of battle; the priest had taken it up, and I had been defeated. The Cross had conquered me. [Applause.] And henceforth,—under what flag soever I may fight,—whenever I see the white banner of the Irish priest pass by, I shall dip my own colors in salutation to it, in memory and in honor of his beneficent devotion to the famishing Irish peasant during the famine of 1880. [Long-continued applause.]

III.

A WELCOME TO AN IRISH STATESMAN.

[On the 22d of May, the Irish-Americans of New York gave a great out-of-door reception in Jones's Woods in honor of Michael Davitt. After speeches by Mr. Davitt, Mr. John Dillon, and Mr. Mooney, editor of the New York *Star*, Mr. Redpath was introduced and received with great enthusiasm. He said:]

Ladies and Gentlemen:

ONE of the great poets of the olden time has said that the gods look down in admiration on every brave man struggling with adversity. If this utterance is a truth, then the men whom the gods most admire are the peasantry of Ireland. [Cheers.] For they have bravely struggled with adversity for seven hundred years. [Cheers.]

The truest test of human greatness is not to be found in the power to rise in the world—for sometimes, you know, both in American society and American politics, the buzzards rise as well as the eagles. [Laughter.] The touchstone of character is not what a man does when he is standing and strong, but what he does when he is weak and on his back. Weak men and weak races are conquered when they are once overthrown; but great men and great races spring to their feet again and fight. [Cheers.] The Irish people have been overwhelmed, the Irish people have been prostrated, again and again, but the Irish people have never yet surrendered—the Irish people have never failed to strike back whenever they have had the opportunity, and they have never failed to make the opportunity. [Cheers.] . . . You all know that the history of Ireland is rich in dramatic episodes. Let me tell you one of them that her coming historians, I think, will chronicle, and her poets of the coming time will sing. During that long reign of terror in Ireland—from 1847 to 1852—when the Irish people fainted and staggered, from hunger and fever, into their graves by tens of thousands and by hundreds of thousands, the landlords of Ireland, pitiless as death, unpitying as famine, armed crowbar brigades to pull down the roofs that still sheltered these gaunt and gasping peasants. [Hisses.] During one of those black years, the crowbar brigade came to the cabin of a farmer in Mayo. He was an honest man and honored by his neighbors, and he had never failed to pay every debt. But the failure of the crops had ruined him. The landlord, deaf to pleas for time, turned this farmer and his wife and their children into the roadside. Down came the roof that had sheltered them, down came the cabin that they had built. [Hisses.] Among the children thus flung into the world penniless, unsheltered, was one bright-eyed boy. He looked on in silence at the work of destruction. This boy had been brought up (as all the boys in the West of Ireland had been brought up) in the belief that the lords of the soil were not the social only but the moral and intellectual superiors of the "common people," and that it was right and proper to respect and even reverence them. But this demonry caused this boy to begin to doubt and think; and when the sons of the people begin to doubt and think it is time for tyrants to begin to pray and tremble. [Cheers.] By and by, that boy's thoughts ripened into aspirations and his aspirations into actions. He soon saw—to use an illustration from recent history—that if to pull down the Vendome Column was an act of vandalism, it was equally an act, and a greater act, of vandalism to pull down the cabin of a peasant. [Cheers.] He saw that if to take property without recompense from the owner of property is communism, then the great landlords of the West of Ireland are the wickedest communists now living. [Cheers.] That boy, when a young man, was arrested and by perjured witnesses he was sent for seven years to prison. In the English house of bondage he served a full apprenticeship to liberty, and he left it a master mechanic in the noble art of destroying despotism. [Cheers.]

Last spring, that boy—now a bearded man—went down to visit the ruins of his father's house. His friends had been there before him. They had built over the ruined walls of his father's cabin a platform, and on that platform, fearless and incorruptible and unconquerable—time's latest incarnation of the indomitable spirit of the Irish peasantry—Michael Davitt stepped forth to unfurl the banner of peasant proprietory! [Cheers.] I do not know in our own American history a more dramatic episode, save one only —and that was when our boys in blue tramped through Virginia and sang, ten thousand voices strong, as they passed the spot where the martyr of Harper's Ferry died for a race oppressed, "John Brown's body lies a-moldering in the grave, but his soul goes marching on!" [Cheers.] That ruined cabin where Michael Davitt threw out the flag of the Irish Land War will be pointed out in time to come as the Runnymede of the Irish people. For a greater victory than Magna Charta was won there. The English barons wrested from King John a compact that has been praised for centuries, and yet it is the charter not of English liberty but of English bondage. It granted privileges to the aristocracy— but not a single right to the people. The barons demanded everything for themselves and granted nothing to their followers. Michael Davitt asked nothing for himself, but everything for the people. [Cheers.] That meeting at Irishtown, in the County Mayo, was the ceremony of the coronation of liberty in Ireland. On that platform, for the first time in Irish history, the Irish people themselves came to the front—no longer looking up to leaders or champions, no longer following men of a higher social order, but marching breast to breast, as if in military array, and receiving the words of command from a man in their own ranks. [Cheers.] It was no longer the Irish patrician claiming rights for his clients. It was the dumb Samson of Ireland himself who had found his voice and was uttering his demands for justice. I congratulate Ireland for having given birth to a man who has taught in liberty what he learned in bondage. He has broken the Irish Samson's fetters and they can never be riveted again! [Cheers.]

But he has a higher claim on your support and admiration. I think he is the greatest statesman that Ireland has ever produced. [Cheers from the audience. Mr. Davitt blushed, and said pleadingly, "Oh don't, don't!"] I mean no blarney—I didn't kiss the stone. [Laughter.] I mean exactly what I say. What is statesmanship? It is not the power to see and to denounce a national evil. That is the function of the reformer or agitator. The statesman is he who has the gift to see a wrong and the cause of it, and to apply a remedy that will cure it. Among all Irish leaders, Michael Davitt, and he only, has clearly seen the cause of Irish misery, and he only has had the courage to prescribe the true remedy. [Cheers.] If you think that I am extolling our honored guest extravagantly, I ask you, when you go to your own homes, to review the history of Ireland, and you will find that while one leader urged that this branch, and another leader urged that another branch of the upas-tree of English misgovernment should be lopped off, Michael Davitt was the first man whose clear eyes saw, and whose brave tongue said: "Cut down the whole tree—trunk and branches [cheers], and then dig up the roots." [Cheers.] Until the power of the Irish landlords is utterly destroyed; until there is not a landlord—good, bad, or indifferent—in all Ireland; until every farmer owns his own land, and tills it—Ireland will never cease to be a rebel at home and a beggar abroad. [Cheers.]

IV.

A SOUPER-JEW'S IRISH POLICY.

[Mr. Redpath was a guest at the banquet given to Mr. Parnell, at Cork, on his return from the United States. He was invited to respond to the toast of "America." Mr. Redpath said:]

Gentlemen:

IF I had been called on to respond to the loyal toast that usually opens British festivities, I should have peremptorily refused to do so, for the reasons that I was a man before I was a guest, and that I am too old a man to become a flunkey. [Applause.] But for a very different reason I must decline with equal peremptoriness to respond to the toast of America. [Cries of " Why ? Why ? "]

MR. REDPATH.—Because America is so great and so good a country that there is no man either great or good enough to represent her. [Cheers.] So, I must speak, if I speak at all, not for America, but as an American. [Applause and cries of " Go on !"]

I am going home. [Cries of " No, no."] British politics are too much for me. In my own country—in the Mark Lane *Express* of the mind market—I think I would have been quoted as ranging "from fair to middling" in intelligence; but here, I confess, I cannot understand even the alpha and omega, the first and the last verbal symbols of British philosophy. I refer to Jingo and Decomposition. [Laughter.]

After a humorous account of the origin of the word Jingo, Mr. Redpath continued:

And now comes that word of direct import — the philological specter, evoked from the tomb of a dead language to frighten Anglo-Saxon men withal, by the distinguished countryman of the Witch of Endor—Beaconsfield's *Decomposition!* Heavens! what a fright it gave England! Irishmen do not get scared quite so easily as Englishmen; for where *banshees* are as common as good landlords are rare it needs a more terrible ghost than Beaconsfield can raise to frighten them. [Laughter.]

But, gentlemen, I cannot talk with levity about this man Beaconsfield. I have no respect for any man who does not love liberty, and who would not fight for liberty—not for himself only, or his own race only, but for all men and for all races. I especially despise men, members of races that have been oppressed, who aid in the oppression of other races. I never met an Irishman in the United States, when slavery existed there, for whom, if he supported the oppression of the black man, I had ever more than two words : *Damn him!* [Loud cheers. Here a priest rose and drank Mr. Redpath's health.]

MR. REDPATH.—I beg the reverend Father's pardon. [Shouts of laughter.] I did not mean to swear, and I did not swear—I only used an American expression to show my contempt for a recreant Irishman, and every Irishman who does not love liberty for all men is a recreant to his race and faith! [Cheers.] But with all my heart and soul and strength I especially despise that man who, by his genius, his fame and his high rank, is entitled to be regarded as the representative Hebrew of our times—the representative of a race that for nineteen centuries has been persecuted for religion's sake— who, false to his adopted creed, and false to the grand traditions of his people, within a few days has sought (as Beaconsfield sought by his letter to the Duke of Marlborough) to arouse against the Irish people, for partisan purposes, the religious animosities of the English nation. [Cheers.] For that is what he tried to do. [Cheers.]

Ireland demands Home Rule.

Beaconsfield asserts that Home Rule means the DECOMPOSITION of the British Empire. All Jingodom replies: "I thank thee, Jew, for teaching us that word," and truly they seem to roll it as a sweet morsel under their tongues.

What *does* it mean? I have traveled in every province of British North America from the ocean to the lakes—in Newfoundland, in Prince Edward's Island, in Nova Scotia, in New Brunswick, in Quebec, and in Ontario. Each of these provinces has an independent legislature, and an independent executive, and five of them have clubbed together to support a sub-imperial Parliament. Newfoundland, with about half the population of Dublin, has not only a legislature and executive for the Island, but a city government for St. John—with such privileges as Dublin never yet has secured—and she refused to join in the New Dominion Confederation, although all the moral and social influence of the Imperial Government was brought to bear to induce her to join it. Is not this Decomposition? Six Home Rule Governments and one Home Rule sub-Imperial Parliament for a population about one-third less than the population of Ireland! And what is the result of this Decomposition policy? The Dominion is largely settled by French Catholics whom England conquered. These original colonists have kept themselves aloof both in social life, in religion, and in politics from British society, British churchianity and British politics. But they never rebel. The Dominion is largely populated by Irishmen from Connaught and Munster. They hate England as cordially as they hated her at home. But they never rebel. Why? They can't invent an excuse. [Laughter.] They have Home Rule. [Applause.] British soldiers and Irish constables are as thick in Ireland as lice and flies were in Egypt during the land agitation there. Ireland is disloyal. There is not a British soldier from the Atlantic to the Pacific—not one; the Canadians know that if they wanted to rebel, men by thousands and money by millions would pour over to their aid; yet Canada and her sisters are loyal. Now, if this is the work of Decomposition, wouldn't it be a wise policy to try the effect of that sort of manure in Ireland [laughter], where the crop of loyalty is a greater failure than the potato crop ever was? [Applause.]

Now, take an aërial trip around the world in forty seconds, and you will find in Van Dieman's Land, in New Zealand, and in Australia, again, independent legislatures and independent executives: Home Rule everywhere and loyalty everywhere, although there are Irishmen everywhere. [Laughter.] There are tens of thousands of men in those colonies who hate the British monarchy, and yet you could not kick the newest world out of the British Empire. Why? Decomposition!

I have been in two disaffected countries under British rule — Jamaica and Ireland. There is no Home Rule in Jamaica and no Home Rule in Ireland. The principle of the Integrity of the Empire (as this souper-Jew calls imperial misgovernment) is enforced in the tropics as well as in this island of yours. No race ever owed so deep a debt of gratitude to a foreign government as the black and brown men of Jamaica owe to the people of England. The people of England forced their Government to stretch its strong right hand across the Atlantic and break the shackles of the Jamaica slave. But the blacks are poor and discontented; and the browns are poor and disaffected; and the whites growl whether they are really discontented or not. Why are the people discontented? Because they do not govern themselves. Why are they poor? Why is Ireland poor? The toiling and hard-fisted absentee landlords and their organs say because you are lazy, and because the soil is poor and overpeopled. Well, the laziest man might make a good living in the tropics, and the negroes are not lazy. It cannot be said that Jamaica is over-peopled or that her soil is poor. If God ever made a more beautiful or a more fertile island than Jamaica, He did not put it on this planet. It is the brightest gem of ocean that ever dropped here from the coronet of the Creator. [Applause.] Jamaica is poor as Ireland is poor, because England maintains there, as she supports here, the power of the absentee landlord, and delegates to him, unquestioned and unchecked, the power of arbitrary taxation in the form of rent. And Jamaica, like Ireland, will never prosper until the absentee is made a permanent absentee; until no man is permitted, under any pretext, to possess land that he does not dwell on and till. [Applause.]

I thought statesmanship was a practical science—to be judged by its fruits; and yet I hear your Prime Minister applauding a policy that everywhere produces poverty and disaffection, and denouncing as Decomposition a policy that yields abundant increase of loyalty and prosperity. I hear great statesmen, so called, extolling his utterances.

I cannot understand it. I am going home. [Laughter.] I am too old to comprehend such statesmanship. [Laughter.] I am going home—to a land where no appeals are made to arouse religious animosities, because even toleration is not tolerated where all men are free and all men are equal; to a land where every poor man can have a home that neither crown nor landlord can confiscate or disturb; to a land—I say it with the profoundest reverence—after God's own heart [cheers], because its government is a government of the people, and for the people, and by the people. [Cheers.]

V.

CONFISCATION AND EXCOMMUNICATION.

[Mr. Redpath was at the village of Leenane, in Connemara, on August 28, 1880. It was a fair day. He was called on to make a speech. "I saw before me," he said in a recent letter, "a roadside full of barefooted women and frieze-coated men; I knew that there was a fierce spirit brooding among them at the exactions of the landlords, and that if some bloodless, but pitiless, policy was not advocated, there would soon be killings of landlords and land agents all over the West; and so I made up my mind to advocate a thorough system of social ostracism—I called it social excommunication—it is now called Boycotting—for the protection of the tenants, whom American charity had kept alive since the preceding autumn. I did not know that there was a short-hand writer present until a full report of my talk appeared in the Dublin papers. This report was immediately telegraphed to all the leading journals of England and Scotland, and if I didn't 'wake up and find myself famous,' it was because I woke *them* up and found myself famous. Even down to the Coercion debate this speech and the Clare Morris speech were represented in England as an appeal to incite an insurrection in Ireland!" The report subjoined is from the Dublin *Nation*. Mr. Redpath, after the cheering had subsided, putting on his hat, after having lifted it to the audience, said:]

YOU will excuse me if I keep on my hat. We Americans never speak with uncovered heads to any one, and never lift our hats except to return a salutation. [Cheers.] There is too much hat-lifting in Ireland. I want you to promise me that you will never lift your hat to any man because he owns land or because he is rich. [Applause.] Never do honor to men who do no honor to human nature.

This is the second time I have visited the West of Ireland. I came over here last winter to find out whether the Irish people were starving, and if they were starving why they were starving. When

I went back, the Americans asked me what was the cause of the misery I described. Was it the potato-blight? No, I said, it is the landlord-blight. [Cheers.] I told the Americans, and I say here to-day, that the exactions of the landlords have done more to ruin the Irish people than the potato-blight and the famine-fever combined. [Cheers.] I do not come to Ireland to make speeches, but to hear them. But now that I'm here——

A Voice.—"You're welcome."

Mr. Redpath.—I will tell you how Irish politics look to an American. The first meeting of this kind that I attended in Ireland was in the Queen's County. I saw there, as I see here, a number of constables in attendance, armed and equipped as soldiers. I asked Michael Davitt——

A Voice.—"Three cheers for Davitt." [Cheers.]

Mr. Redpath.—Whether there was likely to be a riot. No, he said, the constables were there to try and overawe the people. But, he added, they can't do it. [Cheers.] When I described that meeting in the American papers, I think nothing I wrote created more indignation against the British Government than the fact that the people of Ireland cannot assemble peaceably to discuss their wrongs without having a squad of constabulary on the spot to overawe them. I lectured in America about the famine here, and I was the means, simply by telling the truth, of raising money for the starving people of the West. The organ of the Archbishop of Boston said I raised £20,000. Now, I think we Americans have a mortgage on your crops, and I have come over to look after our mortgages. I didn't raise that money for the landlords; and I am here to-day to find out whether you're going to give it to the landlords? [Cries of "No! No!"]

Mr. Redpath.—Faith, I think that if the Irish people pay over American money to the landlords, the best thing that could happen to Ireland would be a blight of the men and let the ould seed die out and wait till the young crop of champions get ripe. [Laughter and cheers.] I know that the young Irish children—the new crop—are going to assert their rights.

At the house where I board in Dublin I heard the lady laughing the other day, and I asked her why she was laughing. She said she had just come from the back-yard where her children, two girls and a boy, were playing. The boy was marching up and down with a broomstick on his shoulder like a gun, and the girls were pretending to be weeping beside a lot of boards that were thrown down.

The lady asked what was the matter.

The boy said: "We're playing at evictions, and the constables have torn down our house, and I'm waiting till the landlord comes to shoot him." ["Hear, hear," and cheers.]

The young crop is all right and I've faith in the ould seed too. [Laughter.]

A Voice.—"Down with the constables."

Mr. Redpath.—No; let them alone. Most of them are right good fellows with Irish hearts; they sympathize with their people; they know they are doing mean work, but it is their duty, and *they* are not the men to blame. [Applause.] Now, I'll tell you how the Irish land agitation looks to an American. When any one asks for money from an American he never gets it unless there is a good reason for giving it. Before we would pay rent we would ask a landlord for his title. Suppose the Irish people were to do that, what would be the result?

There are three good and valid titles to land, and only three. The best title would be a title from the Creator. The Bible tells us that Moses gave that title. Nobody could dispute such a title. But, then, Moses never was in Ireland, and so we needn't discuss this supreme title to land. The next best title to land is founded on the truth that the land of a country belongs to all the people of the country. Now if all the people, by their representatives, give titles to pri-

THOMAS BRENNAN,
Secretary of the Irish National Land League.

vate property in land, that title is absolutely good, subject to whatever subsequent modifications may be needed for the promotion of the general welfare. That is the title by which private property in land is held in the United States. But there is no such title to land in Ireland. The Irish people never agreed to sell their lands to the stranger.

A VOICE.—" Never." [Applause.]

MR. REDPATH.—Before the English invasion the land belonged neither to the Irish kings nor chiefs, but to the sept; and the legal heirs to the old Irish septs are the whole people of Ireland of to-day. The third good title to land is the title conferred by military conquest. That is an absolutely valid title in law—but it is good only until the conquered people re-assert their rights [cheers]—not a day longer! Now, this is not a philosophical theory—it is international law. Two or three hundred years ago, the Germans were at war with France, and France seized and held two German provinces. A few years ago, France and Germany went to war again, and Germany seized and kept its old provinces of Alsace and Lorraine, and every Government in Europe, including the English Government, recognized the right of Germany to hold those provinces. Well, that shuts their mouths when you say that the lands that Cromwell stole are yours, and that the descendants of the psalm-singing savages who butchered men and women and unborn babes and stole their lands have no legal claim either to rent or purchase-money. No man should be paid for property until he can show that he has a just title to it. I have no respect for the Irishman who talks of fair rents and fixity of tenure as a solution of Irish distress. No rent *can* be fair unless the man who claims it has a valid title to the land.

Fixity of tenure is only a pretext for legalizing and perpetuating the curse of Cromwell. The larger part of the soil of Ireland is held by titles given by Elizabeth, Cromwell, or, viler still, by William of Orange—titles rendered possible only by the shameless violation of the treaty of Limerick. Why, the descendants of the men who now hold these lands ought to be right glad to give up their land without money and without price. They should be grateful that you do not insist that they shall pay back all the rent that they have collected for the last two hundred years. [Cheers.] They ought to be made to pay you compensation for disturbance to your ancestors! I suppose there are Fenians here? [Cries of "Yes," and cheers.]

MR. REDPATH.—Well, now, let me talk very plainly about two tender topics. I honor every man who sheds his blood for his country, or who is willing to do it. But there is no need of bloodshed. You can get all your rights without violence. Don't play into the hands of the English Government or the landlords by doing acts of violence. They would like to get you into trouble. They have ruled you for centuries by playing off one party against another—Orangeman against Catholic, and now Catholic against Atheist. Don't be fooled! It is of no sort of consequence to you whether a man goes to the Catholic church, or the Protestant church, or to no church at all—it is none of your business—but no matter what he believes or does not believe, if he fights for Ireland, stand by him. [Cheers.] I despise, from the bottom of my heart, every Irish M. P. who denounced Bradlaugh, who has always been the friend of Ireland, and then supported the souper-Jew, Beaconsfield, who has always been your enemy. Denounce both or neither; but if you must denounce one, curse the man whom O'Connell called the lineal descendant of the impenitent thief. [Cheers.]

Now, I shall talk very plainly about another thing. I understand that an attempt was made to disorganize this meeting or prevent it, because a priest somewhere here did not approve of it. If that is the truth I can afford to speak my mind, and I shall do it. No man in America has uttered such eulogistic words about the Irish priests—words of sincere and heartfelt admiration for their conduct during the famine—as I have written and spoken. But if any priest tells you that it is your religious duty to pay rack-rents, or if he defends the landlords in their exactions—then tell him that you will pay him the duty you owe to him as a Catholic in spiritual affairs, but that you will mind your own business in wordly affairs without his help. I honor the Irish priests because they are Irish patriots, and because, with all the wealth of England and the landlords to bribe them, so very few of them have been muzzled by money or cheap pasturage. But because you must shed no blood and do no violence, you must be men and not allow any human being to dictate to you. If an Irish priest is a patriot also —only a handful of them are not both —then honor him both as a priest and patriot; but if he is not a patriot, obey as a priest only. I have been told that there are in some parts of Mayo priests who say you should pay rents in order to obey the injunction, " Render unto Cæsar the things that are Cæsar's." Why, Cæsar is dead. [Laughter.] He never was in Ireland, and a man of the name of Brutus once rendered unto Cæsar the only tribute justly due to a tyrant—a dagger through his heart. Now, don't render unto any sort of Irish Cæsar such a tribute. There was no sort of need of violence at all. Will any good Catholic tell you that you rightfully owe tribute to the men who hold lands that were stolen from your forefathers because they refused to give up the Catholic faith—because they refused to swear that the Mass was an abomination ? You dishonor your martyred sires by advancing such a plea. Was Cromwell—the demon of Drogheda— a second Moses, empowered for ages to tax this people, and dispose of their lands ? Englishmen will not grant the Crown supplies for more than one year at a time—they know they can't trust the aristocracy—and yet it is claimed that it is right for the dead Cromwell's taxes to be levied in Ireland for two hundred years after his death for the benefit of the descendants of the soldiers who massacred your forefathers— not in battle only, but in cold blood. If any priest teaches such doctrine tell him to go to church and mind his own business—that there, and there only, you will obey him. [Cheers.] It is time for plain talk all round!

We Americans, without regard to Cromwellian theories, do not believe that any class of men, and especially the Irish landlords, have any right to drive the native population off in order to put sheep and bullocks on their homesteads. There will be no prosperity in Ireland until every tenant is his own landlord, and every landlord his own tenant. [Cheers.] How are you going to conquer? I told you not by bloodshed. Don't play into the hands of the landlords in that way. Do nothing that the constables or military can arrest you for doing. If you do England can throw fifty to one against you, and that is what the landlords want. [Cheers.] Organize! If every tenant-farmer in Ireland stood shoulder to shoulder the English Government would be powerless to help the landlords. They could never evict a whole people. Be united, do no violence, and by the operation of the law and the result of your union, the landlords will soon be thrown into the courts of bankruptcy. [Great cheers.]

Call up the terrible power of social excommunication! If any man is evicted from his holding let no man take it. If any man is mean enough to take it don't shoot him, but treat him as a leper. Encircle him with scorn and silence. Let no man or woman talk to him, or to his wife or children. If his children appear in the streets, don't let your children speak to them. If they go to school take your children away. If the man goes to buy goods in a shop, tell the shopkeeper that if he deals with him you will never trade with him again. If the man or his folks go to church leave it as they enter. If even death comes, let the man die unattended, save by the priest, and let him be buried unpitied. The sooner such men die the better for Ireland! If the landlord takes the land himself let no man work for him. Let his potatoes remain undug, his grass uncut, his crop wither in the field. This dreadful power, more potent than armies—the power of social excommunication—has only been used in our time by despots in the interests of despotism. Use it, you, for justice! No man can stand up against it except heroes, and heroes don't take the land from which a man has been evicted. In such a war, the only hope of success is to wage it without a blow—but without pity.

You must act as one man. Bayonets shrivel up like dry grass in presence of a people who will neither fight them nor submit to tyranny.

Americans will never give money again to the Irish tenants if they take it to pay landlords. If the landlords are poor let them work as we do. If some one must starve in Ireland let the landlords starve. [Cheers.] Turn about is fair play, and it is their turn now. But be united; don't quarrel among yourselves. The landlords have ruled you long enough by stimulating dissension in your own ranks. They are united. Every quarrel among patriots is worse than a hundred evictions.

[Cheers.] Act as one man! [Cheers.]

[Mr. Redpath subsequently found that the parish curate at Leenane (although he did not name him) had been unjustly accused of hostility to the Land League; that he was absent on clerical duty in the islands at the time of the meeting; and that he was not only friendly to the movement but president of a local branch. The unpleasantness originated in some hereditary feud between two prominent families in the neighborhood. Mr. Redpath, on being invited by Father Ganly to speak at his meeting at Maam, replied as fellows:

CLONBUR, September 25.

MY DEAR SIR: I regret that my duties will not permit me to accept your invitation to attend the land meeting at Maam on the 3d of October next, and the more especially as I am convinced that I did you an unintentional injustice in believing that you were hostile to the great and beneficent movement that seeks without violence to restore the land of Ireland to the people of Ireland. If priests and people will coöperate and work with a hearty zeal for this noble end, the landlords of Ireland will soon be made to feel that it is impossible to impoverish a race without their consent, and that in the presence of a united people constables are impotent and armies unavailing. Very truly yours,

JAMES REDPATH.]

VI.

"A MOST TREASONABLE SPEECH."

[Mr. Redpath was at Clare Morris, County Mayo, in September, 1880. During his stay, he was told that the more fiery spirits among the Fenians, or "advanced Nationalists," angry at the refusal of the Dublin Land League to appropriate money for the purchase of rifles, had sworn that they would break up the next Land League meetings in that neighborhood. Mr. Redpath was urged by a leading member of the Land League to make a speech at a meeting to which the leading Fenians would be invited, in order to show them that, in his judgment, the only hope for the Irish peasantry lay in the adoption of a bloodless policy, and that to oppose any sincere effort to lighten the burdens of the people would be as disastrous to the hopes of the Separatists as to the methods of the Agitators. The speech had the effect of producing harmony among the people. It was telegraphed quite fully to the English and Scotch journals, and aroused a whirlwind of abuse. It was pronounced "a most treasonable speech." This report is from the Castlebar *Telegraph*, with the passages that had to be suppressed as seditious restored.]

A LARGE meeting of the Clare Morris branch of the Land League was held on Sunday.

The Rev. James Corbett, C. C., was called to the chair. He spoke in very flattering terms of the services of Mr. Redpath, both in arousing American sympathy for the starving tenantry of Ireland during last winter in America, and thereby sending large sums of money to save them from starvation, and also by his vindication of the character of the Irish peasantry against the persistent and malignant aspersions of the English press. [Applause.] No man in Ireland or out of it had done more than Mr. Redpath to expose the iniquities of Irish landlordism, and to bring the Irish land question in its true light before the civilized world, and thereby force a just settlement of it before the English Parliament. [Loud applause.] His name was a household word in every cabin in Ireland, and his tribute to the Irish priests one of the most touching and eloquent vindications of their spiritual guides that had ever appeared in the English language.

MR. REDPATH, on rising, was received with loud cheers, and cries of "A thousand welcomes, and long life to you," and "Three cheers for the Stars and Stripes." He said:

Reverend Father and Gentlemen:—This is my second visit to Clare Morris. I was here last winter to see and to describe the distress that then existed here, and one of the sunniest memories of my life will be the knowledge that my reports of the misery I witnessed in this county were the means of increasing the American contributions for the relief of the starving peasantry of Connaught. I am here now not at the invitation exactly, but at the suggestion of one of your Mayo landlords—a person who carries the double-barreled name of Lord Oranmore and Browne. [Laughter.]

A few weeks since I made a wayside talk to the people of Leenane. I told them that after I went back to America, whenever I was asked whether it was the potato-blight that had brought on the famine, I said, "No; it was the landlord-blight," and I showed them how these landlords who shouted out so fiercely against confiscation owed their property to titles founded on the foulest confiscation, and I told them that not in justice only, but in law, these titles were good only until the Irish people could re-assert their rights and take back their lands. Every lawyer in Christendom knows that this is good law.

Your Lord Oranmore and Browne denounced this argument in the House of Lords. He ended his brainless if not brayless speech by advising me to "attend to my own business." That is why I am here. My business in Ireland, *this* time, is to explain to the American people why the Irish are so poor, although they are, as I say they are, one of the most frugal, and thrifty, and industrious races on the face of this earth to-day. Then why is Ireland the Lazarus Nation of our age—ever showing its wounds, and ever begging at the gates of the world's banqueting halls? I say it is because, under English rule, just as fast as the Irish toiler makes money, he is robbed of it by the lords of the soil, backed by British law. [Applause, and cries of "That's so!"] My business in Ireland is to expose the crimes of the Irish landlords, in order to vindicate the Irish people. [Applause.]

Now, I don't like to be lectured by a social inferior, and every king, queen, and lord in Europe is the inferior in rank of every republican on this globe. [Cheers.] No man is entitled to any respect who lives on the toil of others and renders no service to society. [Applause.] Kings and lords are the human vermin of society, who lurk and feed in its festering sores. [Applause.] I think Lord Oranmore and Browne —one or either or both of them [laughter]—was guilty of gross discourtesy in attacking me in the House of Lords, which no American would degrade himself by entering. [Laughter.] He might have sent me his advice by a half-rate message, or a postal-card that I could have answered without self-abasement. [Laughter.] But, as a cat may look at a king, so even a less worthy creature—an English lord— may give good advice to an American citizen, and therefore I overlooked the impertinence of this person, and came down here to investigate his pretensions to be regarded as the good landlord that he claims to be.

Here I am, in a room so near to Lord Oranmore's castle that the report of a rifle fired at the door could be heard in his bedroom—if he were in it. He said in the House of Lords that he never evicted a tenant. Men of Clare Morris, don't you all know that this is a falsehood? [Cries of "Yes."] Don't you know that, although he has never had the courage to run the risk of forcible evictions, yet he raised the rent so often and so much that he drove out from his estates all the more enterprising tenants? [Cries, "We do, we do."] Don't you know that as fast as the tenants between this village and his demesne improved their land, that he forced them from it, under the torture of the rack-rent, until they were all banished? [Cries of "Yes," and "We all know it."] Don't you know that his estate once supported hundreds of people, where it now supports only a few families? [Cries of "Yes."] Don't you all know that he never paid a shilling for the improvements made by his tenants that he confiscated? [Cries of "Yes."] Don't you know that every acre of his fine grazing farms was reclaimed from the wet bog at the expense of his tenants, and by their own unassisted toil? [Cries of "Yes."] Don't you know that as fast as he drove out men and women and children, he put in cattle and sheep and game? [Cries of "Yes."] Don't you all know how he induced his tenants who had good holdings to remove to the edges of a bog, under the pretext that he would give them fifteen acres of good land; and that he never redeemed his promise, but has reduced the people who were there then and the people who removed there, to one dead level of pauperism? [Cries of "We all know it."] Don't you all know one man who was driven insane, and is mad to-day, by these constant robberies and persecutions? [Cries of "Yes."] Don't you know that he broke all his pledges about cheap pasturage to the people whom he transplanted, and, instead of giving them fifteen acres, took not only half the land of tenants who had ten acres before, but even took half of the cabins, that they had built themselves, and put these "transplanted" tenants into them, without consent of their owners, or compensation? [Cries of "Yes, yes."] Don't you know that he is not content with robbing his tenants under the protection of the law, but that he is constantly annoying them about their religion, although he owes his title to the services of the Catholic clergy rendered to his father? [Cries of "Yes."] And don't you know that, although his tenants were all starving last winter, he never gave a single shilling to relieve them? [Cries of "Yes."]

Well, so do I know these things; and when I get time to "attend to my own business" I shall tell them to the whole world. [Applause.]

[Mr. Redpath here described some scenes that he had witnessed in the County Mayo a few months before.]

Some of these scenes moved me so profoundly last winter that I could not see them, nor speak of them, nor even think of them, in America—three thousand miles away—without tears rushing to my eyes. I have not done so much crying this time. If his reverence wasn't here I might confess that I had done a good deal of private swearing this time [laughter], and if your good priest called me to account for it I would tell him that a Yankee chaplain once saw an act of cruelty in the army and swore at it, and then defended himself at mess next morning by saying that no man could be a good Christian who would not swear in such circumstances. [Laughter and applause.] I can't look on with a pulseless indifference when I see a race of noble women, the wives of hard-working men, the mothers of splendid boys and of comely girls, trudging along without bonnets, without shoes, and thinly clad in all weathers, instead of being dressed as they ought to be dressed—warmly and in good attire all the time—and in purple and fine linen on Sunday and holidays. [Applause.]

Queens have had these feminine trappings quite long enough. I don't begrudge them such luxuries, not because they are queens and ladies, but because they are women, for no woman, I think, ever yet was dressed as well as every good woman ought to be. [Cheers and laughter.] But it is a high crime and misdemeanor for queens or the wives of lordlings to be sumptuously dressed by the robbery of the poor. [Cheers.] It is not the will of God that such things should be. [Cheers.] God tolerates such things as He tolerates other crimes, but it is blasphemy to say that God decrees one class of His creatures—and the meanest class—to live in riotous luxury, while the true nobles—the class who work—go naked and inhabit foul cabins and sleep beneath dirty rags, and live on potatoes and Indian meal all the year round. [Cheers.] Down with the blasphemers who say so! [Long continued cheering.]

It has been asked: "What is the remedy?" Ireland will never be as prosperous as the character and industry of her people entitle her to be until the land is owned by the tillers of the land [cheers] and by nobody else [cheers] —until there is not a man in Ireland who has the right to levy a tax unless he is a member of Parliament. [Cheers.]

Rent in the West of Ireland is a system of taxation by hereditary and irresponsible tax-masters. ["Hear!"] Rent in England, and elsewhere, for the most part is simply an interest on investments. If a landlord in England has a farm to let he improves it, he fences it, he drains it, he builds houses and offices on it at his own expense. The tenant only furnishes the stock in trade to work it. Here the tenant gets a bog that would not raise enough to feed a snipe, and he improves it himself at his own expense, and just as fast as he improves it up goes the rent. Isn't that true? [Cries of "Indeed, it is," from nearly all the audience.]

Talk of compensation to these hereditary robbers of the poor! One day Michael Davitt was listening in America to some talk about compensation to landlords. He asked my opinion. "Well," I said, "the landlords ought to be made to pay back every shilling that they ever took for rent for 200 years, unless they and their ancestors bought the land, and then they ought to be sent to work at hard labor for life to make up the balance due if they had not enough to pay the whole of it"; but as a compromise measure I suggested: "Suppose you sent them to the penitentiary for ten years a head." [Cheers.] If ever they get a shilling, —these men who hold estates by confiscation,—it should be paid, not as their right, for they have no equitable right, but as you would give ransom money for a brother who has fallen into the hands of bandits. ["Hear, hear."] Landlords who bought land or whose ancestors bought land should be paid for it by the state, but no man should be allowed to hold an acre in all Ireland that he does not live on and till. [Cheers.]

Land for the people is not enough; you ought never to cease to insist that Ireland must be ruled by the Irish. [Cheers.] After you have got the land and an Irish Parliament, then, if the people of Ireland demand nationality— a separate nationality—they have the right and it is their duty to work for it. [Cheers.] But this last right should be discussed apart from the other rights of Home Rule and of land for the people. I cannot understand how any Irishman would be satisfied even with the land for the people and Home Rule. If I were an Irishman I should never cease to work for the independence of Ireland. [Cheers.] Yet to me it seems self-evident that you will never achieve independence except by the sword; and if you believe that I am a friend of Ireland I shall tell you why. [Cries of "Go on!" and applause.] You should never allow any one but a friend even to discuss this question with you; for it is an insult to every Irishman to assume, as all arguments against Irish nationality assume, that Ireland has not the right of self-government, in the sense of independence, and that she could not govern herself as well as Switzerland, or France, or Belgium or any other nation. [Cheers.]

As for England, she never has governed herself—a small class has ruled her people always.*

But first let me say that there is a power before which all nations and legislatures now must bow—a power that as Irishmen you ought especially to respect, for it was first called into political action by an Irishman and the greatest of all Irish leaders—Daniel O'Connell. [Cheers.] It is organized public opinion. I think that by that power alone you can secure the land for the people, and secure Home Rule. Let me tell you how.

How has England kept its hold over Ireland for seven hundred years? Just as it got it at the beginning—by the quarrels of the Irish among themselves. How have the landlords been able to keep you all in rags and wretchedness? By your quarrels among yourselves. If Ireland had ever been united, England would have been forced to do justice to her. The remedy for Ireland's ills is so simple that, like the prophet's order—"Go wash in the Jordan and be clean"—I fear it may seem less attractive than learned disquisitions about the Brehon law or Portadown leases, or those quack prescriptions that never cure—commissions of inquiry. *Unite!* Ireland will never secure her full rights unless and until all the great classes and factions of the "common people" are united in one purpose, bloodless in its method, but inflexible in its spirit, until Catholic and Protestant, saint and sinner, Ulster as well as Connaught, are fused into one resistless body to demand that the land of Ireland shall become the property of the people of Ireland, and that the laws of Ireland shall be framed by the people of Ireland in an Irish Parliament. [Applause.]

The toilers of Ireland must do as the English mechanics have done; they

---

*" English liberty," said Mr. Redpath, at Chicago, "is the right that the ruling classes of England enjoy of robbing the toiling classes under the forms of law."

must form an organization that can be wielded as if it were a single body, each member of it loyally protecting every other member, so that the poorest fisherman in Donegal, the hungriest conacre man in Connaught, and the most ragged tenant in Kerry may believe and know that before a rapacious absentee landlord can bring the crowbar to destroy his humble cabin, he must first pass through the solid phalanx of the people of Ireland. [Applause.] You have all heard the trades-unions of England denounced, but whoever has studied their history will tell you that they saved the English mechanic from the condition of a serf.

When an honest tenant, unable to pay his rent on account of bad crops, is evicted from his farm, let no man take it; but if any man does take it, do not speak to him, or buy from him, or sell to him, or work for him, or stand at the same altar with him—let him feel that he is accursed and cast out from all your sympathies, he and every member of his family. Unless you do so, there is no hope for you, because as long as tenants will hire landlords will evict. [Applause.] Until this is done, until you have a solid Ireland, it is idle to believe that the absentee landlords will consent to sell their estates in Ireland. But as soon as this union is made perfect, as soon as all Ireland is a "United Irishman," the landlords will be powerless; for a universal strike against rent will at once force the English Parliament to act, and the world to listen and inquire into the causes of this national action. Irish landlordism is so monstrous an iniquity that it can live only in darkness; drag it to the blazing bar of the world's public opinion, and no plea except the plea of guilty would be entered against it. [Applause.] Suppose, for example, that every peasant in the West of Ireland was moved by one spirit, what could Lord Oranmore and Browne, or the Earl of Lucan, or the Marquis of Sligo do if every man refused to work for him, as a herd, or a laborer, or a gamekeeper? They could not bring in strangers? [Cries of "Oh! no!"] They would be obliged to sell their estates, or restore the tenants to the rich lands from which they were so pitilessly evicted after the famine of 1847! [Applause.] This great reform, as you see, can be achieved without shedding a drop of blood, without violence, without breaking any law—English, human, or divine (and they are three separate and distinct codes over here!)—and by *thus* accomplishing your object you will do more to prove to the world that England has slandered you for generations than if you were to wade to it through a lough of blood and over a causeway of corpses.

[Mr. Redpath then showed the value of resolute Parliamentary action illustrated in the earnest methods of Mr. Parnell and Mr. Biggar as contrasted with the mock-fight tactics of Mr. Shaw and Mr. Mitchell-Henry. "Most of the Home Rule Irish Members," he said, "are mere dress-parade soldiers—there is no fight in them." This part of the speech was not reported.]

Do I tell you in thus speaking to abandon your aspirations for nationality? I would rather that my tongue should wither; for I hope to live long enough to see Ireland an independent republic. [Cheers.] But if you think that independence can be secured by the sword only, then—as I have seen a little war myself—I advise you to deliberate gravely before you act, and to remember that war is a science needing vast supplies and drilled soldiers, experienced generals and a complex and expensive organization, and that steam and the telegraph have annihilated distance—that Kerry is nearer London to day for military purposes than Liverpool was in the days of the illustrious Wolfe Tone. [Cheers.] My friends, it is impossible for Ireland at this time to successfully fight England. The odds are too great against her. Strike out of the list of fighting men in Ireland all the Orangemen, all the landlords and their henchmen, all the well-to-do farmers and the vast majority of the Eastern and Northern tradesmen—the loyalists, the pacific and the indifferent—everybody whom love, or fear, or trade, or religion could influence—and England and Scotland, which would be a military unit against you, would have a terrible advantage, even if it were to be a hand-to-hand fight. But you are unarmed, undrilled, and poor; and England has unequaled facilities to hire men and to impress men, as well as absolutely illimitable resources in the machinery and material of war. Father John, brave as he was, and skillful as he was, could not repeat his career to-day,—nor could Wolfe Tone,—because this is the age of the steam cannon and the *mitrailleuse*, and of vast disciplined armies, and, above all, of the steamer and the locomotive. On Napoleon's estimate of the difference made by machinery in the fighting capacity of nations, you would have to overcome a disparity of eighteen against one. This is not my dictum; it is the dictum of the greatest soldier of modern times.

Be patient! Patience is not cowardice. It needs the highest courage. Seven hundred years of tyranny cannot be overthrown in a day in Ireland. Until the people are planted firmly on their lands, I can see no hope of a successful military revolt against English misrule. For that reason, and that reason only, if I were an Irishman, I might prepare for war, but I would certainly postpone any revolutionary efforts until the men on whom such a movement must rely for success could go forth to do battle consoled by the thought that, if they died for their country in the field, they did not leave their families in the power of petty landed despots, who would be glad to fling them out into the road-side to die. [Cheers.] All great men and all great races have succeeded by obeying the golden rule of success—do one thing at a time.

But, I beg of you, don't fight among yourselves. There is no need of it, and no sense in it. Land Leaguer, Home Ruler, and Nationalist, each in his own way is struggling for the welfare of Ireland, and each of them can have fight enough to satisfy even an Irishman [laughter] by striking at the landlords and the British Government. The land system of Ireland is the keystone of the house of tyranny. Kick it out, and then I hope and I believe that on a free soil, and with a people free, the blood of Ireland's myriads of political martyrs will quicken and blossom into a resplendent Irish nationality. [Cheers.]

["Mr. Redpath," said the report of the *Freeman's Journal*, " spoke rapidly for an hour and a quarter, and his speech was most enthusiastically received by all present. The conclusion especially, in which he urged unity of action between the three parties, many of whom were present, was most warmly applauded."]

VII.

HARVESTING FOR THE LAND LEAGUE.

[Under the head of "An Extraordinary Scene," the following special dispatch appeared in the *Freeman's Journal*, a few days after the report of the foregoing speech:]

(*Special Telegram from our Correspondent.*)
CLARE MORRIS, Tuesday Night.

FOR the last week the following placard has been posted in Clare Morris and some adjoining parishes:

"Hold the harvest! Last spring 2,000 men collected at Ballintaffy to sow the Land League farms. The crops are now ripe, and again the same men are called on to reap them. At his post then, every man! Come without fear and show your pluck, and that you are determined to keep your crops. Bring your scythes and hooks, and let every man who has a horse and cart bring them also to carry away in triumph the fruits of labor free of rent and taxes. The day is coming when every man's crop shall be free. To the front, then, on next Tuesday, the 14th inst. Men of Clare Morris and Gallen! Noble women and brave peasant girls, come you also and help to bind up the first sheaves of corn free of rent and taxes that have ever been reaped in Ireland. The land for the people! The crops for the people! Hold the harvest! God save Ireland!"

About eleven o'clock this morning a brake, in which were seated the members of the Clare Morris brass band, stopped at the presbytery for the Rev. James Corbett, C. C., and then at Ansborough hotel for Mr. Redpath, the American journalist, and Mr. J. P. Quinn, the Land League representative. The brake was driven through the streets of the town, the band playing "God Save Ireland." A large number of cars followed, and as the cavalcade went through the streets toward Ballintaffy, women, men, and children rushed to the doors shouting, "God bless you, Father Corbett!" Ballintaffy is four miles from Clare Morris. On the way the party overtook dozens of carts and large numbers of men on foot carrying scythes and sickles. I arrived at Ballintaffy about noon. More than an acre of "the Land League oats," as they are called here, had already been cut. About one hundred men, women, and young children were employed cutting and binding the oats. The arrival of the Rev. Mr. Corbett was received with loud and long-continued cheering by the reapers and binders. Men and women arrived until there were five or six hundred persons present, each of whom worked. Women apologized for the absence of their husbands by saying they were in England "earning the rint." Men and women were present from Clare Morris and the surrounding parishes, including Kiltinagh, Bohola, Balla, Facefield, Barnacarroll, Lagatample, Cloonconnor, Futagh, Drunikeen, Killeen, Ballyknave, Facefield Blies, Castlegar, Irishtown, Ballindine, Crossboyne, Mayfield, Aughervilla, Drimineen, etc. Quite a delegation of ladies from Clare Morris, Westport, and Balla, elegantly attired, were present to witness and take part in the work. I noticed some ladies dressed in the highest of fashion taking off their kid gloves, going down among the barefooted peasant women, and binding the sheaves.

Mr. Redpath assisted in carrying the sheaves to the carts. Five or six acres of oats were cut and carried to the carts, which conveyed them to Clare Morris in a few hours.

After the work was completed a meeting was held.

The Rev. James Corbett was moved to the chair, which was composed of a stook of oats.

The Rev. Mr. Corbett praised the people for having exhibited such a spirit of independence in coming to the defense of the rights of their own class. He explained some circumstances connected with the holdings, and then introduced Mr. James Redpath, who was received with loud cheers for "the Stars and Stripes," "The land of the free and the home of the brave," etc.

Mr. Redpath praised the patriot priest who had brought out his people last spring and planted these oats under the very shadow of British bayonets— for the constabulary, angry and armed, were there that day. Where were they to-day? Conquered by an unarmed and heroic priest and people. [Cheers.] This should teach the Irish nation a lesson—the irresistible force of moral courage and determination. Mr. Redpath then made an appeal for union of action and harmony among Irishmen of all classes. He reviewed briefly the history of Ireland, and showed that although the Irish were the "fightingest" race on this planet, England had been able to conquer them and maintain its conquest by making Irishmen fight among themselves. Mr. Redpath spoke in eulogistic terms of the noble conduct of the "barefooted ladies" who had shown that, whenever they were called on to do duty-work for Ireland, they would rally, but he hoped they would never do "duty-work, here"* for the landlords again. Mr. Redpath described British rule in Ireland as "the most tyrannical Government on the face of the earth." [Loud cheers.] Why, England could not endure a heptarchy, the rule of seven despots, and yet she insists on putting the Irish under the absolute control, not of seven, but of seven thousand irresponsible despots called landlords! He contrasted in sarcastic terms the conduct of the barefooted ladies before him, who cheerfully worked for their country, with the conduct of the Queen, who gave only one day's wages to the starving poor of Ireland. Landlordism in Ireland must die, if the Irish were ever to be a happy, contented, and prosperous people. [Cheers.] Irish landlordism had better tell its heirs and executors what sized coffin it wore; for the horologe of time had given warning that its hour of doom had come. But Ireland's liberation must come from Irish unity and courage, and not from English justice or patronage. He did not join in the eulogiums of Bright and Forster that some Irishmen uttered. He called them "buck-shot Quakers," and earnestly urged the tenantry to refuse to listen to pleas for fair rents and long leases, but to insist on a peasant proprietary. Half a loaf was *not* better than nothing if they could get the whole loaf—and the loaf was theirs. At the conclusion of Mr. Redpath's speech three cheers were given for him, and three more for the American republic.

A large number of carts were employed all day in carrying the oats to Clare Morris. When the work was done the largest brake, containing the band, followed by a long string of outside cars and a number of carts loaded with oats, moved back to Clare Morris. On passing the residence of a landlord, some one shouted out: "Death to landlordism!" and Mr. Redpath requested the band to play a funeral dirge. The band struck up the "Dead March in Saul," amid great applause. On the seat of the brake was a president of a branch of the Land League, carrying in his arms a sheaf of the oats. Every man in the cars wore an ear of the corn in his hat, and the ladies and

---

* "Duty-work" is a relic of feudal serf labor still enforced in the West of Ireland. By its terms, in addition to exorbitant rents, the hapless and helpless tenants are obliged to work for from one week to one month for their landlord every year without wages, and to feed themselves while working.

children were similarly decorated. On arriving at the outskirts of the town the band struck up "See, the conquering hero comes," and the streets were thickly lined with men, women, and children, who cheered for the Rev. Mr. Corbett and the Irish National League.

VIII.

"BETWEEN TWO LORDS SLAIN."

[Writing to a friend in America from Clonbur, County Galway, on Monday, September 26, 1880, Mr. Redpath told of an exceptional experience as a speaker in the West of Ireland.]

I MADE a speech here yesterday that I intended to be my last speech in Ireland. I was never in a position that needed so much tact and nerve. My friend, Father Conway, the Catholic curate here, had coaxed me to promise to make a speech at a Land Meeting to be held yesterday. I was wretched after I had agreed to speak, because I knew that many of the same people would be here who heard me at Leenane and Claremorris, and I could not think of any speech that it would be proper for a stranger to make, and I would not repeat myself. As I was walking up and down the lane near the church, I noticed the image of St. Patrick and that gave me an idea for a speech. As I was working it out in my mind, a citizen of the place joined me. One after another, seven or eight "outside cars" passed me on their way to the constabulary head-quarters. Each jaunting-car had four armed constables on it. I asked why they were coming?

"Oh!" said my companion, "don't you know the Government has sent down a short-hand writer to report your speech to-morrow, and these constables are here to protect him?"

That information inspired me. As these cars reached the head of the lane, a gentleman dressed in light clothing stopped each of them and spoke to the constables.

"Who is that man?" I asked.

"Lord Montmorris."

"And who is he?"

"A landlord near here," was the answer.

As Father Conway drove up,—he had been at Ballinrobe,—I looked at my watch. It was a quarter before six.

We staid up rather late, as the curate was waiting for a friend. A little after ten o'clock a parishioner came in and announced that Lord Montmorris had been murdered, and his body found on the road-side about a mile from Clonbur!

Next morning,—yesterday,—thousands of people came to Clonbur to attend the Land Meeting. I mingled among them, but heard no expressions of sympathy for the slain lord. The nearest approach to pity was the remark of an old woman, "Sure, he wasn't worth killing!" Lord Montmorris died unwept as he had lived unloved—a corrupt magistrate and a profligate man. He had long since been hated and despised by all classes. Still, I knew how this murder would be regarded in England, and I suggested that the Land Meeting should be postponed. No one agreed with me that it would be wise to postpone it. So, I *must* speak and denounce the murder among a people indifferent to it, and advocate social excommunication after I had been told that this sort of advice *might* possibly be construed as sedition—and there was the Government reporter to take down my words!

A SPEECH BY JAMES REDPATH.

The platform was built inside the church-grounds, and against the walls of the church. Right opposite, on the other side of the lane, were the high walls that inclosed a lawn that had once been Lord Leitrim's estate. Imagine my position—behind me, two miles away, Lord Montmorris, slain; at my back, a reporter, who came as a spy and informer; around me a crowd of people who had hated the murdered lord, and some of whom had just cause to hate him; in front of me, a detachment of the Irish constabulary, and behind them the estate of Lord Leitrim! I stood between two slain lords, and I thought, as I rose to speak, I wonder if the man or men who killed Lord Montmorris are cheering me? Talk about inspiration from audiences—*here* was the regular *poteen* of oratory!

[This report is reprinted from the Castlebar *Telegraph*, with one or two "seditious" passages supplied from memory within a few days after the delivery of the speech.]

Rev. Chairman, Rev. Fathers, Ladies and Gentlemen:

I have noticed that it is the custom of Irish audiences, in a good-natured way, to interrupt a speaker—sometimes by asking questions, and sometimes by interjecting remarks, not always quite in consonance with the views of the speaker. This custom has a tendency to divert the current of a speaker's thought, especially if he is not accustomed (as I am not accustomed) to address public audiences. I ask of you the favor to listen to me in silence. For every man who addresses you should weigh well his words this day. Whatever he says, or may refrain from saying, if a single word he utters, or even if his silence, can be distorted by malice, your enemies will seize on it to seek to injure your cause. He will be charged with inciting a spirit that he reprobates, and approving crimes that he abhors. The dark deed of an individual, or of individuals, will be charged on this community, and whoever is regarded as your friend will be held responsible for offenses of which you are as innocent as your calumniators.

On the other side of that wall in front of us lies one of the estates of the late Lord Leitrim, who was slain in Donegal. Two miles behind us lies the body of Lord Montmorris, who was slain last night. Around us are representatives of the armed constabulary by whom the town is garrisoned. At my side is a reporter, paid by the Government to write down every word we utter here. It is a time to be brave, but to be wise as well; to proclaim the truth, but to give no weapons to your enemies.

Let me congratulate John Bright that at last I see a peaceful audience assembled in Ireland to discuss their grievances without having detachments of constabulary, with loaded muskets, among them; that the time has come when the constabulary, although they are here, attend your meetings as private gentlemen. [Applause.]

It was time that these outrages on the right of free speech should cease, or that John Bright should withdraw from a Government that practiced them, or that Americans should blot out the name of that man, as a lost leader, from the roll of Englishmen whom they have been taught to love.

I hope when next I visit Ireland, I shall be able to report that not only have the constabulary been removed, but that John Bright no longer sullies his once noble record by consenting to belong to a Government that still employs stenographic spies!

The tragic death of the unhappy lord who lies dead to-day will be charged by your enemies to the land agitation. I never heard the name of the dead lord until a day or two ago, and I had already forgotten it when the dreadful crime of last night brought it to every man's lips. But this I do know—that wherever in Ireland the Land League is strong, there not one drop of the blood of sheep or cattle or of man has been shed. Here, as you all know, the Land League was weak, and you know how the landlords in this neighborhood tried to suppress it. Lord Montmorris dead is a stronger ally of Irish landlordism than Lord Montmorris living. The man or the men who slew him have not injured Irish landlordism. They have injured the cause of the Irish tenantry—for although you are innocent, the landlords have still the ear of Europe and your defense will not be heard there. O'Connell said that whoever commits a crime strengthens the enemy. The crimes of the Irish landlords have strengthened your cause in America. Europe is beginning to listen to the story of your wrongs, and, if you avoid crimes and sternly repress them, the verdict of Christendom will soon be rendered in your favor. Every crime delays the day of justice to Ireland. Give violence no countenance, but regard every criminal as your enemy.

But do not submit in silence to slanders! Give blow for blow, and spare no man who libels you! Let me set you an example! In the last number of the *Nineteenth Century*, James Anthony Froude, the most malignant enemy of the Irish race, characterizes the assassination of Lord Leitrim as an agrarian outrage, and then dares, I am told, to call the noble patriots who surround Mr. Parnell " the patrons of anarchy and defenders of assassination." I am talking now, am I not, to hundreds of men and women who knew Lord Leitrim and were his tenants ? [Shouts of " Yes ! " from the audience.] Did Lord Leitrim not bear the reputation of being one of the vilest lepers in social life ? [Shouts of " Yes ! "] Don't his tenants say that he flung a score at least of young girls into the brothels of Liverpool and New York? [" Yes ! "] Was not that his reputation ? [" Yes ! "] Is it not believed by every one that he was killed on account of his personal offenses ? [" Yes ! "] Yes; these facts are as well known in Galway and Donegal as the similar offenses of Nero and of Henry the Eighth. Yet Froude dares to charge the Irish political leaders with being " patrons of assassination," because this leprous Lord Leitrim was slain. I denounce James Anthony Froude before Christendom as the patron of seduction and the defender of debauchery. [Loud cheers.] It is time to talk plainly, and to brand the slanderers of your race as they deserve. [Cheers.] I dare James Anthony Froude to say that he would have introduced his wife or daughter to Lord Leitrim. [Cheers.] [Turning to the Government reporter:] Has John Bright's spy got that down ? [Cheers from the audience.]

I am not defending the slayer of Lord Leitrim : I am only vindicating the Irish character. Assassination helps no good cause. Napoleon said that in war a blunder is worse than a crime; and assassination is not only a crime, but a blunder. I will tell you how to obtain your just rights without a crime, without shedding one drop of blood, without doing anything that the Queen of England does not do, that the aristocracy of England have not done for generations, that the Irish landlords do not countenance at this hour, and that the Catholic Church has not sanctioned and practiced for centuries. I will not tell you to do anything in conflict with British laws and the British Constitution. Now, don't frown when I say British Constitution! My friends, it is true of the British Constitution what the old lady said of the doctrine of total depravity: " It's a very good thing if it's only lived up to ! " [Laughter.] The trouble in Ireland has been that only the landlords have been able to take advantage of the British Constitution !

Why have the landlords so much greater power in Ireland than in any other civilized country ? You know, but the world does not know, and, therefore, it is so hard for foreign nations to understand your wrongs. The despotic power of the Irish landlords comes from the fact that there is no diversity of industry in Ireland—that in this western country every one must live by the soil, or *die*. Why are there no manufactures here? Because England destroyed the woolen manufactures in William of Orange's time, and then prohibited the establishment of other industries for long generations. She has given the soil of Ireland to aliens; her laws have imperiously prevented the transfer of the soil; and she has thus made it impossible to develop the mineral and even the fishing resources of the West. Her evil eye has blighted every industry, excepting agriculture only, and that industry she suffers to exist at the price of the serfdom of the tillers of the soil. She makes the landlord the absolute master of the lives and fortunes of her people. He can drive them into the road-side, or into the poor-house, or into exile, or into the grave; leaving the land a desert, or a game-cover, or a grazing farm; destroying every village trade, and every calling, and every profession at his sovereign will and pleasure, and then blaspheming the God who made this earth for the people thereof by calling this heartless, this heathen system, the enforcement of the rights of property. The landlord confiscates not the wages of toil only, but the visible results of it; and this is not defended by English opinion only, but enforced by English law. Whoever dares to deny the right of any man to drive an innocent people into exile is called a communist by these brawling parasites of the greatest communists on earth!

To destroy the power of the landlord you must refuse to help him in his cruel work of eviction and confiscation. If a landlord evicts a poor tenant, do not take that farm, nor work on it for any one; you violate no law in refusing to take or to labor on such a farm, but you do rivet the chains of your people if you do *not* refuse to take it, or do not refuse to work on it. [To the reporter:] Has John Bright's spy got that down? [Laughter.]

But if a man *does* take a farm from which a poor tenant has been evicted, I conjure you to do him no bodily harm. [To the reporter:] Get ready, John Bright's spy! Act toward him as the Queen of England would act to you if she lived in Clonbur! Act toward his wife as the Queen of England would act toward your good wife if she lived in Clonbur! Act toward his children as the Queen of England would act toward your children! The Queen of England would not speak to you, she would not speak to your wife, she would not speak to your children. She would not regard you, your wife, nor your children as her equals. Now, imitate the Queen of England, and don't speak to a land-grabber, nor to a land-grabber's wife, nor to a land-grabber's children. [Cheers.] *They* are not *your* equals! Do as the Queen of England does, and you will violate no law of England! [To the reporter:] Has John Bright's spy got that down? [Laughter.] Oh! my friends, be loyal! [Laughter.]

If a land-grabber comes to town, and wants to sell anything, don't do him any bodily harm; only act as the rich landlords in Mayo and Galway have acted toward my friend from Clare Morris here [pointing to Mr. Gordon, who stood on the platform]. You all know that Mr. Gordon is the best boot-maker in Connaught [cries of "Sure we do!" "He is, indeed"], and that he once employed about a dozen workmen. He made all the boots and shoes for the gentry in this part of the country. Just as soon as he addressed a Land League meeting, his custom fell off, the landlords wouldn't buy shoes from him, and my friend Gordon was almost ruined. Now, imitate these landlords. If you see a land-grabber going to a shop to buy bread, or clothing, or even whisky, go you to the shop-keeper at once; don't threaten him; it is illegal to threaten any one, you know; just say to him that under

British law he has the undoubted right, that you wont dispute, to sell his goods to any one,—don't forget to say all that,—but that there is no British law to compel you to buy another penny's worth from him, and that you will never again do it as long as you live, if he sells anything to a land-grabber. The landlords wont buy their boots from Mr. Gordon because he is *your* friend; now, don't you buy your goods from any shop-keeper who is their friend. [Cheers.] [To the reporter:] Has John Bright's spy got that down?

Don't buy anything from a land-grabber. This policy is truly loyal and conservative British policy. The British laws make it almost impossible for you to buy a lot of ground from a landlord—so don't buy anything from his friends until they repeal their laws. Imitate the landlords! [To the reporter:] Has John Bright's spy got that down? [Laughter.]

If the land-grabber sends his children to school, don't drive them away. They have the right to go there. Act as the Queen of England would act if your children forced their way to the same school with her children. Take your children away. [Applause.] You have a right to do so, and if you did so it would soon cause some of the teachers who have been muzzled by the landlords to become advocates of your rights. [Cheers.] [To the reporter:] Has John Bright's spy got that down? [Laughter.]

If the land-grabber goes to the Mass, don't drive him away. One by one, quietly and decently, without disturbing the services, go out of the church, and leave him and his family alone with the priest. They need praying for. [Laughter.] If a noisy and drunken man entered the church, the priest would tell you to withdraw, so that there might be no disturbance in the chapel. Act in the same way when the land-grabber enters it—for he is worse than a drunkard and a brawler.

For centuries the royal families and the aristocracies of Europe and the landed gentry of Ireland have socially excommunicated—they call it ostracized—whole classes and professions, and even races. Follow their example, not in the interests of social pride, but in the interests of sacred principle—and they will find that this sword is two-edged, and that they have no longer a monopoly of the hilt! [Cheers.] Surely, my friends, if kings can do no wrong, and if aristocracies *are* the nobility, and if the gentry are in fact, as well as pretense, a superior class—you would not only violate no law, but you would be entitled to great praise for imitating their illustrious example. [Cheers.] [To the reporter:] Has John Bright's spy got that down? [Laughter.]

This is no new policy. I am advocating only a new application of an ancient policy. Once Europe was a vast camp of armed men. And yet we read that the haughtiest emperor of Europe was once forced to kneel in the snow, a suppliant, for three days and nights at the door of a priest who had not an armed soldier to obey his orders. What power brought the armored prince to the feet of the unarmed Pope? It was the terrible weapon of religious excommunication. That weapon you cannot wield in defense of your rights; but the next keenest weapon—the power of social excommunication—is yours, and no law of the state nor of the church forbids you to draw it. [To the reporter:] Has John Bright's spy got that down?

[Pointing to the statue of St. Patrick over the church door, Mr. Redpath continued:]

Since the sandals of St. Patrick first pressed the soil of pagan Ireland—since he planted here, never more to be overthrown, the radiant banner of the Christian faith, there never yet has sprung from the illumined heart of any Irish patriot a project so worthy of that flag and that faith as the movement that the Land League is now sending forth its heralds to summon you to join,

Its creed is pure; its ways are wise; its aim is divine. It is the latest and the ripest fruit of the sacred seeds that St. Patrick sowed. [Applause.] The saints and heroes of a century that has been dead for centuries devoutly prayed and bravely fought for the recovery of the Holy Sepulcher and the rescue of the Holy Land from the "infidel Saracens." You are called to a kindred crusade—to rescue the holy land of Ireland from the infidel Saracens of the nineteenth century—the Irish landlords! Never has "The Isle of Saints" given birth to a man so saintly that his white robes would have been sullied by fighting the battles of this new crusade. Ah, no! they would have shone with a more luminous purity thereby. [Cheers and applause.]

And in this holy land there is a prize more precious than even that empty sepulcher, forever sacred, in which once lay buried the Holy Body. You know Who it was Who said that whoso feeds the hungry, and clothes the naked, and breaks the chains of the captive, gives bread to, and raiment, and liberates, not the earthly disciple needy, but the Heavenly Master in want. This sublime and sacred utterance consecrates and sanctifies the West of Ireland—this old home of wrinkled sorrow—as the Holy Land of our day, the Holy Land in which, ragged and hungry, and at the mercy of men without mercy, the living Lord Himself inhabits every wretched hovel in these sterile hill-foots and these stony mountain-slopes. [Loud cheers.]

It is a heroic Christian crusade—this bloodless warfare that you are waging—for the recovery of the holy land of Ireland for the people of Ireland.

The Saracens were called robbers because they held a Holy Land by virtue of a military conquest. The Saracens were called infidels because they did not believe in the truths of the Christian religion. For the same reasons, and by the same token, are not the great landlords of the West of Ireland the infidel Saracens of our day? You can tell a man's real religion in one way only—not by listening to what he says, but by looking at what he does. By a cuttle-fish rhetoric a man may hide the truth, but his acts will betray him. [Cheers.]

What is the real religion of the great landlords of the West of Ireland? Translated into words—not by their lips, but by their deeds—the religion of these landlords is the most purely pagan religion of any age or of any race on this planet to-day. [Loud applause.]

I shall not sully my lips by repeating every article of the landlord's creed, but I shall quote two or three of the more fundamental dogmas of it.

The first article of the landlord's creed is this: "I believe that the Creator intended that the land of a country should be owned, not by the native inhabitants of the country, but by any accidental conqueror of the country, and that it should be divided, not even among the soldiers who made that confiscation possible, but exclusively among a few favorite officers who strengthened and extended the power of a foreign king, or among the parasites of a regal court, who served his selfish purposes, or flattered his vanity, or yielded to his lust." On these two dead branches of a upas-tree hang most of the titles of the great landed proprietors of Ireland to-day.

The second article of the landlord's creed is like unto the first article. It reads: "I believe that the land of Ireland and the people of Ireland were created for the sole purpose of administering to the comfort and convenience of the Irish landlords." [Loud applause.] You all know, men of Galway, with how remorseless a thoroughness the great landlords of the West of Ireland have enforced this article of their heathen creed. Thousands of schools, and churches, and villages in the West of Ireland; tens of thousands of the cabins of the toilers of the soil and of the sea; and hundreds of thousands of laborers, and mechanics, and artisans, and teachers, and scholars, and priests—by individuals, and by districts—have been swept away as if a pestilence had passed over them, throughout all this Land of Sighs, by these hereditary "Huns and Vandals," who use not the flaming sword of a "scourge of God," but the civil decree of the process-server — Huns who hide their cowardly heads in foreign gambling hells; Vandals who hire a native constabulary to destroy the homes of the people of Ireland. [Loud cheers.]

The third article of the landlord's creed is that the Irish family has no rights that the Irish gamekeeper is bound to respect; that whenever the little holding of the farmer, by his own toil, or by the toil of his forefathers, reclaimed from barrenness, is necessary for the welfare of his hares and rabbits and grouse, the fathers, and mothers, and little ones must be driven out that the ground game and wild fowl may fatten. [Applause.] Every one of you can testify that the tourist traveling from the sea in any direction in this county must pass through a wild and deserted country, desolated not by conquerors in the interest of their race, but by landlords in the interest of their rabbits.

Americans regard their Government as an organization for the protection of the rights of men. The Irish landlords regard the British Government as an institution, not for the protection of human rights, but for the more perfect conservation of feudal prerogatives—prerogatives everywhere, elsewhere, even in England, either so tempered by usage that they have lost their ancient power to oppress, or abolished by law, or abrogated by custom or contempt.

The people of England and Scotland are governed by the laws of England. If the people of Ireland were governed by the laws of England, then their grievances might be justly, however ungenerously, classified as sentimental grievances.

But the West of Ireland is not governed by the people nor by the laws of England, excepting as they are auxiliaries to the despotic government of the landlords. The people of England would not endure the wrongs you suffer from the tyranny of the landlords; nor, I believe, would they permit you to endure them if they knew the true story of your wrongs. But, breathing the moral malaria of London social life, that so soon poisons even Irish Parliamentary patriots, the leaders of the British parties and the British press—and especially the self-named "Liberal" journals—papers like the *Daily News*, for example, and the London *Times*, edited by intellectual eunuchs for intellectual serfs—one and all persistently refuse to report the whole truth about Ireland, or to listen with patience to her story.

And yet, there is no more important question for England than the Irish question, whether it is regarded from a national or an international point of view. The Irish landlords have made a tool of the British Government and a fool of the British people for generations. When I go back to America, I shall say, and I shall prove by examples—giving names and dates, and figures and estates—that there is no parallel to the oppression that the Irish peasantry endure in all Europe to-day, excepting in the Christian provinces of Turkey, where the taxes are farmed out to Mohammedans. [Loud cheers.] These landlords have escaped exposure before Christendom, because by their law of libel they can ruin any editor who tells of their cruelties. [Applause.] Standing at my side is a Mayo editor who received a threatening letter from the great landlord in this parish, warning him of the consequences if he did not publish a paragraph that the statements of your honored and heroic curate were false.* That letter was a legal letter, written in legal terms; not in a disguised hand, but by a solicitor. The laws of England protect Lord Ardilaun in sending it. But the law of English libel does not run in America, and my Lord Double X will find that journalists are an international fraternity, and will stand by each other against any invader of their rights. [Cheers.]

What would England have said if three millions of Christians had been expelled from Turkey, or starved into the grave, for no offense except that for a single famine year they could not pay extortionate taxation? England would have flung the Sultan and his hosts out of Europe headlong into Asia. But the Irish landlords have driven three millions of Irish Christians into their graves and from *their* native country, and England has looked on and helped them, and sternly punished every effort of the people to resist this expulsion. [Cheers.] For three centuries, the rule of the landlord has been one long record of ruin and disaster; and yet to-day, as in the days of Cromwell, the only remedy of the lords of the soil is—exile or exterminate the Irish! Once their cry was, "To hell or Connaught!" Now it is, "To the poor-house or America!"

Do the British statesmen never pause to ask themselves whether, in continuing to be the lackeys and executioners of the Irish landlords—whether, in driving away these sore-hearted Irish exiles—they may not be sowing the winds that will ripen into a hurricane of hatred against England? Where do these peasants go, who have been expelled to give place to pheasants? I will tell them. They go to a land that has not one cause to love the British Government, and many reasons to hate it. Every Irish exile becomes a missionary of hate, to quicken, to keep alive, and to fan every spark of animosity against England. [Cheers.] There are already in America, at the lowest computation, sixteen millions of citizens of Irish birth and Irish descent. Their numbers and their influence are daily increasing. If there is any man in America of Irish descent who does not hate the British Government—barring here and there a solitary Orangeman—I never met that man, nor ever heard of him.

How is it with the native Americans? The Americans have a kindly regard for the English people; but, North and South, they have no good-will to the British Government. American flunkeys in England often fawn on English society, and our embassadors, as in duty bound, prophesy smooth things. Do you know why we send poets to England? Because poets are of imagination all compact; and when an American talks in England of American friendship for the British Government, he needs must depend wholly for his facts on his imagination. [Applause.] But British statesmen should know the truth; and, however distasteful the truth may be, it is a fact that the leaders of the South hate the British Government, because they believe that they would have succeeded if England had recognized their Confederacy, and that the people of the North have neither forgotten nor forgiven the destruction of our commerce and the hostile spirit of British statesmen and the British press during our long years of national agony. [Applause.]

Is it wise to drive missionaries of hatred by the millions to America?

---

* The editor was Mr. James Daley, of the Castlebar *Telegraph*, who—like Mr. Gordon, previously referred to—is now [May 1, 1881] in jail, without trial or accusation, at the instance of the recreant Quakers, Mr. Secretary Forster and Mr. John Bright, who act as the pious figure-heads for this infamous suppression of free speech and a free press in Ireland. The Lord Ardilaun is Sir Arthur Guiness, whose family was "ennobled" by Beaconsfield. The Guinesses have always been partisans and parasites of English tyranny in Ireland; they have grown rich—and "noble"—by selling Dublin porter, and thereby debauching five generations of Irishmen.

Would it not be better, looking to the long future, to abolish the system that furnishes fresh fuel to such a smoldering fire? But what care the Irish landlords? What care they for an American alliance? They must keep their rabbits and get their rents, even should races perish or empires grapple in the strife.

The creed of the landlord is paganism. The fruit of his rule is serfdom. Don't be afraid of hard names. These pagans call you communists, because you demand peasant proprietary. Why, all the great minds of modern political science have advocated the institution of peasant proprietary; and, what is better even than their approval, the example of a prosperity unparalleled before, wherever peasant proprietary has been established, is the conclusive and irrefutable answer to these brawling inanities. What was statesmanship with Hardenburg and Stein in Germany cannot be communism with Parnell and Davitt in Connaught. [Cheers.]

Who opposes the landlords? The Land League. [Cheers for the Land League.]

What is its creed? The Land League teaches that God endowed all men with equal rights to the soil; that the land of a country is the property of the whole people of the country, which they alone can alienate, and then only in perpetual trust, always subject to such laws as shall promote, not the selfish interests of a class, but the general prosperity; that the system that breeds, and for centuries has bred, hunger in hovels, wretchedness in rags, indigence and ignorance—empty stomachs and empty heads—to the end that rich brewers may hunt over the sites of ancestral homesteads, and rich brokers * may mock Heaven by attempting to revive feudalism in the nineteenth century—that pheasants may fatten and peasants grow gaunt—that the existing system of feudal land tenure in the West of Ireland is in its origin immoral, despotic in its government, and by its influence destructive alike of material prosperity and intellectual development—and that, therefore, having being weighed in the balances of time and found wanting, it shall be thrown down and destroyed utterly and forever. [Cheers.] The triumph of the Land League will be a triumph of civilization over barbarism—a triumph of democracy over feudalism—a triumph of human rights over blood-rusted prerogatives.

Again, men of Galway, it is the old battle with new banners and new warcries, but waged against the same old foe.

Again, it is the auroral dawn of a civilization of liberty and light that is dispelling the Egyptian darkness of an ancient despotism.

Again, it is the people against the aristocracy.

Again, it is the spirit of St. Patrick, with unlifted hands, invoking the aid of Heaven against the oppressors of God's poor.

Under which banner, men of Galway, will you fight—under the green banner of the Irish saint, or under the black flag of the Irish lord? [Cries of "St. Patrick," and cheers.] "Choose ye this day whom ye will serve," and having chosen, stand firm, listening to the voice of no charmer, charm he ever so wisely; and, ere long, without a crime, but without a doubt, Ireland will be held by her people and tilled for her people, and, once thus held, this prayer-perfumed Isle of Saints, the home and altar of the Virgin Mother of the Nations, who has wept for centuries in grief, but never once blushed in shame, at the slaughter of her firstborn, slain for the sweet love of her—this Holy Land of Ireland, for a thousand generations to come, liberated from tyranny and luminous with virtue, will be the chosen heritage and

---

* Many of Mr. Mitchell-Henry's tenants were at this meeting.

CHARLES STEWART PARNELL,
President of the Irish National Land League.

perpetual inheritance of the Irish race. [Loud and long-continued cheering.]

"Mr. Redpath," says the Dublin *Nation*, "was serenaded at the residence of Father Conway in the evening by two bands and a great concourse of people. He made a second speech, which he announced would be his farewell speech in Ireland."

IX.
ST. BRIDGET AND BRIDGET.

[This speech, published in the Boston *Pilot*, is preceded by a letter from Mr. Redpath, dated New York, December 3, 1880, in which he writes: "MY DEAR BOYLE O'REILLY: As you have published the speeches that I delivered in Ireland, I send you a speech that I wrote *to be* delivered in America, but which must remain an unspoken speech, because I cannot read it aloud. *You* liked my other speeches, but this is the speech *I* like. I intended to make it in response to the toast of 'St. Bridget and Bridget,' at the little supper you and my other Irish friends promised me at my next visit to Boston. I wrote it one day in Dublin, about three months ago, after I had come back from Mayo, and had again seen the agonies of separation at the railway stations—scenes that nearly drove me wild last winter, and that I can never recall without keen suffering. The thoughts these scenes give rise to I noted down, intending, by and by, to put them into a more perfect form. But I send them as I wrote them, with only two or three slight alterations. I can never deliver the speech, because when I come to tell of the partings I do not see the words I wrote, but the agonies I witnessed, and my heart chokes. If you care to publish it, you can do so and welcome. Ever your friend, JAMES REDPATH."]

THERE was once a saint in Ireland who bore the name of Bridget. From the nature of the discussions, largely carried on by American ladies, that appear from time to time in the Boston dailies, I long ago came to the conclusion that, if a consensus of Yankee opinion could be obtained, it would be found to be a quite common belief in our beloved land that St. Bridget left no successor of her own name.

"One-half of the world does not know how the other half lives." This famous utterance is the dim shadow of a finger-post that shows how far away yet is the good time coming, foreseen by the poets and the prophets. A century often separates our kitchens and our parlors. The struggle that is going on in Europe to-day between the Coming and the Past, between Democracy and Feudalism, is felt, in another form, in almost every wealthy household in America. There, in the Old World, Feudal Oppression still strives to conserve its power to dominate and debase; here, in the New World, the homes of the nineteenth century are often made unhappy by the mischief that it has already wrought. There, the oppression of the feudal classes has driven millions into hovels so wretched, and has kept them in squalor so foul; it has forced them to lodge in cabins, without other floors than the damp earth, without stoves, without grates, without mirrors, without wash-stands, without wash-tubs, without towels, without sheets, without blankets, often without windows and without chimneys; it has doomed the young Irish peasant girls and Irish peasant mothers, and the gray-haired Irish grandmothers, and even the great-grandmothers, to go for months, and sometimes for years, without shoes and stockings, without decent underclothing, without any single article of feminine adornment or luxury; it has fed them for generations on a diet fit only for the beasts that perish—on potatoes or Indian meal and skim-milk thrice a day, with meat only once or twice a year; it has kept them in compulsory ignorance for so many centuries past, and up to a period within the memory of men still living, by every device that selfishness could devise and cruelty could enforce, feudal England has so pitilessly suppressed the Irish intellect and oppressed the Irish heart that, when it coronates its crimes by expelling the Irish poor by city-fulls from the land of their birth, her champions have found it easy to convert other nations, and especially our people, to their own infamous creed that the sufferings of the Irish people are the natural result of their own vices and faults of character. England, by her policy in Ireland,—not for this or any one generation only, but for seven red centuries,—has fed and lodged the Irish peasantry as we feed our pigs—although American farmers house their pigs in greater comfort. England has sternly and remorselessly, for seven hundred years, kept the Irish peasantry outside the pale of European civilization, by a wall made of bayonets; and now, when she hurls them by the million into our complex and affluent civilization, when we find their children awkward in the handling of utensils that they had never even heard of at home, careless as to a cleanliness that it was impossible to cultivate in their dark and smoky cabins, and apt—as all newly emancipated people are apt—to forget that discipline is not only not incompatible with social democracy, but essential to an order based on liberty,—England, by her hirelings and parasites, pointing to poor "Patrick's" and "Bridget's" short-comings, plays the part of "Dick Deadeye" with the pomp of a "Turveydrop," and says: "I told you so! I told you so!"

When I was in Ireland I found that whatever the British tourists said about the Irish peasants, as a general rule, was the exact opposite of the truth. When the Southern "Ku-Klux" shouted that the negroes were committing outrages, everybody knew, if he had studied the history of the ten years after Appomattox, that the haters of the blacks had been doing some mischief, and were trying to conceal it. It is the same in Ireland. The methods and the apologies for tyranny are essentially the same in every country. It is always the rich robber who shouts "Stop thief." In Ireland, it is the landed class who commit agrarian outrages—who accuse the landless toilers of agrarian outrages. And, in the case of Bridget, it is the class who have kept her in enforced ignorance at home, and in compulsory penury, who should be held responsible for her ignorance of the machinery of opulence in America. She is not to blame, and she ought not to be blamed for it. When our American ladies suffer annoyance at Bridget's want of skill, they should not be angry at their servant, but at feudal England, for it. And, if they would take the trouble to try and learn from their "Irish servant-girls" the true story of their life at home, they would sometimes make a discovery that would surely astound them—that St. Bridget *had* left successors who bore her name; that many of these Irish servant-girls, who so often "try" American patience by their ignorance, and provoke American petulance by their awkwardness, have braved dangers of the sea and perils of the unknown lands that the Puritan saints have been almost canonized for confronting; and that they have faced and overthrown temptations which Catholic saints *have* been canonized for resisting. They might discover at the same moment that some of the traits that American ladies most strongly condemn in the character of their "hired girls" are neither vices nor faults, but only the reverse sides of the medals of the heart that bear on the other sides the sacred figures of self-sacrifice and filial affection.

New England, on its "Forefathers' Day," celebrates the heroism of the Puritans who crossed unknown seas to a land unknown—who faced the known terrors of the ocean and the unknown terrors of the wilderness—

"that they might worship God according to the dictates of their conscience." I honor New England for honoring these heroes, and I do not condemn New England for forgetting to remember that these Puritans had their faults; that they, too—these fugitives from religious oppression—became in their turn the oppressors of other men who sought to worship God according to the dictates of *their* consciences. But, if ever the Irish race in America establish a "Foremothers' Day," I shall regard them as cowards if they do not place side by side with the Pilgrim fathers of the seventeenth century the Irish servant-girls of the nineteenth century. Heroism is heroism, whether it sings psalms or says its beads; whether it lands on Plymouth Rock or at Castle Garden; whether the motive that inspires it is love of God or love of man, of Heaven or home.

We have all seen the "Departure of the Pilgrims from Holland." New England genius has drawn aside the thick curtain, woven by the jealous spirit of three centuries to conceal it; and, throwing on that immortal scene the tender lights of poetry and painting, it has exhibited that kneeling group, with bended knees and hands clasped in prayer, as they were ready to embark on a stormy sea for an inhospitable shore.

In the West of Ireland, this very year, I have witnessed many scenes more pathetic and as noble: groups of young Irish maidens clinging to their sobbing mothers, and weeping, and shrieking, and quivering in anguish, and tearing themselves away; and then trying to enter the cars, but instantly rushing back again, and wildly clasping the desolate old women to their bursting hearts once more. Suddenly, the whistle of the engine sounded; and then arose such a chorus of sobs and shrieks and moans; there was such a frantic flinging up of trembling and wrinkled arms to Heaven; there were such tumultuous outbursts of passionate despair in that ancient tongue that centuries of sorrow have consecrated to the holy sacrament of human suffering, that I have been forced again and again to rush away and hide from the appalling spectacle of hopeless anguish. And yet I was only a looker-on; and yet I knew that these young girls were going from a worse than an Egyptian house of bondage to a better than a Hebrew Land of Promise.

Why did they go? Not to escape religious persecution, nor even to advance their worldly ambition; not from the love of adventure, nor from a hatred of home; for no Irish girl would ever leave her native land if she could live in comfort in it. They went, these young girls, unguarded and untaught in the ways of the world, into the dread unknown of earthly life, most of them never having seen a steamer, nor the sea; some of them without a friend to welcome them on the foreign shores on which they would be landed almost penniless. Why did they go? Often it is to save their aged parents from the terrors of impending eviction—that the white-haired woman who bore them might die in peace beneath the old cabin roof.

The Pilgrims were men of tough fiber, and inured to hardship. They went with their families. They emigrated in colonies. They preferred exile to oppression. They acted from principle. I honor them for it. I recognize their courage. But I honor still more these Irish girls who go alone from the land they love—not at the dictation of the manly intellect, but from the promptings of the womanly heart.

I have heard it said that Bridget, fresh from the bogs of Connemara, is more of a Yankee than the Yankees themselves in driving a sharp bargain for her services. I have always regarded this charge as a compliment to the Irish girl. I have looked on it as an augury of good omen to our republic, for it seemed to me to show that she was quick to adapt herself to the spirit of American institutions. It appeared to me a guarantee that her children would be sure to assimilate themselves with American nationality. But in Ireland I discovered the true reason for this promptitude, so to speak, of financial naturalization; that it came not from her intellect, but her memory; because she knew, what the American lady did not know, that the old folks at home were at the mercy of a class without pity, but with despotic power. No American who has ever come in contact with landlord power in Ireland will blame Bridget for her dread of it, even if it is shown, as he may think, at his own expense. Let it teach us that no race can be oppressed anywhere without every race being forced to suffer from it. We are taxed in America to-day by the same class that oppresses the Irish at home. The Irish in America pay the rents of thousands of farms in the West of Ireland. Every dollar that is sent there is abstracted from our national wealth, and hence we Americans have a vital interest in the liberation of Ireland from landlord tyranny. Having driven the old Irish from all the fertile lands of Ireland into the once desolate Connaught, and then driven them by thousands out of Connemara beyond the sea, the landlords still pursue them across the Atlantic, and tax them beneath the "Stars and Stripes." "Taxation without representation is tyranny," and as we are not represented in Parliament we owe it to our great national principle to help to destroy the landlord tyranny of Ireland.

If I did not know that Bridget would forgive me without the asking, I should beg her pardon for keeping her waiting during this political digression, but I know that she hates the Irish landlords with such a hearty Irish hatred that she would be willing to stand for hours and hear them denounced.

There is a class of women in Ireland whose purity of life and self-sacrificing devotion to the poor have evoked the admiration of every honest heart that ever beat in their presence. St. Bridget is their representative in the past, and my saintly friend, the Nun of Kenmare, is their representative to-day. I mean the Irish nuns. Not a Catholic nor Irishman among you honors them more than I do, although I am neither Irishman nor Catholic. Not one of you would more quickly or more indignantly resent any imputation on their saintly fame. Not by the millionth degree of a hair's breadth would I lower the lofty pedestal on which Irish piety and Irish gratitude have placed their images. But I ask you to remember —if there is one among you who needs public recognition as a standard by which you must measure human worthiness—that there is another and a larger class of Irish women, not secluded from the world, and enveloped by reverence and guarded by traditional sanctity, but fighting in the thickest and murkiest smoke of the battle of life,—solitary, often tempted, always poor,—who, in every land and among every class, have done an equal credit to Irish character and to womanly virtue and to their religious faith; I mean the "Irish servant-girls." Now, if I were a Catholic, I should still be a republican, and I should insist, if I were placed where my voice had authority, that there should be a democracy in canonization; that if any one man—St. Anthony, for example—was entitled to have his name enrolled on the list of saints for his resistance to one temptation, then, that Ireland should be known in the calendar of the Church, not as the Island of St. Bridget, but the Island of the saints called Bridget.

X.

"PARNELL AND HIS ASSOCIATES."

[Mr. Redpath responded to the toast of "Parnell and his Associates," at the banquet on St. Patrick's Day, 1881, at Brooklyn, N. Y. The report is from the Brooklyn *Daily Eagle*.]

Mr. Chairman and Gentlemen:

THERE could be no more appropriate day than St. Patrick's Day, save one—the sacred day of the Nativity—on which to send a message of thanks and of cheer to Mr. Parnell and his associates, for they are carrying on the work of St. Patrick in the spirit of St. Patrick, as he carried forward the work of his Master in the spirit of the Master.

What is the Irish struggle? It is not a mere squeaking squabble about rent; it is not a selfish contest for selfish ends between classes or between creeds. It is a noble crusade for human rights; it is a holy war to break the chains of the oppressed, to feed the hungry, to clothe the naked, and to uplift the down-trodden people of Ireland. Never in our time has there been a grander fight for a grander cause.

The spirit of the leaders in this war is worthy of its lofty aim. They do not seek to array class against class, or race against race, or religion against religion. They issue no appeals to the baser instincts of men. They make no unrighteous demands. They ask only for justice and for equality of rights.

Their creed is a bouquet gathered from the gardens of modern thought, containing not a single flower that liberty has not planted, and philosophy watered, and the love of mankind wooed into beauty. [Applause.]

It is rarely that any honest American citizen can give an unstinted approval of the principles and the leaders of his party. He often feels forced to make a choice of evils—to strike an average—and to cast his ballots, not from his heart, but from his head. There is no such necessity in Ireland to-day. The leaders and the principles of the Land League are alike and equally worthy of approval and acceptance. I respond with all my heart to the toast of "Mr. Parnell and his associates." I went to Ireland prejudiced against them, but I soon learned there to honor and admire them. They are the advance-guard of American liberty on its conquering tour around the world. [Applause.] It is idle now to question Mr. Parnell's capacity for such leadership as these times demand—which is not the intellectual autocracy of an O'Connell, but the organizing intuitions of a Lincoln. "New times demand new measures and new men"; and the era of autocrats has vanished, or is rapidly vanishing. The new leaders must be content to organize existing forces, and to obey the will of the people—not to create parties and to command them. That nation is not fit for liberty which depends for victory on any one leader. During our war, general after general failed, and our President was slain, but the republic, although it wept, never faltered for an hour. My hope of Ireland to-day is chiefly founded on the belief that if Mr. Parnell and all of his associates in leadership were to die or to be imprisoned to-night, the Irish nation would arise sadder, but as resolute as now, to renew the fight to-morrow morning. [Applause.] No living man is entitled to the credit of organizing the mighty moral forces of Ireland to-day. The Irish people organized themselves. [Applause.] I had the happiness to be a spectator of their work. For the first time in hundreds of years, from the day of Brian Boroihme, the victor, to the day of

Victoria, the evictor [laughter], the Irish people themselves have come to the front. The Land League is the organization of the Irish Democracy. Yet even in a democracy, although leaders are no longer kings, they can largely influence for a time the progress of the popular aspirations. Mr. Parnell and his associates, thus far, have shown great skill and wisdom and courage. They have not yet made a single mistake. The frantic efforts of the monarchical press to proclaim errors only serve to point out where another saber-thrust has penetrated the royal coat of armor. [Applause.] I have watched every movement in Parliament and in Ireland, and I repeat that the Land League leaders, up to the present hour, have not committed a solitary blunder.

Obstruction has not only delayed the triumph of despotism in Ireland, but it has torn off its mask and drawn out most of its fangs. England to-day stands, not arraigned only, but convicted, of tyranny and hypocrisy. When last the coercion laws were enacted, Irish patriots were swept by thousands into the prisons, if not unwept, unchronicled. To-day they can be counted by units, and the British Government has declared that less than one hundred shall be arrested. Only one of the great Irish leaders has been sacrificed—a man so pure, so noble, so self-sacrificing, so patriotic, that the British Government does not dare to leave him at large—a man who loves Ireland and liberty so fervently that he would kiss the scaffold with more than the rapture of a lover if he thought that by doing so he could marry liberty to Ireland—Michael Davitt. [Enthusiastic cheering.]

Boycotting has brought the landlords to bay, almost to reason—the first time that either event has occurred in their history. [Applause.]

I have no time to speak of the more conspicuous leaders associated with Mr. Parnell. It must suffice to say that, knowing them well, I regard them as the most noteworthy and the noblest group of public men on this planet to-day.

But, gentlemen, Mr. Parnell has other associates greater than they. When I think of his associates I see behind him the united Irish nation—the center of his army—of which the right and left wings are the Irish race of two hemispheres, while away at the antipodes there is an Irish reserve, eager, liberal, and alert, ready to sustain him if his main army should waver. England cannot evict a whole nation; England cannot imprison a whole race; England cannot coerce the lovers of liberty among every race, and, therefore, if we shall keep step, refusing to quarrel among ourselves, I believe that we shall all live to see the dawn of liberty in Ireland. [Applause.]

I praise the present leaders of Ireland because they are men of our day, with modern ideas—they look ahead, not behind; they do not waste their lives in eulogizing the old chiefs and kings of Ireland, but in preparing the way for the good time coming, when there shall be neither chiefs nor kings on this earth. The man who follows a ghost lands at last in a graveyard. The Irish leaders of to-day have their faces set toward the Zion of republicanism. They are looking forward, and leading their people to the promised land, foretold by so many Irish poets and prophets—the free republic of Ireland. [Applause.]

XI.

WILLIAM BENCE JONES, MARTYR.

["Mr. James Redpath," says the Boston *Globe*, "whose letters from Ireland to the New York *Tribune* during the late famine in that unhappy country were read by so many persons in America, and created such a practical sympathy in behalf of the grief and hunger stricken people of that unfortunate isle, is staying at the Parker House, where he arrived after lecturing in Portland, Maine. In view of the Queen's speech to the British Parliament, and its references to Irish affairs, and also in view of several newspaper articles which have recently appeared in this city on the Irish question, the *Globe* desired to lay before its readers some accurate information upon this important subject. Not knowing any person more competent to speak upon it with authority and without prejudice, both from personal observation and from extensive reading,—as all who heard that gentleman's recent lecture in Music Hall in defense of the Irish Land League will admit,—a representative of the *Globe* called upon Mr. Redpath yesterday, and found him conversing upon Irish affairs with the genial editor of the Boston *Pilot*, John Boyle O'Reilly. Receiving a cordial greeting from the host, the reporter explained the object of his call, when the following interesting conversation ensued: "]

REPORTER.—"Mr. Redpath, what do you think of the Queen's speech?"

MR. REDPATH.—"Well, it shows that although his intentions toward Ireland may be as good as any of the good intentions with which Hell is said to be paved, yet Mr. Gladstone thoroughly misconceives the situation in Ireland, and is incapable of conferring on it any lasting benefit. For example: She, that is, he, says that the act of 1870 has conferred great benefits on Ireland, or words to that effect. I quote from memory. Now, the truth is that the law of 1870, which was honestly intended by its author, Gladstone, and its improver, John Bright, to benefit the tenants outside of Ulster, was of no service whatever to them. The reason for this is, that in the West of Ireland the people were too poor to fight before the landlord courts for the rights it conferred on them, while in the east of the island the great landlords, following the Duke of Leinster's example, compelled their tenants to take leases in which they were forced to waive their rights under that act."

REP.—"Was that custom really general?"

J. R.—"Yes, it was almost universal. Take, for example, the case of William Bence Jones, on whom two Boston journals have had editorials within a week. He never granted a lease until 1870; but since that time he has insisted that those tenants who had largely improved their farms should take leases for thirty-one years. The reason why he granted leases on those terms was that his rents were excessively high, and therefore he could easily evict his tenants if a bad season came. By eviction for non-payment of rent, he confiscated all the tenant's improvements, and was not liable under the Gladstone act for any compensation to be paid the tenant. In this way, 'he unjustly contrived,' to use the language of Father O'Leary, a priest in one of the parishes in which Jones's estates are located, 'to make the act of 1870 a dead letter.'"

REP.—"You say that Mr. Jones compelled his tenants to take out leases for a term of thirty-one years. Am I to understand you to mean that the Gladstone act of 1870 only applied to leases drawn for certain periods, and not to those drawn for other periods, as, for instance, the leases drawn for thirty-one years?"

J. R.—"No. It was intended to extend a fraction of the Ulster custom over the Catholic counties of Ireland. It provided that if a tenant was capriciously evicted by his landlord, that the landlord should pay him seven years' rent; that is to say, if the rent was £10 per annum, the tenant should receive £70, with a reasonable compensation for improvements made within twenty-one years, and that he should also be recompensed for unexhausted manures; but if he was evicted for non-payment of rent, he got no compensation whatever. Under the Ulster custom a tenant gets compensation under any circumstances, and for improvements made both by himself and predecessors, and he could not be evicted at all as long as he paid his rent. Now, by these leases, the wealthy tenants waived their rights under that law, and, therefore, Jones and the others insisted upon their tenants, to whom formerly they would give no leases, taking them out."

REP.—"Mr. Jones seems to be praised as a model landlord, and the *Herald* says that 'he is beyond question one of the ablest and most authoritative exponents of the views of his class, and that his opinion on agrarian issues carries whatever weight should be granted to an experience of forty years both as a land-owner and as a farmer in Ireland."

J. R.—" For more than thirty years Mr. Jones has maintained the reputation in the County Cork of being one of the worst landlords in the South of Ireland. It was said of him that he had raised rack-renting to the level of a science. More than twenty years ago, his life was threatened, and he would have been killed but for the interference of the parish priest. Mr. Jones, in his essays, speaks about his own farm and how much money he has spent on it. He forgot to mention, doubtless in the haste of composition, that his own thousand acres were made into one farm by evicting, without compensation, scores of families whose children are now in exile. His tenants pay the highest rents of any in the County Cork, and, I have heard it said by responsible men, the highest in the South of Ireland. He says in his article in *Macmillan*, 'I never raised any man's rent except at long intervals, or thirty-one years, or his life.' Note that phrase—' or his life.' Whenever one of his tenants dies, his successor, son, wife, or brother must pay an increase of rent, sometimes to the extent of nearly one hundred per cent. Take two or three examples: When Michael White of Cloheen died, a few years ago, Jones raised the rent on White's widow from £50 to £80. When Patrick Hayes died, Jones raised the rent on the farm from twenty-five shillings to £2 an acre, and compelled the new tenant, under threat of eviction, to take a lease of twenty-one years, which confiscated the improvements that his father had made, although those improvements included a dwelling-house and out-buildings costing fifteen hundred dollars. Only two or three months ago, when a widow named Walsh died, he caused her son to consent to an increase of £15 per annum. Some of his farms were held at such high rates that one after another tenant was ruined. As an illustration, take the Dempsey farm. The Government valuation was ten shillings per acre. Remember that was estimated on the farm as it had been improved by the tenant. Remember that when a tenant in Ireland pays 'Griffith's [that is the Government] valuation,' he is paying a tax on his own industry, improvements, and capital—because the tenant has reclaimed the land at his own sole expense from barren bog or sterile hill-slopes, and ' Griffith's valuation' was based in every case, not on the land as the tenant received it from the landlord, but as the assessor found it when improved at the tenant's cost. Griffith's valuation is a Shylock rental, and yet last winter every landlord who *only* charged fifty per cent. over Griffith's valuation was regarded by his impoverished tenants as a good landlord! On Dempsey's death Jones raised the rent to £2 per acre, and now it is vacant and growing weeds. Three different tenants were ruined by it. Why, a gentleman of Cork recently told a priest, a friend of mine, that he had asked one of Mr. Jones's tenants the name of his landlord, and the peasant replied, 'Un Diabhoil'—a devil. As to the *Herald's* statement that Mr. Jones is an authority, the *Herald*, among the rest of its vast and varied misinformation on Irish affairs, does not seem to know that the most eminent solicitor in the County Cork, Mr. Wright, in open court more than once, to the entire satisfaction of the magistrates, denounced William Bence Jones as a liar. Jones has always been thoroughly unpopular, not only with the peasantry but with the magistrates also. He has taken so much pleasure in denouncing the Irish people that, when he was asked to subscribe toward the erection of a Protestant cathedral in Cork, he promised a subscription of £500, on the condition that "no Irish architect should be employed." Every magistrate in that district, Catholic and Protestant, denounces him as a dogmatic, insolent snob. A correspondent of the London *Standard*, a Tory paper, who went down to Cork to defend Jones, wrote: 'In Cork I have met, at different times, at least half a dozen magistrates, of Protestant and Catholic, Conservative and Liberal views, who are in accord as to one point only, viz., that Mr. Bence Jones, because of certain peremptory behavior, intentional or constitutional, as the case may be, is not beloved by them.' This is a very mild way of stating that he is universally execrated by the gentry as well as by the common people of Cork. Jones says that, under his administration, whenever there were no leases the rents were considerably raised. 'I was under no engagement, expressed or implied, with these tenants, and therefore felt at liberty to make my own terms with them. I accordingly let them the land at the highest rent it was in my opinion worth to them. This was very often a very considerable advance on the former rent, but it was still less than in my judgment the land was intrinsically worth.' That is cool, but he was still more frank in his conversations in Ireland. He said to a well-known Protestant clergyman in County Cork: 'I can deal with my farms as with any other chattels.' This remark was made in a conversation about the farm held by Edward Lucy in Castle Liskey, County Cork. This farm fell into Jones's possession, and the first thing he did was to demand an increase in the rent of six shillings per acre, and to tell the old man, Edward Lucy, who had lived all his life on that farm, that he would add at least another six shillings per acre. What was the result of this action of Jones? It is pathetically told in a few simple words by Father O'Leary: 'Lucy gave up the farm and died of a broken heart.' Not only as a landlord but as a magistrate also, Mr. Jones has made himself excessively unpopular by his harsh and despotic decisions. Instances are given in which his arbitrary and excessive findings were appealed from and overruled. Last winter, he made himself especially obnoxious by first denying in England that there was any distress in the district, and by seeking, on his return home, 'to put a stop to the relief works which had kept many families in the town from either dying of starvation or being thrown on the rates.' This is the expression of a resident of the district. He himself did not contribute one shilling to the relief fund."

Rep.—"Why should a landlord do those things?"

J. R.—"Lord Lansdowne's agent, Mr. Trench, did precisely the same thing. The landlords do those things because they want to drive out large numbers of poor tenants and confiscate their improvements without compensation, and add them to their grazing farms. This Jones is the sort of man who is held up as a model landlord. Now, the *Journal* states, if I remember correctly, that this man's life was threatened, and that a grave was dug opposite his door, and at the close of its article that paper charges those threats and outrages on the leaders of the Land League. The *Journal* seems not to have known a meeting of the

Land League was promptly called and that it publicly denounced a threatening letter, or notice, which had been served on Jones. The *Journal* also charges on the leaders of the Land League the maiming of cattle and other agrarian outrages. Why, Mr. Parnell is just as incapable of giving any such advice, direct or indirect, as Mr. Stockwell himself. Mr. Dillon is a man as sensitive and refined as the editor of the *Advertiser*, and Davitt is quite as incapable of any such action as Mr. Haskell of the *Herald*. The truth is that not a solitary outrage has occurred in Ireland, except where the Land League was weak."

REP.—" I see, Mr. Redpath, that the *Journal* last week said: ' Mr. Smalley, of the New York *Tribune*,' for which you wrote so many interesting letters on this Land question, ' a correspondent of exceptional information, declares that since the beginning of the disturbance no week has witnessed greater political excitement or more flagrant instances of lawlessness than the week before last.' "

J. R.—" No man who knows Mr. Smalley would doubt any statement made on his personal authority, but, instead of being in a position where he can procure 'exceptional information,' he is in precisely the worst place in Europe to learn the truth about Ireland—London. I know myself, of my own knowledge, that some of the statements telegraphed to the New York *Tribune* by Mr. Smalley when I was in Ireland were false. He simply took his ' exceptional information' from the London press, and nine out of every ten of their accounts of outrages in Ireland were utterly untrue."

REP.—" Mr. Redpath, it has been reported that the Fenians are joining the Land League in great numbers. What do you think of those rumors ? "

J. R.—" I think it is quite likely that they are correct. The Fenians, or Nationalists, frequently belong, as individuals, to the Land League, although some of the old leaders are what we call ' sore-heads.' The young men of Ireland, as a class, believe not only in peasant proprietorship, but in independence, and they are only working for the Land League with the hope that it will prove a sort of base of supplies. They not only are not hostile to it, but they are coöperating with it heartily. But they do not mean to be satisfied with its triumphs when they come, as come they will. They will be accepted only as a part of what justice to Ireland demands."

REP.—" The *Journal*, in one of its articles on this movement, says that ' the Land League leaders have disclaimed the intention of precipitating a collision, and admit that the people are not prepared for such a movement; and yet, with a fatuity which is incomprehensible, they have persisted in a course which promises to bring upon Ireland the curse of an unorganized and abortive revolt.' What do you say about those statements ? "

J. R.—" I say that that statement is untrue. The Land League leaders have held the people in check. They have permitted no outbreak, and each and every statement that there was an outbreak, and every prediction that there would be one, came from the hopes of the English press, and not from the intentions of the Land League leaders."

REP.—" But, after all, Mr. Redpath, would it not be better, as a practical measure, for the leaders of the Land League to accept a modified system of reform, such as Gladstone and Bright propose ? "

J. R.—" No, it would not. The radical wrong of Irish landlordism—a wrong that cannot be overcome by any compromise—lies in the facts that the landlords are absentees ; that whether they get rack-rents or more reasonable rents, the money is always drained out of the country, and that the machinery for the enforcement of those laws is in the hands of the landlords. It is not a question of whether rack-rents or moderate rents shall continue. The question is: Shall Ireland bleed at every pore or only at half of them, or not be bled at all? English legislation is always founded on a firm faith in phlebotomy. Now Ireland can never prosper until this wound is stopped—until absentee landlordism abdicates in favor of peasant proprietorship."

XII.

IRISH CRIMES AND OUTRAGES.

[From an interview published in the Chicago *Tribune* of February 7, 1881, the subjoined passages on Irish outrages are quoted. "In the course of the conversation," says the *Tribune*, "the reporter asked for Mr. Redpath's opinion as to the probable effect of Michael Davitt's arrest and the suspension of the Irish Obstructionists. Mr. Redpath said:"]

THE arrest of Mr. Davitt, I think, will result in a solid Ireland. It will drive thousands of the Protestant farmers of Ulster into the Land League. Of late the Land League has been making rapid progress in Ulster, because the farmers find that they have no adequate protection under the Ulster custom against a constant increase of rent, and they have come to see that their only security lies in a peasant proprietary. They have enjoyed, many of them for over two hundred years, greater rights than Gladstone proposes to extend to the rest of Ireland, and yet they find these rights powerless to protect them against the exactions of the landlords.

REPORTER.—" Is Davitt still as popular as ever?"

MR. REDPATH.—" He has a stronger hold on the hearts of the people than any man in Ireland. His arrest will produce a belligerent animosity against the Gladstone Government, because everybody in Ireland knows that, while Mr. Davitt has maintained the right of free speech, he has never uttered a word urging violence. On the contrary, he has done more to restrain the people from committing violence than all the British troops and constabulary put together. He is the idol of the peasantry. But, even if the British Government should arrest every leader, the movement would go on, because the rising generation in Ireland are as well educated as the people of Illinois. The national schools there are quite as good as our public schools, and the people are all republicans. This is emphatically a people's movement. It is not the result of agitation by the leaders. This is shown by the fact that the Land League made its most rapid strides while Davitt, Parnell, and Dillon were not directing its movements,—while some of them were in America and others in London."

REP.—" What is your view as to the obstructive tactics adopted by Parnell and his associates in Parliament, which resulted in their suspension?"

J. R.—" The Speaker himself, I was told, has often expressed the opinion that Parnell is one of the ablest Parliamentarians in the House of Commons, and it is certain that he has never been at fault in his motions and objections. This is an English opinion of Parnell, you understand. His action was simply what is known among us as 'filibustering.' By this system of obstruction, the Irish members compelled all Europe to listen to the story of their wrongs, instead of submitting, as they had done before, to be voted down with the silent insolence of a sneering majority of English members. It was a masterly system of advertising the wrongs of Ireland."

REP.—" Have you seen the statement made in the correspondence of one of the Chicago papers relative to the alleged increase of outrages in Ireland of late years?"

J. R.—"Yes; and I have carefully analyzed it. The best answer to it is a telegraphic dispatch by the London correspondent of the Dublin *Freeman's Journal*, published in November last. I sometimes read it at my lectures. Here it is: 'The outcry against crime in Ireland ought to be pretty considerably checked by the results of a return just issued. The proportion of the criminal classes, in and out of prison, taken together, is about half as large in Ireland as in England and Scotland. The proportion of convicts is considerably below one-half, and persons in places of punishment not more than one-half. As regards peculiar classes of crime, I find that, under the heads of offenses against property with violence, Scotland is about six times, and England and Wales about two and one-half times, as criminal as Ireland; and that, under the head of 'offenses against morality,' the proportion is as twelve to five against Scotland. Yet *they* tell *us* that we are the most criminal race on the face of the globe!' This is the answer furnished by the British Government itself to its slanders on the Irish people—slanders now translated into coercion acts.

"Now, as regards the Government report, published in the Chicago paper, official comparative statistics — also gathered and published by the British Government—show that in 1845 there were 2,477 more outrages than were reported last year; that in 1846, 12,374 crimes were committed, as against 5,609 crimes last year; that in 1847 there were four times as many outrages —that is, nearly 21,000 — recorded against the Irish people as there were last year; that the crimes committed were, in 1848, 18,080; in 1849, 14,908; in 1850, 10,039; in 1851, 9,144; and in 1852, 7,824. So you see that, according to British official returns, the crime reported in Ireland is far below what it used to be, although the papers report in general terms more crimes last year than were ever known before, and they attribute these crimes to the influence of the Land League. Thirty-five years ago, when these returns began, there were 21,000 crimes committed. Last year there were about one-fourth of that number.

"That is the final answer furnished by the British Government to its own impeachment of the Land League."

REP.—"Are these crimes specially attributable to the land agitation?"

J. R.—"If you will analyze the report of the crimes of last year, you will find that one-half of the cases of outrage reported in Ulster are threatening letters, in the proportion of seventy-seven to one hundred and forty-nine; and that the next highest item in the catalogue is published under the marvelous heading of 'otherwise.' Now, it is notorious to every one who has studied modern Irish history, and it has been proved again and again, that the most of these threatening letters are written by land-agents and bailiffs, in order to keep the landlords out of the country, so that they may have a better chance to steal from the tenants. There is no pretense that these threatening letters were written by the Land League.

"Take the next province. The number of outrages reported is two hundred and twenty-eight, and of these one hundred and fifty-one were threatening letters. So much for Leinster.

"Take Munster next. There six hundred and forty-three outrages were reported, and of these, three hundred and fifty-six were threatening letters.

"In Connaught, under the head of 'letters and otherwise,' there are three hundred and fifty-seven outrages out of six hundred and ninety-eight reported.

"This is the best showing that the British Government has ever been able to make. The authorities for these reports of outrages are the magistrates, and the magistracy of

Ireland, from Lord Chief Justice May down to the lowest stipendiary magistrate, are all landlords and their partisans. The English-Irish bench is the most corrupt judiciary in Europe. Even the moderate *Freeman's Journal*, which was hostile to Parnell while he was in America, and which is owned by the Lord Mayor of Dublin, says that whatever little confidence the people of Ireland might have had in the magistracy of the country as a body, is being rapidly undermined by the course which members of that institution are now taking by giving exaggerated ideas as to the condition of their localities.

"Take the County Cavan, for example. The statements of the magistracy there are emphatically denied by the town commissioners, and by leading citizens who are not members of the Land League. The bishop of the diocese publicly challenged Mr. Forster to name the localities in which outrages had occurred. All unite in saying that the county was enjoying absolute peace. My experience of last summer convinced me that there were fewer crimes in Ireland than among any similar population in Europe. That correspondent who sends these stories to the Chicago paper is an ultra-Orangeman. That is to say, he is a religious Ku-klux, and his statements about Irish outrages are about as reliable as those of a Cyclops of the Ku-klux Klan would be in relation to outrages by negroes in our own South."

REP.—"Yet the London papers often report outrages."

J. R.—"Yes, and never correct them. Here is a specimen of their lies about Ireland, a paragraph from a recent number of the Dublin *Nation:*

"'We have this week a fresh crop of bogus agrarian outrages exposed in a manner which the landlord party will, no doubt, think extremely inconsiderate. Thus, a Parsonstown correspondent telegraphed some days since that a Galway landlord, named Gardiner, had been tarred and feathered by a body of masked men in his own house. It was a capital story from the coercionist point of view, but Mr. Gardiner has stupidly spoiled the effect of it by asserting that it does not contain a word of truth! Another Galway landlord, Mr. Edward Kennedy, Abbey Lodge, Loughrea, was said to have been fired at as he was walking in his garden. Another good story: but then Mr. Kennedy, following the example of Mr. Gardiner, contradicts it. He even adds that he had no difference with his tenantry, and that he is himself a member of the Land League! Again, on Saturday last it was reported that "a bailiff, named John McManus, on Lord Greville's property, near Drumshambo," had been fired at; but Mr. Philip O'Reilly, agent to Lord Greville, writes from Colamber, Rathowen, Westmeath, that that nobleman has no property near Drumshambo, and no bailiff of the name of McManus in his employment! One more: The *Freeman* of Tuesday announces with reference to an alleged slitting of a man's ears at Doon, County Clare, because he paid his rent, that it is enabled authoritively to say that the outrage never took place. Now, this is too bad. Contradicting "outrage" stories may serve the cause of the tenantry and their friends, but how is it likely to serve that of the landlords? There is, however, one consolation left for the lords. The English public, for whom chiefly the manufactured outrages are prepared, are not allowed to hear of the exposures. The English newspapers, so far as we can find out, have not dared to "spoil trade" by correcting any one of the four falsehoods to which we have referred!'"

REP.—"Then there are few agrarian outrages in Ireland?"

J. R.—"No, sir; there are many agrarian outrages in Ireland. Let me give you a specimen of the real agrarian outrages, as reported in a late letter from Michael Davitt, just before he was flung into jail. He writes:

"'The following particulars of the

estate of Ballinamore, County Mayo, the property of Mr. Anthony Ormsby, which were published by the League yesterday, will show what an industrious people have to bear under this infamous system of landlordism, and explain the determined stand which they are now taking against its acts and supporters: In seventy-three holdings upon this estate (numbering five hundred and four persons) the Government valuation is £595 19s., while the present rent is £924 5s., or close upon *double* the rent which should be legally exacted. *Almost the entire of these lands consist of mountain slopes, and were all reclaimed by the tenants without any aid from the landlord !* They are also compelled to do duty-work— that is, employ their families and horses for a certain number of days per annum in gratuitous labor for the landlord. Tenants must obtain consent from him ere any of their children are married, under penalty of a fine being added to the rent. J. Casey was fined ten shillings for a stone on the top of a gate not being whitewashed to the landlord's liking. John Ruane was compelled to remove from where he lived and to build a new house on some waste land in order to have it reclaimed. When the house was finished, the landlord made him pull it down again and erect it *ten yards farther away*. When the land was reclaimed Ruane was again removed higher up the mountain, where he shortly afterward died. Pat Walsh, a mason, worked at a building for thirty-five days, but would only be paid for twenty, and upon protesting against this treatment, Mr. Ormsby made him throw down the wall, and then evicted him from his holding without compensation. Thomas Cavanagh was compelled to throw down his cabin and build a new one. After a few years' time he was forced to change to a bog, where he had to build again. When the bog was reclaimed he was changed again, and, upon remonstrating against a *fourth* removal, he was evicted without compensation, and had to enter the work-house, where himself and wife soon after died. Other instances of similar treatment were also given and published, the truth of which I can vouch for, as I have had the same statements repeated to me on my visit to that part of the West of Ireland during the recent famine.'

"I discovered many similar outrages in the West of Ireland—quite as bad as the cases reported by Mr. Davitt. The London press rarely tell the truth about Ireland. I never read but one true statement about Ireland in the London *Times*—in the number for March 12, 1847. It was exasperated because the Irish famine was taxing the English exchequer, and it rose for a moment to the level of truth. It said:

"'Ireland, then, is at the same time rich and poor. It produces a vast superabundance of food, but that food is drained from its shores. It is not, however, drained by the state. It is drained in a great measure by the landlords and their creditors, who, the more they get, the more they will drain. Now what does mercy to Ireland require under these circumstances? Is it mercy to let the landlords go on, drain, drain, drain, forever? Is it mercy to let him go on squeezing the hapless peasant down to the skin of his potato? Is it of any use—has it been of any use—to remit rates and taxes and lend money to the landlords? No ! the only mercy is to keep in the island and upon the spot the gracious gifts of Providence and rewards of human toil, and to compel the land-owner to spend them in the employment of the laborer and the relief of the poor.'

"That is sound sense. But there is only one way to carry out that policy— by abolishing Irish landlordism; by making every farmer the owner of the soil he tills; and yet, because Davitt and Parnell and his associates advocated that wise measure of statesmanship, the London *Times* howled until Davitt was imprisoned, and Parnell and his associates brought into court, and the coercion law enacted ! "

XIII.

AN EXILE OF ERIN.

[There will be few names more famous in the history of Ireland in 1880 than the name of "Capt." Boycott, a land-agent of the County Mayo, against whom the terrible power of ostracism, or social excommunication, was evoked by the peasantry whom he had pitilessly oppressed. "Capt." Boycott, as he called himself, landed in New-York in April, 1881. He was interviewed by the reporters of the New-York *Sun*, New-York *Herald*, and New-York *Tribune*. Mr. Redpath was interviewed about these Boycott interviews by the Chicago *Inter-Ocean*, and from that journal of April 14 the subjoined report is taken. It is somewhat elaborated by extracts from Mr. Redpath's lecture on "What I know about Boycotting."]

MR. JAMES REDPATH, the well-known correspondent in Ireland of *The Inter-Ocean*, being temporarily in the city, the opportunity was seized to interview him on the subject of the recent interviews with Captain Boycott, published in the New-York papers, but more particularly in reference to one which appeared in the New-York *Herald*. The result of the interview with Mr. Redpath will be seen in the following report, which cannot fail to be interesting, both on account of the subject and of the person who granted the interview:

REPORTER.—"Mr. Redpath, have you seen the interviews with Captain Boycott, published in the New-York papers?"

MR. REDPATH.—"Yes, I have read the reports in the *Sun*, *Tribune*, and *Herald*."

REP.—"Have you any objection to making comments upon them?"

J. R.—"No. To begin with, the *Tribune* reports Captain Boycott as saying 'the Irish people had been spoiled by being humored. They declared that they were determined to get rid of the landlords, but had no idea what they would then do with the land.'

"My answer to that is, that the Irish people have been humored for seven hundred years by being compelled to submit to the most oppressive laws that any civilized people ever endured without rebellion, and that there is not in all Europe a system of land tenure so degrading to the people as the land tenure of Ireland, for which England is responsible. The Irish people are determined to get rid of the landlords, but they *have* a clear idea of what they will then do with the land. *They will cultivate it!* Captain Boycott says that the Land League would ruin the people. Now, no popular movement in Ireland has ever done so much before, as has been done by the Land League in two years, to raise the character and relieve the sufferings of the Irish people."

REP.—"As, for example?"

J. R.—"By saving thousands of the Irish people from death by hunger and fevers brought on by hunger. John Mitchell shows that one million and a half of the Irish people perished from hunger, or by the famine fever that was brought on by hunger, from 1847 to 1852. *Then*, in spite of repeated warnings and prayers from every part of Ireland, the British Government did not move until it was too late. Three millions of the Irish people were driven into their graves or out of Ireland, in consequence of that appalling apathy; and in England, when one man, listening to a speech by Disraeli, proposed three cheers for the Irish famine, that Jewish miscreant said, 'There are worse things than the Irish famine.' Its horrors were welcomed by many Tories as a Providential solution of the Irish question. There were hundreds of parishes in the West of Ireland last year where, if no relief had come, and constant relief had not been given, nearly the whole population would have been swept away. Before Mr. Parnell sailed for America, the English and Irish landlord press and every organ of the British Government, including Mr. Lowther, the Home Secretary for Ireland, denied that there was any famine. Famine would have driven the Irish, by hundreds of thousands, into exile, and thereby carried out the English policy in Ireland for two centuries. When Parnell sailed, the British Government saw that it would be disgraced by any further inaction, and so the Duchess of Marlborough issued an appeal for help. Then the Mansion House, offended at the action of the Castle in undertaking a work of charity that precedent had always confided to the Lord Mayor of Dublin, issued another appeal; and the New-York *Herald*, to conciliate the Irish-Americans whom its assaults on Mr. Parnell had alienated, issued an independent American call for aid. Money poured in from every civilized nation, and there were not more than a dozen deaths from hunger in all Ireland. But I hold that the Land League is entitled to the credit of all the relief, from whatever source it came and through whatever agency it was disbursed; because, but for its action, no relief would have reached the starving peasantry in time to save them. That's the first great service rendered to the Irish people by the Land League.

"The second service is, by so uniting the Irish tenantry that landlord outrages have been rendered equally difficult and odious—such outrages as exacting rack-rents after two years of bad crops and one year of famine, and then, on the failure of the poor people to pay them, throwing them into the road-side to die, as the landlords did after the great famine of 1847. The more impecunious landlords have been forced to reduce their Shylock rentals, in many cases down to Griffith's valuation. The amount of money thus saved to the tenantry is vastly larger than the amount contributed by all the world for the relief of the Irish peasantry last year. I have seen this sum estimated at fifteen millions of dollars, but I do not know whether this sum is correct, from any personal study. It is certain that it is quite large.

"The third service that the Land League rendered the Irish people was in preventing an insurrection or widespread agrarian homicides. The Irish peasantry in 1847, believing that Providence sent the famine, lay down and died without a murmur. But the young generation in Ireland are better educated than their forefathers, and the belief is general that it was the landlords and not Providence who blighted the potatoes. And they are right. For, while under any system of land-tenure there would be occasional bad seasons, the inevitable result, in every climate and in every soil, of planting the same crop year in and year out in the same field is the final ruin of the crop. Now why do the peasantry plant potatoes only on their little holdings? Because, after the great famine, the people were driven out of the good lands that they had reclaimed at their own expense and by their own labor, and those who did not die or emigrate were driven to little patches on the edges of bogs or on the sterile slopes of mountains—holdings so small that the poor people could *not* rotate their crops. So, blight became inevitable. But even the peasantry who never thought of this cause of blight, knowing that they could not pay their rack-rents from extreme poverty, but would gladly have done so if they were able, were determined not to be murdered or banished for it even under the pretext of the 'enforcement of the rights of property.' They believe that peasants have rights as well as landlords, and that the men through whose unaided toil the bogs and hill-sides of the West of Ireland were made arable have in justice and in law the first equitable title for support from the soil. This is not a 'communistic' doctrine. Gladstone himself has taught it, and John Stuart Mill, and John Bright.

So, if, last spring, the landlords had enforced their Shylock 'rights,' they and their agents would have been killed by hundreds from Donegal to Cork. The Land League taught them a better way, and where fifty thousand British soldiers and Irish constables were unavailing to keep the peace, the leaders of the Land League preserved order in Ireland.

"If the leaders of the Land League had accomplished nothing more than these three reforms, its leaders would have been entitled to rank side by side in the Pantheon of Irish Gratitude with the greatest Irishman, in my opinion, who ever lived—Daniel O'Connell.

"Here is a report of a passage in my lecture that gives another reason for my admiration of the action of the Land League:

"'You know that, in Ireland, whenever a Cork man and a Kerry man meet, they quarrel, and sometimes fight. [Laughter.] I heard of a dispute between a Cork man and a Kerry man, when I was in Ireland, that illustrates their traditional antagonisms. The Kerry man advanced a theory which the Cork man repelled by saying that it was contrary to the principles of human nature. The Kerry man wasn't going to be bluffed in that style by a Cork man, and so he said:

"'Human natur'! Human natur'—human natur's a damned scoundrel, anyhow.' [Laughter.]

"'Now, I don't believe in that theory; I think human nature is a pretty good fellow; at any rate it isn't in my nature to disparage human nature—but, ladies and gentlemen, when I visited the wretched hovels of the West of Ireland last winter, and saw the broken-hearted women and broken-spirited men there, —for the poor people not only did not know where the money was to come from to feed their children till the spring, but they expected to be driven out of their homes into the poor-house when the spring came,—after I had learned how pitiless the landlords were, and how helpless the tenantry, I went back to Dublin and said to Michael Davitt:

"'I'm afraid it is too late to save your people; the hunger has crushed their souls, and I believe nothing will restore their manhood except emigration to a land where they will have equal rights.'

"'Michael Davitt told me to wait and see.

"'I did wait, and I did see. On my second visit to Ireland, I visited the same baronies, the same parishes, the same counties that I had visited last winter, and lo! there, where I had left a class of cowering serfs, I found a race of resolute freemen! [Cheers.] That resurrection of the manhood of Ireland is the beneficent work of the Irish National Land League. [Cheers.]'"

REP.—"In an interview with the *Sun*, Captain Boycott says that he has never had any personal trouble with his neighbors and tenants, and that the charges circulated against him were an after-thought, and that the Earl of Erne, his landlord, refused to believe them and has declined to remove him from the agency."

J. R.—"That's true. The boot was on the other leg then. The first account of Boycott ever written was my letter to the *Inter-Ocean*, dated October 12, 1880. You had better quote a part of it:

"'My last letter ended with the story of a "farmer" who was "terrorized" into paying sixty cents a day to men for harvesting, and thirty-two cents to women. Mr. Bennett, the well-disposed correspondent of the London *Telegraph*, from whom I quoted, showed that he regarded the conduct of the peasantry as an interference with "the rights of property." But who was this "peaceful farmer?" Boycott—one of the most merciless miscreants in the County Mayo—a man who never hesitated to fling families out of their little farms into the poor-house if, from any cause, they failed to pay their rents—even although they had themselves reclaimed the land from absolute sterility, and drained it, and fenced it, and built the houses on it. He held a rod of iron over his tenants always. They were his serfs—not as "a figure of speech in Parliament," but as a fact of life in Ireland. If they refused to obey his behests he had the power to ruin them, and he did not falter in using his power.'

"Captain Boycott came into that country seventeen years ago, but had not lived there five years before he had won the reputation of being the worst land-agent in the County Mayo. He raised the rents of the poor tenants, in many cases, to double Griffith's valuation, and when a tenant in Ireland pays 'only' Griffith's valuation he pays a rent not merely on the land as the landlord gave it to him, but also on the houses, fences, offices, and reclamations that he himself has created.

"In addition to charging exorbitant rents, Captain Boycott compelled the tenants of the landlords for whom he was agent to work for him on his own farm at his own terms, and he paid men one shilling and sixpence (about thirty-six cents), and women a shilling (about twenty-four cents) a day. Eighteen pence a day is about two and a quarter dollars per week. But he always managed to fine men for violating the rules of the estate, so that they never actually receive more than a dollar and seventy-five cents a week, on which they are expected to support a large family and 'find themselves.'

"These 'rules of the estate' are a code of laws made by the landlords themselves, for the violation of which they inflict fines at their own pleasure. For example, Captain Boycott would fine a man sixpence—one-third of his day's wages—for coming five minutes late in the morning; sixpence for walking on the grass instead of on the gravel; sixpence for putting a wheelbarrow out of its place. He had so many of these arbitrary rules that it was utterly impossible for any tenant to work a week without violating two or three of them.

"Captain Boycott was one of the most brutal and foul-mouthed ruffians in the West of Ireland. He never addressed a poor man without an oath—without calling him a d——d Mick. Captain Boycott himself is an Englishman. He never met one of his tenants without compelling him to stand with his hat in his hand if he passed him on the road-side, and as long as he talked with him, even if it was raining. This has been the custom for generations in the West of Ireland; but the Land League has abolished that degrading habit. If a poor man went to his office he compelled him to stand as far off as the room would admit of. He was an Irish Legree, without the lash, but with the equally terrible power of eviction, which Gladstone in Parliament pronounced to be equivalent to a sentence of starvation in the West of Ireland.

"The land agitation suddenly aroused the tenantry to a sense of their power, which they could wield without violating any law, if they would combine and act as one man. The first use of this power against Boycott was made when he sent last summer for the tenantry of the estates for which he was agent, to cut the oats on his own farm. He expected them to work, the men for thirty-two cents a day (and feed themselves), and the women for twenty-four cents a day. They asked respectfully that he should pay the ordinary harvest wages—2s. 6d. for men and 1s. 6d. for women. He refused with the most brutal insolence to make this reasonable advance. The whole neighborhood declined to work for him. The willful old fellow swore that he would not be dictated to—*he* who had always dictated to them. So he and his nephews and nieces and three servant-girls and herdsmen and car-driver went down to the fields and began to reap and bind. He held out three hours, but could not stand it. He was heard to curse Father John O'Malley as the cause of the 'insubordination' of the peasantry, and to say that although 'they had got him now he would be even with them soon.' Mrs. Boycott went from cabin to cabin that night to coax the people to come and work for her husband at their own very moderate terms. They came. Mind, these laborers work from ten to twelve hours a day, and yet this strike to get sixty cents instead of thirty-two cents a day—a demand to be paid only five cents an hour—was heralded even by an honest English journalist as an unwarrantable interference with the relations of employer and employed, and by others as one of the lawless and treasonable actions of the Land League! The New-York papers speak of Boycott as a 'pleasant-spoken man'; but in the County Mayo he is known as a bully.

"When November came he sent for the tenants. His day of vengeance had dawned—*he* thought so; but it proved to be his day of doom. The tenants asked a moderate reduction of rents. He refused to abate the Shylock rents one farthing; although nearly all the tenants of the Earl of Erne had been supported for months by foreign charity and although the Earl himself had not given a shilling for their relief. The Earl is an old man, —it is said in his dotage,—who lives in the County Fermanagh."

REP.—"Could the tenants have paid their rent?"

J. R.—"Some of them could have paid it, but if they had done so they would have been at the mercy of the shop-keepers and the gombeen men. Remember, 1879–'80 was the third bad season. During the first two years, the peasantry, after paying their rents, managed to get through the summer by their credit at the shop-keepers, but all credit was stopped as soon as it was known that the third season would see another failure of crops. The peasantry then borrowed money from the gombeen men or money-lenders and the pawnbrokers, to pay their rents. They were only in arrears one year. Whoever goes unpaid, the landlord insists on his pound of flesh first. Now, some of these tenants had been in England harvesting and had earned money enough to pay even Boycott's rents, but if they had paid them they could not have paid the gombeen men and shop-keepers, and they would have been prosecuted by them. So they refused to pay the rent if no abatement was made. Boycott threatened them with evictions, but they left his office without paying the rent.

"Boycott issued the eviction papers, and hired a process-server and got eighteen constables to protect him. In Ireland, a constable is not a policeman but a soldier armed with a musket, buck-shot, and bayonet, and under military drill and orders. There are nearly twelve thousand of them in Ireland. The finest cottages and houses in the rural districts of Ireland are the head-quarters of these Irish mercenaries. This process-server served three writs on the women in three different cabins before the purpose of the expedition was known. Note my expression—on the women. In Ireland, if a shop-keeper or any one but a landlord issues a writ for debt, it must be served on the head of the family, but if the landlord is the creditor, the law says—as the landlords make the laws—that the writ may be served on the women, or if they can't be found or shut the door in the officer's face it may be nailed on the door, and recently, I see, it has been decided that the writ may be sent by mail. When this process-server reached the fourth cabin, the woman, a Mrs. Fitzmorris, told the process-server that she would lose her life before she would allow him to serve a process on her. She shouted and raised the signals."

REP.—"What do you mean by that?"

J. R.—"In some parts of the West of Ireland the peasantry have a secret code of signals. By waving a flag (you may call it petticoat if you like) of a certain color, the neighbors come to a cabin to assist the signaling party, who thus signifies that he is in distress. If I remember rightly, the red flag means that the process-server has come. These signals caused all the women and girls in the neighborhood to assemble."

REP.—"Didn't the men come?"

J. R.—"Such of them as had returned from England. But the women wont allow the men to resist the process-server because they are sent to jail so long for doing so, and, besides, these women think they can take care of the process-server themselves. I saw one woman near Clare Morris, a pregnant woman, who was defending the hovel that sheltered her little family, who had a bayonet thrust into her breast by these loyal servants of a woman,—the richest woman in Europe,—the 'royal lady' who gave only one day's income to relieve these her starving subjects. Do you remember, when Haynau visited Barclay & Perkins's brewery, in London, about 1850, when the workmen found that he was the man who ordered Austrian women to be whipped for political offenses, that he was kicked out of the brewery, and that all England applauded? Is it worse to whip women than to bayonet them?"

REP.—"The men didn't fight?"

J. R.—"No; they looked on. The women gave cheers for the Earl of Erne (he had been a decent landlord before Boycott was his agent), and they gave cheers for the constables (who hate this work as a rule), and they gave groans for Boycott and the process-server. Suddenly they threw mud and manure and stones at him, and he ran off with the crowd of women after him—the constables vainly trying to protect him from the violence of the infuriated women."

REP.—"Why didn't they fire?"

J. R.—"They had no magistrate with them to read the riot act. The process-server was knocked down several times. There were a couple of hundred women and girls pursuing him, and they never halted until they reached the boundary line of the parish.

"Boycott was furious. He went to Ballinrobe and secured a force of one hundred constables to protect the process-server next day, as it was the last day on which these writs could be issued if the cases were to be brought before the next session of the court. Next day the process-server refused to go, and nobody could be hired to take his place. The reason of his refusal was a visit from a woman of the parish of the Neale to his wife. This friend had told his wife that the women had found out that a process-server had no legal right to nail his writs on a cabin door, unless it was closed against him, nor to take in a constable unless he was resisted, and that they had determined to leave the doors partly open and not to fight him until he should enter, 'and, then, every woman of them 'll have a kettle of hot water handy, and fling it in his face.' Near Westport, last winter, I saw several cabin doors covered up with manure, and near Balla, last summer, I saw cabins all stoned up so as to prevent the process-server from nailing the writs on them. The family expected a visit from the process-server in the morning —he had been resisted in both instances the day before—and the people had slept out all night to be ready for a renewal of his efforts to evict them.

"'Captain' Boycott was now completely baffled, and he was wild with rage. He wrote a letter to the London *Times*, in which he said that his fences were destroyed, the gate of his demesne demolished, and his own life in danger, and that he was thus persecuted because he was a Protestant.

"Meanwhile, the people at the Neale assembled. Brass bands from Ballinrobe brought together all the people of the parish. There is a priest there greatly beloved by his people,—a man of resolute character and highly educated,—and, although he is naturally conservative, he has unbounded influence over every member of his con-

SISTER MARY FRANCIS CLARE
(The Nun of Kenmare),
Author of "The Present Case of Ireland Plainly Stated."

gregation, from the fact that he neither tolerates outrages by his parishioners on landlords, nor outrages on them by the landlords. He addressed the meeting, praised them for asserting their rights to their homes; but urged them, if the constables should come again in force, to offer them no resistance. It is Father John O'Malley.

"I was told by —— —— (it would ruin him if I were to give his name) that, after Father John had left, he told the people about my prediction of the effects of a strike against landlords, in my Clare Morris speech, and advised them to try it on Boycott at once. The advice was taken. The men advised Boycott's herdsmen and car-drivers to strike, and the women advised Boycott's servant-girls to strike, and that evening every one of them left his house.

"Next morning, when Mrs. Boycott went to buy bread, the shop-keeper told her that, although *she* was a dacent woman, and they all liked *her*, yet the people couldn't stand that 'baste of a husband of hers any longer,' and she really couldn't sell them any more bread!

"The Boycotts had to send to Ballinrobe for provisions. They would not have been ostracized by the shopkeepers there, but for Boycott's letter. Every statement in that letter was a lie. I rode past Boycott's estate shortly after it was published, and his fences and gates were in perfect order, and if his life was in danger, it must have been in danger from the armed constables who were protecting his cowardly life night and day. It exasperated the people, and they issued a decree of social excommunication against him. No shop-keeper in Ballinrobe now dared to sell him a mouthful of anything to eat, nor a yard of anything to wear."

REP.—"If the shop-keeper had ventured to defy the decree, what would have become of him?"

J. R.—"He would have been ruined. Nobody would have crossed his threshold. Since I left the County Mayo, I heard of one shop-keeper so rich that he thought he could defy the peasantry. He took a farm from which a poor tenant had been evicted. For three months nobody entered his shop. Whether this story is true or not,—I have no personal knowledge of it,—it is certain that this has been done in the West of Ireland.

"Boycott was isolated. He had to take care of his own cattle. His farm is of four hundred acres. As long ago as October 12, 1880, I wrote to the *Inter-Ocean* that the people were 'determined to drive him out of the county,' and you see they have done it, and that he admitted in New-York that no one could resist such excommunication."

REP.—"You call it sometimes isolation, sometimes excommunication, and sometimes Boycotting. How did the word Boycotting come into use?"

J. R.—"It was invented by Father John O'Malley about three days after the decree of social excommunication was issued against Boycott. Up to that time it had been called sometimes moral and sometimes social excommunication when ostracism was applied to a 'land-grabber,' as a man is called who takes a farm from which a tenant has been evicted. I was dining with Father John, at the Presbytery of the Neale, and he asked me why I was not eating.

"I said, 'I'm bothered about a word.'

"'What is it?' asked Father John.

"'Well,' I said, 'when the people ostracize a land-grabber we call it social excommunication, but we ought to have an entirely different word to signify ostracism applied to a landlord or a land-agent like Boycott. Ostracism wont do—the peasantry would not know the meaning of the word—and I can't think of any other.'

"'No,' said Father John, 'ostracism wouldn't do.'

"He looked down, tapped his big forehead, and said:

"'How would it do to call it to Boycott him?'"

"I was delighted and said, 'Tell your people to call it Boycotting, so that when the reporters come down from Dublin and London they will hear the word: use it yourself in the Castlebar *Telegraph;* I'm going to Dublin and will ask the young orators of the Land League to give it that name; I will use it in my correspondence, and between us we will make it as famous as the similar word "Lynching" in the United States.' Lynch was the name of a Virginia backwoods 'extra-judicial judge,' you know. Father John and I kept our compact; he was the first man who uttered the word and I the first who wrote it. But Father John is entitled to more credit than the mere christening of the policy. If he had not had so great an influence with his people, Boycott's conduct would have— I have not a bit of doubt of it—so exasperated the people that he would have met the fate of Feerick and Lord Montmorris, both of whom were killed within three miles of Boycott's farm, and both of them within a mile of constabulary stations. By his firmness and his popularity he 'held the fort' until Boycott quietly sneaked out of the parish, and this surrender inspired the people all over the West of Ireland with a faith in the policy of Boycotting that they had never had before and might never have held. To be perfectly just, Boycott is entitled to some credit himself; for even Father John's influence would have been powerless, I think—some compromise might have been made—if Captain Boycott had not been such an insolent tyrant, and hated by every man and woman in the neighborhood who ever had any dealings with him."

REP.—"Did the Earl of Erne get his rents?"

J. R.—"No. He had been popular before Boycott became his agent, and after Boycott was Boycotted—on the very next evening—the tenantry of the Earl assembled, every man of them, and sent him a letter, apologizing for their treatment of his agent, but stating that they would hold no further communication with him, either officially or otherwise, and that they would never pay him a shilling, but that, as soon as they conveniently could do so, they would pay any other person whom the Earl should appoint to receive the rent. They said that they had come to this resolution because they were convinced that his agent had been prejudicing his lordship against them, and that for their own protection they had determined to refuse to have any further dealings with him.

"'*The majority of these people,*' said Father John,—I am now reading from a letter that I wrote on October 12, and that you published in the *Inter-Ocean*,—' *these tenants of the Earl, had been supported for nine months previously on charity. They got no help of any kind from the landlord.* They attributed his neglect of them to ' Captain ' Boycott. The Earl stood by his agent, and he has got no rent yet.

"But Boycott's letter to the London *Times* had a great result. The English Government and the Irish landlords were paralyzed by this new policy. Although the London *Times*, in commenting on my Leenane speech, sneeringly said that the Government would 'know how to deal with this policy of passive resistance with which they were threatened,' it found that it did *not* know what to do about it—because no laws could force any man to deal with a shop-keeper whom he disliked, nor to speak to a man whom he hated. The blasphemous Boycott's suggestion that he was persecuted because he was a Protestant, gave the landlords a cue. They thought they could arouse the old feud between the Protestants and Catholics, by which England has been enabled to divide and ruin Ireland for two centuries. So, they called for subscriptions to organize what they termed a 'Relief Expedition'—to dig Boycott's potatoes. The Earl of Erne anonymously headed the subscription with £50. Money poured in from landlords. Fifty loafers from Fermanagh were hired—these were heralded as champions of the Protestant faith. The scheme aroused only ridicule in Mayo, because Mayo is the most Catholic county in Ireland, and yet it elected Rev. Mr. Neilson, a Protestant preacher from Belfast, as one of its two representatives in Parliament. Erne owns 31,389 acres in Fermanagh, and only 2184 in Mayo.

"Seven regiments of soldiers were sent to protect the potato-diggers. Nobody would sell them anything to eat. The landlords had paid these men's expenses and their wages. They went to Boycott and asked what they should do for something to eat? He said, in a surly tone, that he supposed they must eat some of the potatoes they were digging. You've heard of Irish hospitality? Boycott invented a new variety. He charged these men, his 'rescuers,' fourpence a stone for all the potatoes that they ate. He incurred the hatred of the troops and the constabulary by treating them with similar hospitality.

"It was published that it cost the British Government £5,000 sterling to dig £500 worth of potatoes, but I see that Captain Boycott says, preserving the same proportion, that he had only £350 sterling worth of potatoes; and that it cost the British Government £3,500 sterling to gather them. In fact it taught the people of the West of Ireland that, without bloodshed or outrage, they could successfully resist the aggressions of the landlord.

"So far from Father John O'Malley encouraging violence, as Boycott charges, he simply sanctioned the scheme of ostracism which is now called Boycottism, in order to secure the rights of the tenants, and prevent them from resorting to violence.

"The English Government has charged the expense to the County Mayo,—punishing every one alike, those who, in its opinion, were guilty and those who were innocent,—but as the landlords will exact as rent everything inside of the skin of the potato if the British Government does not, it makes no practical difference to the people whether the Earl of Erne's agent or John Bright's associates vent their Dick Turpin spleen on the poor tenantry. If it costs the British Government £3,500 to dig £350 of potatoes, how much will it cost it to dig all the potatoes and cut down all the crops belonging to landlords in Ireland next harvest if the Land League advises a strike?

"Captain Boycott goes on to say that he has been made a scape-goat for the uprising against the agents because he was more prominent than the others. Translated into plain English, this means that he was more odious than the others, because he was the greatest tyrant in the West of Ireland, with the possible exception of Trench, the agent for Lansdowne, and Mr. Hussey. 'No matter what the business of a peasant with Boycott might be,'—I am quoting the words of a gentleman. of Ballinrobe as I wrote them down in short-hand at the time,—'the poor man was sure to be cursed and abused by him. He did not treat them as human beings at all: he so exasperated them by his brutal tongue and conduct that when they got a chance they just rose against him as one man. But,' he added, 'Boycott is well tamed now!'

"I see that Captain Boycott says that the tenants have paid more money to their leaders than their rent would cost. The Land League has already reduced the rentals of Ireland, as I have already stated, some $15,000,000 per annum. In a large number of cases, it has already brought the rental down to Griffith's valuation, whereas last winter, when I was in the West of Ireland, every landlord who '*only*' charged fifty per cent. over Griffith's valuation was accounted a good landlord. The money contributed by the people of Ireland to the support of the Land League does not amount to probably more than one-thousandth part of the reduction made through the influence of the Land League in the rentals of Ireland. There were not more than half a dozen men paid for their services by the Land League—at least while I was in Ireland—and they were men of education, who were content to receive the salaries of second-class clerks in Chicago. There is not one of them who could not have doubled or quadrupled his salary by returning to the business in which he was formerly engaged before entering the service of the Land League. The expenses of the Land League are occasioned by supporting tenants who have been arbitrarily evicted owing to an inability to pay rent after a year of famine, during six months of which they were supported by the credit of the shopkeepers, and during the other six months of which they were supported by the charity of America."

Rep.—" Captain Boycott says that the average profits of the landlord at the existing rents have not been four per cent. of the value of the land, and yet he says that he thinks the average abatement of rents has been at least seventeen and a half per cent., and that some of the landlords have abated as much as twenty-five per cent. How do you reconcile these statements?"

J. R.—" My answer is that Captain Boycott, himself, was charging as rent more than any American farmer would give for the fee simple to the soil, and that when he says that the profits have been four per cent. on the value of the land, he ingeniously remembers to forget that ninety-nine-hundredths of the renting value of the land was created by the tenants by their own labor, at their own sole expense. For example, in this very parish of Neale, the land is mostly rock and the thinnest of thin soil, which can only be cultivated by incessant manuring and by spade tillage. Such land in Illinois could not be given away.

"The Earl of Erne, and other landlords for whom Boycott was agent, never spent any money on the improvement of their estates. They compelled their tenants to make all the improvements themselves, and under Boycott's management, as fast as they created what he calls the 'value' of the lands, the rents were raised. The lands of the Earl of Erne, as nature made them, were not worth a shilling an acre, and the exorbitant rents that he was compelling the tenants to pay for them were a tax on their own industry. The best answer to Boycott's statement that he had never any trouble with his neighbors before Father John O'Malley's speech, is the fact that he was obliged to be attended by two constables for a long time before that date, and that after one of the rises of rent he speaks of he was very glad to escape with his life. I don't know any community in the Western States where he would not have been lynched years ago if he had been guilty of one-tenth part of the insolence and tyranny which were reported to me about him by his own tenants in the County Mayo; and yet the people in that county would die for any decent landlord. For example, while Boycott dare not return there, while Lord Sligo dare not live there, while Oranmore and Browne does not dare to live there, Thomas Tyghe and one or two landlords who live between Clare Morris and Boycott's house, a distance of less than ten miles, could raise a thousand men to protect them. They have no need whatever of police protection, while Rourke, another land-agent within three miles of Boycott's place, is obliged to go around with two constables guarding him whenever he leaves his home, and Feerick, another land-agent who imitated Boycott, was killed last spring within three miles of Captain Boycott's house. That part of the county is inhabited by Fenians, and, therefore, is not a safe country for a tyrant to live in. Yet nothing can exceed the loyalty and devotion of the Irish peasantry to any landlord who treats them decently."

Rep.—" I notice that Captain Boycott says that he is in favor of such a revision of the land laws as will secure to the tenant the value of his permanent improvements."

J. R.—" Boycott himself, ever since he was an agent in the West of Ireland, has taxed his tenantry to the full value of all the improvements they have made on them, and he has persistently opposed, as communism, any attempt to vest in the tenant the value of the improvement he has made. This declaration of Boycott is one of the strongest proofs that I have met of the beneficent influence of the Land League."

REP.—" Boycott further says in the New-York *Herald's* interview, that 'if the land bill of Gladstone should include the three F's, it would not materially improve the condition of the mass of the Irish people, because if they had the land for nothing it would not support them, as it is the sole ambition of an Irishman to get a portion of the land, or even a cow-house, as a homestead; that in mountain districts and on the western sea-board there are large populations gathered together in villages, composed of families having houses and from three to five acres of land, mostly of inferior quality, and they are all the time complaining that from the produce of these patches they are unable to support themselves. Now, how can a man reasonably expect,' he asks, ' to feed and clothe a wife, himself, and, perchance, half a dozen children on the produce of three, four, or even half a dozen acres ? The fact is that all the trouble in Ireland is caused by the insane desire of the people to farm land at all hazards. The demand is greater than the supply, and that is all about it.' So says Captain Boycott; what say you, Mr. Redpath, to that ? "

J. R.—" English writers, statisticians, and agricultural and political economists, have demonstrated that Ireland can support, with comfort, at least fifteen millions of people, while the population of Ireland to-day is, probably, not more than five millions. The County Mayo, for example, could support, in comfort, probably five times its present population. But it cannot support the present population, in comfort, when all the good land in the county—nine-tenths of the good land —is held by men like Lord Lucan and agents like Captain Boycott (by the by, his title of captain is a fraud; he is not a captain); by men who take all the good land as grazing farms and throw the poor people into bogs and barren mountain-sides. Remember that all of these good lands were reclaimed from sterility by the people themselves, and that when the famine of 1847 came they were driven from them, either into the grave or the poorhouse, or into exile, when they failed to pay a single year's rent. What Boycott calls the insane desire of the people to farm is simply the instinct of self-preservation, because in the West of Ireland there are no manufactures and no industries, and no means by which the people can live, and it should be borne in mind that the manufactures of Ireland were prohibited by the British legislature for generations, and that since the repeal of these laws by the triumph of Catholic emancipation, when any companies undertake to carry on a manufactory in Ireland, outside of Belfast or the Protestant counties of Ulster, which are a part of the ' English garrison,' a combination of British manufacturers ruin them. That is the reason why I am urging the Irish in America to Boycott all British manufactures, and especially Irish linen, because these manufacturers, British and ' West Britons,' are the bitterest enemies of the Irish people, and leave them the land as their sole resource; while, at the same time, they encourage the landlords to confiscate without compensation all the improvements of this wretched peasantry, and to drive them from the farms. Ireland is too small a country to support three sets of feeders—vampires, namely, the landlords; leeches, namely, the land-agents; and the toilers, namely, the common people."

Rep.—"Boycott was asked by the New-York *Herald* reporter 'whether the land laws of Ireland will, in all important points, compare unfavorably with those in France, in England, and other countries, as affecting the interest of the tenant,' and he answered, 'certainly not; that the Irish tenant enjoys a greater freedom in dealing with his land than does his brother farmer in England; that, as a rule, no yearly tenant in Ireland is bound down as to how he shall crop and dispose of the products of his land, and that in England there is a hard and fast rule as to the routine of cropping, and what produce may be sold.' What are your views on this subject, Mr. Redpath?"

J. R.—"The system of land tenure in the Protestant counties of Ireland and in England and Scotland is radically different from the system of land tenure in the West of Ireland. There is no grave injustice in an English landlord evicting his tenant when he is unable to pay his rent, because the landlord built the farm-house and the houses of the farm laborers, the barns, stables, fences, and, as a rule, at his own expense subsoiled and reclaimed the land, or else made an allowance to the tenant for so doing. Properly speaking, there are no peasantry in England. The farmers are capitalists, and employ laborers, who are the most degraded class of workingmen in all Europe, excepting, possibly, the serfs of Russia before their emancipation.

"The English and Scotch landlords live on their estates, and have a personal interest in their tenants, and, as a rule, they are indulgent to them; whereas most of the Irish landlords are either English absentees, or they live in remote parts of Ireland and know nothing whatever about the condition of their tenantry, while the land-agents are paid a percentage of the rents which they collect, and consequently have a selfish interest in squeezing the last penny from them. There is no parallel between the land system of Ireland and the rest of Europe to-day. Even the late Russian serfs are infinitely better off than the peasantry of Ireland under Queen Victoria. The best proof that the misery of Ireland is caused by the land-tenure system is shown by the fact that since Hardenberg and Stein abolished the feudal system of land tenure in Germany,—and the same may be said of France,—the peasantry of those countries are now the most prosperous working people in Europe, whereas formerly they were as wretched as the Irish. Most of the erroneous and unjust judgments passed by the American press on the Irish Land League movement come from the belief that the Irish land system resembles the land system of America, England, and other civilized countries, whereas it is feudalism stripped of all the features that rendered feudalism tolerable. It represents the most grasping form of the commercial spirit. It recognizes no duty whatever on the part of the landlord. Many of the rents were so high that if the little holding raised a big crop of potatoes, and they should be sold at the highest market price, the amount obtained would not pay the rent."

Rep.—"Then how is the rent paid?"

J. R.—"The poor men have to leave their wives early in the spring and work all summer in England in order to make money enough to pay the landlords. Boycott conveniently forgot to say that those very tenants who Boycotted him were supported for nearly nine months last year by American charity."

Rep.—"Captain Boycott says that the only remedy for the Irish trouble is emigration. What do you say about that?"

J. R.—"I think he is right, and more than that, he is honest, for once, because he has set the example himself. Ireland will be prosperous just as soon as all the landlords and all the agents are forced to emigrate, and not till then.

"Captain Boycott's other plan for the regeneration of Ireland is the introduction of outside capital to carry on manufacturing industries. He says that there is no reason why Ireland should not have her own manufactories for glass, wool, and many other articles of domestic consumption. He attributes the fact that there are no such manufactories to the faults of the people, themselves; because, at the present time, no capitalist could be found to invest money in its disaffected condition. Why are the people disaffected? Landlordism is the cause of it, and English hatred of the Irish. The Irish who come to America fill our manufactories, and yet while they are well paid here—paid double what they would ever have expected to receive there—our manufactories flourish. Ireland has coal-beds, marble quarries, and vast mineral resources, but it has been utterly impossible for any capitalists to work them, owing to the exorbitant exactions of the landlords. Irish absentee landlordism blights every industry as well as the country itself."

REP.—" Captain Boycott says that he considers that the constabulary is thoroughly reliable, and that the Irish element in the British army would never betray their trust in the event of a rising of the people. Do you think so?."

J. R.—" Yes, I do! The constabulary are not policemen. They are armed and drilled soldiers; armed with muskets, buck-shot, and bayonets, and under military discipline, and whatever their sympathies may be, they are obliged to obey orders. Last year and this year, they have again and again bayoneted and shot down women, and when soldiers do that, they can be 'implicitly relied on' by any form of despotism. I, myself, saw a woman into whose breast a constable ran a bayonet for seeking to defend her own home. As far as the regular army goes, of course, they are trustworthy, because the English Government took special care to eliminate all Irish soldiers from the regiments sent into Ireland. They are all English and Scotch."

REP.—" Captain Boycott says that Parnell is a very good leading man, but denies that his programme has the adherence of the people at large; that the masses are with him, it is true, but that the intellect of the country is against him. How is that?"

J. R.—" I have always supposed that the masses of the people meant the people at large, and as for the 'intellect' of the country being against him, I never read in history of a single instance in which the owners of despotic power were not against the masses of the people."

REP.—" Why did the people cheer the constabulary, and yet maltreat the process-server? Were they not equally guilty?"

J. R.—" Because the people regard the constables as only doing their duty, however degrading that duty may be, while they execrate the process-servers because they are volunteers—*they* are not obliged by law to serve ejectment notices; they are only obliged to serve civil decrees."

REP. — " What proportion of the landlords in Mayo and Galway are absentees?"

J. R.—" Father John O'Malley told me that there are more absentees in Mayo than in Galway. 'In Galway,'* he said, 'I should say that one-fourth are absentees; but in Mayo, fully one-half, on the average. Dillon, Sligo, Lucan, Erne, Cooper, Farmer, Farroll, Jameson, Kilmaine, De Clifford, and several others—all large landlords, owners of two-thirds of the County Mayo—are absentees. Nearly one-half of Galway is owned by absentees. Many of them never visit their estates at all, and have never seen them. In the parish of the Neale (where Boycott lived), there is not now, and there has not been for the last half-century, a single resident landlord.'

"I asked Father John whether this

---

* These quotations are from short-hand notes taken at the time, and subsequently revised by the priest.

absenteeism was owing to the reason assigned by the English press, that agrarian outrages made it impossible for the landlords to live on their estates. The priest said:

"'For the last twenty-five years there has not been a single agrarian assassination, or an attempt at one, in this parish, either on landlords or their agents. Some of these landlords come over once in a while, for a few days, and never one of them has been, or pretended to be, in any danger.'"

REP.—"What is the condition of the peasantry of Ireland?"

J. R.—"I never yet saw a single cabin in the Southern States so wretched; I never met a slave so badly dressed; I never saw a slave so poorly fed—as three millions of the industrious people of Ireland are lodged, clothed, and fed to-day. Southern slavery, with the single exception,—and that was a very important exception,—of the right to sell vested in the slaveholder, was a system, infernal as it was, vastly superior to the system of Irish tenantry at this very hour. But I have my notes of a conversation with Father John O'Malley, in Boycott's own parish, and it is specific in its details. I will read them, only omitting my preliminary questions:

"'As to their indolence,' said Father John, "from my own experience of them, and from what I have heard from so many high authorities about the peasantry in other countries, I consider the Irish peasantry as the most industrious and hard-working race on the face of the earth. What do you think now that you have seen them at home?'

"'With the sole exception of the Chinese,' I answered, 'I think they are not excelled in industry by any race in America, and that they are only equaled by the Germans.'

"'Not only all over the West,' continued Father John, 'does the head of the family himself work, and his grown boys, and all the women, but even the youngest females, as soon as they are able to do any work—not only in the house, but hard work in the fields, as you have seen everywhere. They are so industrious in their habits, and so soon are they set to work as children, that unless I make it a point to secure the attendance of the children at school between the ages of five and eleven, I might bid farewell to all hopes of teaching them at all. If the people did not work as incessantly as they do, how could they procure even the commonest sustenance for their large families after paying such exorbitant rents and taxes? From my experience and observation, all over this West of Ireland (and I have had a large experience, and seen most of it thoroughly), I can truly say that, in ninety-nine cases out of a hundred, whenever you see any Irish peasant not at work it is simply because he can find nothing to do.

"'Now, then, as to his improvidence,' continued Father John, 'why, Mr. Redpath, the very idea of charging these struggling peasants of Ireland with improvidence is cruel sarcasm. Let me tell you how the ordinary peasant lives. But, after all, I need not tell you how he lives—you have seen enough of it; but possibly you have had no opportunity to see how they are fed?'

"'No, sir.'

"'Well,' said the priest, 'let me give you the daily bill of fare of these peasant families: For breakfast, potatoes. If they are pretty comfortable, they have a little milk and butter with it. But, in the great majority of cases, they have nothing but the potatoes, or possibly a salt herring. The dinner and the supper are only a repetition of the breakfast. That is their bill of fare all the year round excepting at Easter and Christmas, when even the poorest try hard to get a few pounds of meat—generally "American meat."

"'You have seen everywhere that the clothing of the peasantry is made by themselves from the wool. They shear it, spin it, get it woven and dyed themselves into flannel and frieze. "Frieze?" Frieze is home-made cloth. How *can* any people be more provident than people who live on the meanest diet that can support life, and who not only make their own clothing but make and dye the cloth itself?'

"Would you like some more?"

REP.—"Go on."

J. R.—"Well, let me read the rest of my report:

"'Well, Father John, now as to intemperance—I am not asking for my own information, for I know the truth about it—how do you answer the statement that in Ireland, with all its poverty, there is so much consumption of alcoholic drinks?'"

"'In the first place,' said Father John, 'the amount consumed in Ireland is not all drank by the peasantry, which the argument assumes. You must take away, in the first place, all that is consumed by the upper and middle classes, by the Government officials, and in strictly temperate families—for drinking in Ireland, as in England, is a universal social usage—and you must remember that the expensive wines and liquors are consumed by these classes. The poorer classes never drink any liquors that are costly. You must also deduct what is consumed by the working classes—by *all* classes—in the towns and cities, because no complaint has ever been made by Irish reformers about their poverty being *specially* caused by bad laws. They may be affected by an expensive form of government causing heavy taxes—but so are the laboring classes of England; and the Irish worker of the cities has also the additional wrong done him that English legislation destroyed Irish manufactures, while the land laws, by driving out the rural population, ruined all the minor home industries. But to keep strictly to the point, it is against the peasantry that this charge is made—for they are the only class whose grievances at this time are specifically championed. Now I assert, from my personal knowledge and from the concurring testimony of hundreds of priests in different parts of Ireland—as well as by other trustworthy evidence—that, excepting on very rare occasions, such as a fair-day, the Irish peasant rarely drinks at all. On fair-days he does drink, because it is the custom of the country for the seller to treat the buyer to a drink after the sale of sheep or a cow. The charge that the Irish peasant is a constant drinker is a gross and cruel calumny. Of course, there are a few rash, foolish creatures who are an exception, but as a rule, the Irish peasant is temperate both from necessity and from religious influences. Drunkenness is exceedingly rare in rural Ireland.'"

REP.—"I see that Boycott says he came to America only on a visit, and he is going down to Virginia to see a friend in Amelia County."

J. R.—"Yes: 'birds of a feather.' I was asked by Father Corbett, of Clare Morris, if I could not have an absentee Irish landlord in Amelia County, Virginia, Boycotted! Little did I ever think that Boycott himself would go there! Father James gave me seven writs of ejectment that this Irish-Virginian had issued against some of the most famished peasants near Clare Morris. I gave them to Major Conyngham, editor of the New-York *Tablet*. They are brought by 'Murray Magregor Blacker, of Haw Branch, Amelia Court House, Virginia, U. S. A., against Thomas Mullee, of Kilcolman, for £6 6s. rent; against Michael Prendergast, of Kilcolman, for £7 10s.; against Patrick Nevin, of Cuilbeg, for £4 10s.; against Patrick Clarke, of Cuilbeg, for £3; against Martin Mudlany, of Lisnaborla, for £12 10s.; against Michael Flannigan, of Boherduff, for £7 10s., and against Thomas Mullee, of Boherduff, for £15 10s.'

"This man, Blacker, never gave a shilling for the relief of these tenants, who were kept out of their graves by foreign charity. Their lands are wretched holdings, and the rents are extortionate, but 'Captain' Boycott's friend, Mr. Blacker, is as pitiless as his guest. Since the yellow fever met the cholera at New Orleans a few years since, there has never been such an illustration of the law that like seeks like, as the meeting of Boycott and Blacker will be!"

XIV.

IRISH LANDLORDS AND IRISH LAND LEAGUERS.

[The Omaha (Nebraska) *Herald* of February 15 says: "James Redpath, journalist and the advocate of liberty, lectured at the Academy of Music last night under the auspices of the Irish Land League. The house was filled in spite of inclement weather with a most intelligent and eager audience. Mayor Chase presided and introduced the speaker, who was enthusiastically received. He is a forcible and magnetic speaker. A brief or hasty outline of his speech, which continued nearly three hours, can give but little idea of the graphic pictures that Mr. Redpath drew of Irish life, purity, and fortitude, as he had seen it last year. At the close of the speech, Mr. John Rush read a series of resolutions which were adopted, thanking Mr. Redpath, whom they termed 'the Lafayette of Irish Land Reform.' Rousing cheers were given for Parnell, Redpath, and Davitt. A dispatch was read from the Irish-American members of the Senate and House of Representatives of the State, greeting and welcoming Mr. Redpath to Nebraska. In order to obtain his views more fully, a *Herald* reporter interviewed Mr. Redpath yesterday afternoon and was accorded a free expression from that gentleman: "]

REPORTER.—" What, in your opinion, will be the result of the present agitation in Ireland?"

MR. REDPATH.—"The establishment of peasant proprietorship. Of course I do not expect that this result will be reached at once. The landed proprietors will make a desperate struggle— first to resist any change in the present relations of landlord and tenant; then to make as few changes as possible; then to defeat peasant proprietorship. The struggle may last two or three years, but if the Irish peasantry stand firm, and are not provoked into insurrection, I have no doubt that, first, the London companies and all corporations will be forced by Parliament to sell; then that the absentees will have to let go their grip of the soil—and then the rest will be easy. There are only eight thousand landlords of all grades in Ireland, including owners of one acre, and also I believe including the holders of long leases; but two thousand out of these eight thousand hold more land than all the rest put together, and three thousand out of the eight thousand are absentees. They draw—these absentees—$60,000,000 every year from Ireland, and do absolutely no service in return either to their tenants or to the country—except to slander the Irish people throughout the world, and to call for coercion laws."

REP.—" What do you mean by the London companies and the corporations?"

J. R.—" James the First confiscated six out of the thirty-two counties of Ireland and granted them to favorites and corporations. The Protestant Bishop of Ulster got forty-three thousand acres, Trinity College got thirty thousand acres, and the Trades-Unions of London got two hundred and ten thousand acres, on condition of planting them with English tenants and driving out the native inhabitants. The city of Derry, in the North, was granted to these companies, rebuilt and called Londonderry. Now these companies are all bad landlords. Corporations have no souls, as Blackstone says, to be damned, nor, he adds, the portion of the body that is kicked, but I think they will be kicked out of Ireland. I visited the estates of the Trinity College in the island of Valencia, and at

Cahirciveen, in the County Kerry, and I nowhere saw more horrible spectacles of human wretchedness."

REP.—" You mean their estates will be confiscated?"

J. R.—" No; they ought to be. But they may be purchased by the state and then sold to the tenants."

REP.—" Would not this be an unprecedented action?"

J. R.—" No; it was done in Belgium and in Germany within the present century—not from motives of philanthropy, but as a measure of safety to the state. It is only in Ireland that feudal landlordism exists. It does not exist in England or Scotland. In fact the Irish tenant-at-will is a serf of the soil, and even Russia has abolished that system. Irish landlordism is worse than feudalism,—I might almost say it is the opposite,—for a feudal lord had to feed, clothe, lodge, and protect his tenant in return for his service, while in Ireland the lord of the soil does nothing but starve him, clothe him in rags, pass penal and coercion laws against him, and defame him. These absentees care no more about their tenants than if they were beasts—less, in fact, because they do feed and keep their horses and cattle in prime order."

REP.—" Can you give the exact figures of Irish landlordism?"

J. R.—" Yes, 6,000 are small proprietors; 1,198 own from 2,000 to 5,000 acres each—in all one-sixth of the soil of Ireland; 185 own from 10,000 to 20,000 acres each; 90 own from 20,000 to 50,000 each; 24 own from 50,000 to 100,000, while 3 own over 100,000; over 36,000 own only one acre each. The Devon commission found—in 1844—681,000 farms exceeding one acre. In Connaught, several proprietors had over 100,000 acres each; while, out of 155,842 farms in that province, 100,254 had from one to four acres each. In 1871, the absentee proprietors owned 5,120,169 acres of the soil of Ireland."

REP.—" What is a tenant-at-will?"

J. R —" A man who can be evicted at the will or caprice of the landlord and have all of his improvements confiscated. There are 682,237 tenants in Ireland. Now out of these, 626,628,' or about 73 per cent., are tenants-at-will."

REP.—" Did not Gladstone's act of 1870 protect these tenants?"

J. R.—" It was intended to do so, but it has been a dead letter because the landlords conspired to defeat it, and every case between a landlord and tenant is tried before a court of landlords, and they always construe every doubt in favor of the landlord. The judiciary of Ireland is more corrupt, from Chief Justice May down, than the judiciary of New-York was under Boss Tweed's rule in New-York. The large farmers of the East were cheated out of their rights under the Gladstone act by being compelled to sign leases under which they waived all the rights intended to be conferred on them by the law of 1870, and in the West the tenants were too poor to fight the landlords, as law proceedings are not only tedious but excessively expensive."

REP.—" In the Queen's speech it was said that this law had been of great benefit to Ireland."

J. R.—" It was never enforced until last summer, when the Land League took up the cases brought before them and had them tried before the courts by their own lawyers."

REP.—" What is the quickest way to learn the truth about Ireland on this side of the Big Pond?"

J. R.—" Read what the English papers and books say about Ireland, and then believe the exact opposite. In nine cases out of ten, you will hit the mark by adopting this plan. Remember that all the cable dispatches are sent over here by the bitterest enemies of the Irish people—the most servile parasites of the Irish landlords and the British Government."

REP.—" Why doesn't Parnell go in and support Gladstone and the English liberals?"

J. R.—"Why, because as far as the Irish are concerned, there is no essential difference between English tories and English liberals, or even English republicans. What the Irish want is the abolition of landlordism, that every tenant shall own the soil he tills, and that Ireland shall have home rule—which does not mean independence, but the same right that every State in this Union has, and every province in Canada has, and every colony in the Australian group has—the right to regulate its own local affairs. Gladstone and Bright believe that the relation of landlord and tenant in Ireland should exist, but be modified—and they equally believe in the right of the English to govern the Irish. The Irish don't want landlordism modified but abolished. The Irish don't want the English to rule them but to rule themselves. No compromise is possible between these positions. They are inherently antagonistic. Besides, how do you expect Parnell and his party to support the so-called 'liberal' government when that same government has done its best to put him and his associates into jail? Would any party in America support a government that was trying to put its leaders into jail?"

REP.—"You don't take any stock, then, in the liberal professions of the British Government?"

J. R.—"None. The British Government is the most cruel, the most corrupt, the most tyrannical government on this globe to-day, among nations that have even the semblance of liberty. When has it ever done justice, except under fear of compulsion? It grants home rule to Australia, because the Australians are so far away that they could throw off British trammels; it grants home rule to Canada, because Canada is so near the United States; and yet, when Ireland asks for home rule, England yells out that such a policy would be the 'decomposition' of the empire. It was forced by the philanthropic classes of England to abolish slavery in Jamaica, but it refused to abolish there the curse which renders its amazing fertility of no service to its people—the same curse which blights Ireland—absentee proprietorship. No, England will do nothing for Ireland that is worth doing until it is worried into doing it. Parnell knows his people and his enemy, and he is taking the only course that is likely to succeed."

REP.—"Do you think there will be an insurrection in Ireland?"

J. R.—"No, I hope not; it would only end in disaster at this time. The young Irish are well educated, and they know that it would please England if there was an insurrection, and they have no intention of gratifying her."

REP.—"How often have you lectured, since you came from Ireland?"

J. R.—"About 60 times in 60 different cities, east, west, and south."

REP.—"What is the feeling about Ireland?"

J. R.—"The Irish-Americans everywhere are enthusiastic over the Land League programme, and the Americans of the West are solid in their sympathy for the Irish people in this struggle; while in the East the vast majority of the Americans who care anything at all about Irish problems are pleased with it. England imagines that we have forgotten the *Alabama* and the English sneers against us during the late war; but she will find that we have better memories than she gives us the credit of. The Americans only want to understand this Irish land question to be, heart and soul, everywhere—as they are now nearly everywhere—in sympathy with the Land League movement."

[In a letter describing the famous obstruction debate over the constabulary estimates in the English House of Commons, Mr. Redpath elaborates the same opinion expressed in this interview respecting English liberalism that he has everywhere advocated in America. He wrote:]

"I have lost faith in English Radicalism. The English Radical *thinks in English;* he seems incapable of discussing Irish questions from the point of view of equality or even of justice; he is always arguing whether it is expedient for England to '*concede*' this right or that measure; and, if he has written an article or two in some London weekly or monthly, the English Radical regards himself as entitled to distinguished consideration from the Irish race. John Bright's speech was a coruscation of this sentiment. He did not deny, he said, his utterances in behalf of Ireland; he took not one of them back, but re-affirmed each one of them; he had been, and he was, a friend of Ireland, and of Irish aspirations. And having said all this—not in these words, but with elaborate skill —he asked, *what?* That the Irish members would kindly offer no obstacle against arming a force of twelve thousand constabulary with rifles and buckshot to shoot down the Irish people! There is no more need of an armed police in Ireland than in England— because, as every week's criminal calendar shows, there are fewer crimes committed, in proportion to population, in Ireland than in England.

"'Call me brother!' said the French Jacobins, 'or I will kill thee!'

"'I have called thee brother, Paddy,' says Quaker Bright, 'and now let me shoot thee.'

"'I will not be the instrument of injustice,' quoth Quaker Forster, 'but I refuse to substitute batons for buckshot!'

"Buckshot Quakers, or British Liberals, or English republicans—they are all alike; there is no sense in trying to conciliate them. They must be fought with their own weapons. I trust that as soon as public opinion is so ripe in Ireland that the present timeserving Home Rulers and Liberals will be compelled to act under Mr. Parnell's lead, that, then, obstruction will be advanced one step further, and that Irish members will 'interfere' at *every* stage with *every* English measure, and introduce *every* reform bill, one by one, that *any* class of Englishmen demand— making themselves the organs and exponents of English disaffection, just in order to teach the English Government and the English 'liberal' members to attend to their own business, and let the Irish rule Ireland, or else showing them that the Irish will rule England through the machinery of her own self-enacted parliamentary rules."

XV.

THE TRUE REMEDY.

[This is a speech by proxy. It was sent by Mr. Redpath to several Land League meetings and read, in response to large numbers of invitations to speak, after the British press had denounced his addresses at Leenane and Clare Morris. "This letter," says the Kerry *Sentinel*, "was written in reply to an invitation to speak at a Land meeting, but our readers will find in it an exposition so thorough and masterly that we have little doubt it will call forth admiration even from many who may differ in some respects from the theories which it propounds. Only a few months ago, Mr. Redpath came to this country an utter stranger, having no knowledge of the country save, of course, that which one of his education and attainments must have gathered of it in the course of his reading. How prejudiced were the sources from which that information was in most instances derived, he himself has very truly described. But this extensive knowledge, his keen insight, and his long acquaintance with other nations and other peoples, enabled him to see at a glance the enormities of the system of legislation under which the Irish people battle for existence; and he required but to travel amongst them, to see their homes, and judge for himself of the evil effects of the system, when his most generous sympathies were enlisted on behalf of the people of Erin, and we say—truly say—of him that he is now *ipsis Hibernis, Hibernior*—more Irish than the Irish themselves." Here is the letter as read, only two sentences having been added to make the meaning more clear:]

My dear Sir:

IT would give me great pleasure to attend your meeting, but my duties elsewhere prevent me from accepting any more invitations to speak for the people—numerous and very cordial as these invitations are. The same duties prevent me from complying with the recommendations of the London and Dublin landlord press to return to America, nor to stand upon the order of my going, but to go at once—many and really sincere as these suggestions are. By priests, and leagues, and audiences in the West of Ireland I have been urged to speak, but in London, in Ulster, and in Dublin I find myself charged, both on public platforms and in the press, with " abusing the hospitality of the country " by having yielded to these requests. If I spoke again I should answer these toadies and parasites of the landlords; and perhaps you will read to your friends a summary of my reply to them?

What right has an American citizen to talk in Ireland on Irish politics? Because Americans believe that taxation without representation is tyranny; and because America is taxed every year to pay the rack-rents of the West of Ireland landlords; and because America, whenever there is a famine, is expected to pay the expense of saving tens of thousands of Irish tenants from starvation, although Mr. Gladstone has admitted that the property of the landlords is legally liable for this charge. As nearly as I can ascertain, more than half of the rents of the small holdings along the Atlantic coast of Ireland are paid by the exiled sons and daughters of their tillers, now in America. That is one reason why the landlords are so anxious to send out the young people—because their earnings enable the old folks at home to pay rents out of all proportion to the value of the produce that can be raised on their farms. When the landed Shylocks of Ireland cease to take half of their pound of flesh from America, then (and not till then) Americans will have no right to discuss the character of their exactions.

But consider the supreme arrogance of these cockneys and landlord parasites! The free people of Ireland are not to be permitted to invite any gentleman, traveling in their country, to address them, unless what he says shall be acceptable to the monarchical flunkeys of London and the religious bigots of Belfast! As if *any* honest American *could* speak pleasant words about the petty tyrants called landlords who rule Ireland! As if every American—Protestant, Catholic, Rationalist, Materialist, Spiritualist—without regard to religious belief or non-belief in religion—did not despise every form and phase of religious intolerance! Oh, yes! England is the "land of the free and the home of the brave"; but if any stranger tells the truth in Ireland —really, you know, "it's outrageous, you know," "pure Socialism, you know," —and Lord Montmorris died of it,— although, to be sure, he lay stark and cold long before the "seditious language" was uttered! "Conscience makes cowards of us all," and it is because the landlords know their own crimes that one feeble voice crying in the wilderness thus alarms them.

If I had the gift of eloquence, and could postpone other duties in America, I should never leave Ireland until I had addressed the people wherever they invited me—to pay back to England the great gift she made us, with the applause of her aristocracy, in sending George Thompson, one of her most brilliant orators, to denounce and help to destroy American slavery, before that twin monster of Irish landlordism died the death it merited. Our tyrants denounced him, as your tyrants denounced me; but John Bright applauded him across the Atlantic, and preached the same doctrine to us that Wendell Phillips preaches to you— "Destroy the evil. No compromise with it." The English aristocracy sent money to help on our anti-slavery movement, and the American democracy will pay it back in contributions to help the anti-landlordism movement.

There is a perfect parallel between the development of the anti-slavery movement in America and the growth —albeit the more rapid growth—of the anti-landlordism movement in Ireland. If the parallel shall continue, judging from the past, you are threatened by three dangers—violence, disunion, and compromise.

The young men must be taught that violence is not criminal only, but stupid; that this great reform must be accomplished by moral, social, and political agencies; and next, that patriotic projects never hinder, but always help each other; and that, although their methods may, and even *must* differ, they never can conflict.

It seems to me, as a friendly and impartial looker-on, that the Land League movement is Ireland's last hope of saving her race and her nationality from an absorption which, however it might benefit other races and nations, would enable and force the coming historian to tell her story in one sad word—*failed*. For, until O'Connell rose, and after he fell, every patriotic movement has—*failed*. Irish hero-worship is the worship of unsuccess. Think of it: in 1,400 years, two men only have succeeded in their efforts until death overtook them—St. Patrick and Daniel O'Connell. I do not mention the military hero who rose on the ruin of the constitution of his country—for successes such as *his* have always proven to be more disastrous than defeats.

There is a new element in the Irish problem that makes further quarreling fatal. I mean *steam*. While Nationalists, Home Rulers, and Land Leaguers quarrel, young Ireland is buying tickets for America and Australia. It is union or death for old Ireland now.

But greater than the dangers from violence and dissensions is the danger of compromise. Already I see symptoms of this disease of politics. Already I see efforts made to discriminate between good landlords and bad landlords, and I hear pleas made for "perpetual leases," or leases with "security of tenure."

Let every leader who talks in this fashion suddenly find himself in the center of a silent solitude. Never denounce any man who has ever done even one good act for Ireland—it would be ungracious and ungrateful to do so, and besides time is too precious to be wasted in dissensions; but let every public man know that the one condition he *must* submit to, in leading even a single company of Irish tenants, is to keep afloat the oriflamb of "land for the people," of "free farms for free men," and not the pawnbroker's flag of long leases for peasant serfs, with security of tenure to landlords. This is not a petty scramble for cheap rents, but a grand crusade for free homes.

Rent is the whip with which usurers and usurpers have scourged the backs of the Irish people for centuries, and leases is only another name for lashes. *No compromise!* This crusade is not a Donnybrook Fair fight, to break the heads of the landlords, more or fewer, but a democratic uprising for the immediate and total abolition of landlordism in Ireland. It is not a mad riot against men, but a holy war against a system. The men are bad enough, but the system is worse, and the inherent and ineradicable fault of the system is that if the landlord is bad he can call on the whole power of the British empire to enforce his tyranny; whereas, if he is good, his kindness depends on personal caprice; it is not secured by law; and while his authority is hereditary, his benevolence may die with him.

Quacks had better leave this question to be dealt with by competent men. As high as the heavens are above the earth, it soars above the range of demagogues and politicians. Cromwell was merciless, Cromwell was bloody, but Cromwell was a great statesman as well as a great soldier, and he accomplished, by demoniac methods, his demoniac purpose. He meant to cripple the Irish, and he *did* cripple them for centuries.

As I said about social excommunication, I again say about the Cromwellian settlement: there is no reason why despotism should monopolize all the most effective methods of achievement. Cromwell drove the Irish into Connaught—*now* the Irish must return to the lands from which he expelled them. Landlords and bullocks must go—to Connaught or England, as they please; but the rich midland and eastern counties of Ireland must cease to be grazing farms, and become the homes of the people of Ireland. The landlords have driven the people into the edges of wet bogs and up the slopes of stony mountains, and they have given the best lands to beasts. *Now*, the brutes must leave and make way for the people. To leave the people in the lands they now live on would be to perpetuate, not the curse of Cromwell only, but the crimes of the landlords for generations since he died.

I do not believe that any large proportion of the Irish landlords have equitable titles. I advanced this theory at Leenane—just to admonish my Lord Shylock that the pound of flesh theory is a dangerous one in law as well as in morals. I talked to a road-side full of peasants, but Shylock's howls were heard in every city of England and Scotland, and they even crossed the Channel to France and were reverberated in America. Now that this argument has served its purpose, I feel it due to my friends among the tenantry to say that England, without a revolution, would never accept it as a guide to action. If the people of Ireland are to be peacefully restored to their ancestral lands, the revolution must be accomplished by purchase.

But I do most earnestly protest against some of the propositions that have been advanced regarding purchase. Without referring to their authors—which might cause needless controversy—I hold that the true theory of purchase must first take cognizance only of the landlords' original possession, and carefully credit to the tenants' account all improvements made by him or by his predecessors. Griffith's valuation is often referred to by well-meaning men as a fair estimate (on the average) of the letting price of farms. While it is quite unequal in certain sections—because Griffith had to trust largely to subordinates—on the whole it is approximately correct, *if we utterly ignore the right of the workingman to any property in the improvements and reclamations made at his own sole expense*, and if we admit that the landlord is justly entitled to confiscate the value of these improvements and reclamations. Not otherwise—by the God of Justice, not otherwise! For Griffith's valuation was made (on the average) at thirty per cent. below " the full" or *highest* (that is the rack-rent) letting value of the farms; BUT this valuation was made on the holdings as they were when the valuator saw them, *not* as they were when the landlord let them. Why, if the tenant is to buy his farms, should he pay the landlord for *his own* improvements?

No race and no class of men were ever yet found just enough or good enough to have unchecked control over any other race or any other class. There is safety only in the government of all by all—security only when every man is the guardian of his own property and rights. The rights of peasants and the rights of landlords—that is to say, the prerogatives or demands of classes—must clear the way for the reign of the equal rights of all the people.

Quacks talk of the "impossibility" and "impracticability" of planting the people on free farms, or of inducing the British Government—a body of landlords—to "consent to a confiscation of the estates of the landlords." "The Government of England will *never* do it," they say, "without a revolution, and a revolution means bloodshed." Well, the British Government *can* do it, and it *has* done equally "impossible" tasks without bloodshed. When the British Government says *never*, history shows that (like Sir Joseph Porter of the *Pinafore*) it means "*hardly* ever." It once said that it would never grant Catholic Emancipation—but it did grant it. It said—this body of landlords—that it would never repeal the Corn Laws—but it did repeal them. And, besides, the official Englishman cares quite as little for the interests of the Irish landlord as he cares for the demands of the Irish tenant. He did not hesitate to disestablish the Irish Church, although he was told that it would lead to the disestablishment of the English Church; and he will not hesitate to disestablish Irish landlordism, if he sees that it is for his interest to do so, even if it should be argued that it would end in the Nationalization of the Land of England.

To the average official Englishman, Irish tenants and Irish landlords are only rival nuisances that he would like to abate in any way that would restore quiet. "A plague on both your houses" is his normal opinion of both parties to the Irish Land War. Irish landlords are resting on a broken reed when they fancy that England will support them in their hour of need, if the people of Ireland refuse to yield to state force or to be seduced by state craft. England begins to see that it does not pay to tax herself to support a class of runaway landlords, to whom she gave the lands originally on condition that *they* should support *her*. When the English find that anything does not pay, its greatest moral prop is gone. And, of all unprofitable institutions to England, Irish landlordism is the chief.

The only "impracticable" and "impossible" idea in planting and transplanting the Irish people lies in the insane idea that this sick Ireland can be cured without abolishing her disease. That *is* impracticable. Landlordism must go, or Ireland must go. Ireland is going as fast as steam can carry her, and I hope there will be a *universal* exodus if any attempt is made to save the despicable despots of her soil. *Out with them!* Better that the whole Irish race should be merged in our composite nationality *in America*, than that the Irish race *in Ireland* should continue to remain a race of perpetual tax-payers to men who got their lands by confiscation and by perjury, or because the forefathers of their present tenants refused to serve man rather than God, and become false to the faith in which they had been reared, and by which alone they hoped for the life everlasting.

Let it be repeated and repeated, and remembered and remembered, that if the tenant purchased his holding at Griffith's valuation, he would be paying sometimes double, and quite as often quadruple, the price to which the landlord would have been equitably entitled, *even if he had originally come honestly into the possession of his farm.*

Now, I often argued last winter, both in public and in private, that when the time came for universal purchase, in order to establish people's proprietorship, every landlord should be compelled to deduct from the amount to be otherwise paid to him, every shilling that he had received for rent over Griffith's valuation. The landlords pay their share of taxes on the basis of Griffith's valuation, and therefore they should be compelled to disgorge every shilling that they exacted from their tenants since that valuation was made. I am glad to see that a distinguished Catholic bishop has recently advocated the same doctrine. Its extreme moderation is seen from the fact that his lordship is content to ignore the tenants' rights in his improvements, at the time when Griffith's valuation was made.

The next lion in the way of peasant proprietorship is the vast sum that would be needed " to buy out the landlords and pay them at once." Why should they be " paid at once " ? Are they " paid at once " now ? As soon as the Land League is strong enough, not all the power of England will make it possible for the landlords to be paid *at all!* A strike among the tenants in Ireland would be quite as effective as among the English workingmen; and all the power of the English Government does not dare to lay one finger on the trades-unions. The Queen might die at St. Helena if such an attempt to coerce the British worker should be seriously made.

If, after a careful examination, it shall be determined to compel the landlords to sell (I use the word compel for the sake of clearness, and because I mean it) at, say ten or fifteen years of Griffith's valuation, then—*after* the deductions of rack-renting shall have been made—the Government should simply guarantee the payment of ten or fifteen annual installments, holding the lands in its own name and absolute sovereignty until the full amount was paid. The installments would probably be about one-third of the present rents.

THE END.

www.ingramcontent.com/pod-product-compliance
Lightning Source LLC
Chambersburg PA
CBHW022147160426
43197CB00009B/1458

THE LIFE

OF

PAUL SEIGNERET,

SEMINARIST OF SAINT SULPICE;

SHOT AT BELLEVILLE, PARIS, MAY 26, 1871.

TRANSLATED AND ABRIDGED BY
E. A. M.

LONDON:
R. WASHBOURNE, 18 PATERNOSTER ROW.
1873.

PREFACE.

In perusing the following account of Paul Seigneret, the reader may, perhaps, be inclined to ask why a life so simple, and, until the approach of its close, so devoid of anything remarkable, was written.

The answer is, because in that life there was an integrity and consistency which turned every circumstance into a means of preparation for its end. It is the noviciate of a saint which is presented for contemplation; the story of one who "being made perfect in a short time, fulfilled a long time," and whose spirit of self-devotion, whether for life or death, together with his generous love of suffering, so fitted him for his early crown.

E. A. M.

PARIS, 1873.

CONTENTS.

CHAPTER		PAGE
I.	CHILDHOOD AND EARLY YOUTH	1
II.	THE CHATEAU DU DRENEUC	17
III.	THE ABBEY OF SOLESMES	39
IV.	SAINT SULPICE	46
V.	THE PRISON	60
VI.	DEATH	86

THE LIFE OF PAUL SEIGNERET.

CHAPTER I.

CHILDHOOD AND EARLY YOUTH.

PAUL-MARIE-JOSEPH-CLAUDE SEIGNERET was born at Angers, December the 23rd 1845. His father was a professor at the "Lycée," or Government School of that city, a circumstance which secured to the young Paul the benefit of a careful education. He was an affectionate and intelligent child, and had from his earliest years the advantage of a Christian training from his excellent parents.

The first fifteen years of his life were spent peacefully at home; but in May 1861, his father being appointed to direct the college at Epinal, Paul was sent to the Lycée at Nancy. He was at this time still a child in appearance, impressionable and sensitive to excess. It is easy to imagine the effect produced upon a boy of this temperament by a sudden change from home-life to the uncongenial atmosphere of a public school; his first letters therefore are naturally full of sadness. But the very event which might have overwhelmed him with discouragement, awoke in him new energy and life. No longer sheltered and surrounded by the Christian safeguards of his father's house, he felt his danger, and sought from God the assistance of which he had need. Shortly before the vacation of 1861, he wrote: —" I have had a greater longing than I can express to see you all again, ever since I have been living here alone in the midst of strangers. I am so weary of hearing nothing but coarse and revolting conversation. Ah, if you only knew in what society I find myself! Everywhere blasphemies and other nameless horrors surround me."

The previous year, at the "Petit Séminaire" at Angers, he had been present, when, as was customary, all the pupils before taking their departure for the holidays, had assembled round the statue of the Blessed Virgin, and sung an adieu to the house which was almost as dear to them as another home; and he adds, 'Oh, happy house! oh, happy inmates, who live under so Christian, so gentle, so paternal a rule, and where the emulation in evil which reigns in the Lycée is unknown!"

At the same time he mentions with affectionate gratitude the kindness he received from several of the masters, who quickly began to understand the requirements of this exceptional disposition.

The persevering ardour with which he applied himself to his studies, resulted in his being raised to the rank of "Premier," in June 1861, and he writes to tell his father of "the good place which God had allowed him to take, that he might not be discouraged." However, a week later he announces "a catastrophe in Latin verses," where he was the seventeenth of twenty, and says that what most distresses him is the thought of his father's pain at his being "in so deplorable a place," adding, "and yet, do not suppose that I am discouraged. No, just as I thanked God, when I was successful, so have I offered this reverse to Him. Our chaplain has lent me the 'Imitation of Jesus Christ,' and this book has taught me to offer all my troubles to God."

The best proof of Paul's sincerity is the determination with which he combated his weaknesses. Children generally have a fondness for sweatmeats, and the young Paul was not free from this inclination. No sooner, however, had he entered the Lycée than "to punish himself," as he says, "for his greediness," he made a vow not to permit himself to spend a halfpenny on this sort of pleasure all the time he was there. And this did not satisfy him. A few weeks afterwards he was discovered in the practice of some excessive austerity, with reference to which, in answer to a letter from his mother, he writes:—"I very sincerely beg your pardon, my dear mother, for the anxiety which I have caused you. I own that I have gone too far, but it was the desire to overcome completely my inclination to greediness which led me to impose various privations on myself, that I might become indifferent about food. . . . . So you will pardon me, dear mother, and I will be careful to obey your injunctions."

A foible striven against with so much energy and constancy could not long retain its hold; but his extreme sensitiveness cost him more sustained efforts. This, however, he set himself to control by the acquirement of greater self-command.

After the holidays Paul returned, in October, 1861, better prepared to meet the trials which he had found so painful; but up to the close of his career at the Lycée, he continued to lead the same solitary life which his timidity and modesty had led him to adopt from the first; not because his gentle spirit was capable of indifference or disdain, but, with one passing exception, none in the busy throng around him shared his tastes, ambitions, feelings, or desires. Their thoughts were bent on other things. Whenever he could do so unobserved, he would absent himself from the walks and recreations of his comrades, to kneel before the Tabernacle, or say the Rosary, in the college chapel. With regard to these practices, he writes:—" I am told that I shall grow egotistical, if I do not associate more with my companions. I assure you that I love them with all my heart, and would do anything to serve them ; but what good would come of my joining in conversations which I abhor, and which, instead of giving me the peace I find with God, would leave me nothing but emptiness and disgust ?"

Towards the end of his studies, Paul met with one among his schoolfellows, a Protestant, whose tastes corresponded in many respects with his own; and whom, with all the energy of his ardent nature, he set himself to convert to the Catholic faith. That his efforts were not, however, successful, we find from a letter dated January 11th 1866, in which he says:— "My poor N—— has enrolled himself in a company of former scholars of Nancy, fine gentlemen, who announce themselves to be affected by a grand Byronic doubt, and take upon themselves to judge, reject, accept, whatever may be for the moment the fancy of their despicable reason, with regard to the divine and mysterious verities which one ought only to approach with a devout respect. It is they who have lost me my friend. Earthly friendships are like buds, which can only bloom to perfection in the sunshine of the love of God."

Notwithstanding his reserve, and the comparative solitude in which he kept himself, Paul won the esteem of his comrades, and the sincere affection of those of the masters whose functions gave them frequent opportunities of appreciating his character. "M. le Proviseur," or "Head Master," showed him the most affectionate regard, and had him at his house every Sunday, thus enabling him to share, from time to time, in the pleasures he so much missed of

CHILDHOOD AND EARLY YOUTH.

family life. More than once the humble-minded scholar wonders at the interest he inspires, and says, "These gentlemen must indeed be very kind, if they can manage to love, even a little, one who is always melancholy, bashful, and reserved;—for this is my portrait."

But he was alone in this opinion, for no one who approached him could fail to be attracted by a nature so singularly gentle, so feeling, and refined.

During the whole of the time he was at the Lycée, Paul was remarkable for his steady love of work; and by his conscientious and well-directed studies he acquired an amount of varied information by no means commonly to be found in a young man on leaving college.

He was there regarded as one of the best pupils, and was more than once the object of flattering distinctions, which made him happy, less on his own account than for the sake of the pleasure they occasioned to his parents, whose gratification was his greatest ambition.

His ordinary labours were always the best. The anticipation of any special ordeal, perhaps in public, would usually so disturb him, that he gained " nothing for his compositions but a good headache and a bad place." These partial checks did not hinder his " Year of Rhetoric " from being crowned with success, in November 1863; nor his passing with honour the examination for the " Baccalauréat ès Lettres." He says:—"The subject of the Latin discourse, which was disliked by all the rest, I found most delightful. It was a letter from S. Basil to S. Gregory, inviting him to come and share his retreat in the Thracian Bosphorus, and speaking of his feelings and of his joys. In literature, I had to appreciate the Cid; and in Philosophy, to treat upon Liberty. With these admirable subjects I forgot everything—examiners and audience—and troubled myself about nothing, if only I could shed upon the hearts of others any words that should tend to the glory of God and their own good."

In these last lines we see an indication of the thought for the future which already occupied the mind of Paul Seigneret, for it was in the unfavourable soil of the Lycée that first arose the desire for the sacerdotal life, which increased within him until his last hour.

A noticeable feature in this young scholar's

CHILDHOOD AND EARLY YOUTH.

life is the amount of time he gave to prayer. It is his comfort at all hours. Whatever has any sort of importance to him, he recommends at once to God and the Blessed Virgin. His gaze towards heaven has the promptitude, simplicity, and reverent familiarity which are the privilege of innocent souls.

It was his habit to communicate every month, and to prepare himself carefully for some time before the days which to him were such great and happy festivals.

Two characteristics, apparently opposed to each other, are particularly noticeable in Paul. To an effusion of sentiment and a poetry of expression, which might occasion a doubt whether imagination had not too large a share in his piety, he joined a comprehension of the supernatural beauty of the Cross, and a love of suffering, which would be worthy of the most austere inmate of a cloister.

His moral sufferings at the Lycée were not his only trial. His patience was often exercised by illness, against which he invariably struggled to the utmost of his strength. In December 1862, he writes from the infirmary: —" For a long time past I have been unable to get any warmth in bed, but have lain shivering most of the night. I said nothing, however, *hoping that I might have the happiness to suffer in this way without falling ill.* But a week ago, in addition to the cold, frightful internal pains began at midnight, and lasted until morning—(for I did not wish to disturb anybody)—when I had no strength left, and they carried me to the infirmary." After this illness he was allowed a separate bedroom, instead of being required to sleep in the common dormitory—a privilege which he considered inestimable.

During the earlier part of the time he was at Nancy, the military career seems rather to have attracted Paul, until, after reflecting on the moral dangers to be encountered in a soldier's life, he writes to his brother:—" Pray to the Holy Virgin for me, that I may give up the thought, if unhappily I should not have strength to keep myself pure and unspotted in this career." Also, after speaking strongly of the evils which daily shocked him at the Lycée, he adds:—" And yet this is but the image of a regiment in miniature."

Thus the young Paul found himself, though unawares, much nearer to the seminary than the barrack. He delighted in the sacred ceremonies of the Catholic faith; and was often heard to speak in raptures of the grand services at the Abbey of Solesmes, as, later on, of the magnificent solemnities of S. Sulpice; but it was not until the commencement of his third year at Nancy that he writes to his father, from whom he had no secrets, of his new aspirations.

He begins:—"I am going to write to you, my dear father, the most serious and important letter that I have ever written in my life. .... For three years, without any one knowing it, I have felt an ever-increasing desire to be a priest. At first I dared not speak of it, feeling that every one would say to me, 'You, so weak in mind and character; you, so unworthy, so unsteadfast, in the love of God; you would be a priest!' .... But the idea has never left me, and it is in vain that I have wished to put it aside; it follows me everywhere, at all hours, day and night. I would fain dedicate myself to God, who is so good, who loves us so much, and who died for us, and who receives so much contempt from His creatures. But then a cry escapes my heart: 'Lord, I am not worthy that Thou should'st enter into my house, nor even that Thou should'st look upon me; but say the word only, and my soul shall be healed, my stains effaced, and I shall be purified, and made worthy to be Thy servant.' "

Without making any opposition to a vocation which gave so much promise of reality, Paul's father advised him to take time for mature consideration, adding that silence was to be recommended for the present, as most agreeable to God,—a rule of conduct which was accepted with grateful submission by this most docile of sons.

From this time it is only in letters addressed to his father that he makes any allusion to his vocation for the ecclesiastical life, but to him, whom he calls "the mirror of his heart," he often recalls these thoughts upon which he delights to dwell.

In answer to certain objections, he writes, "I know, my dear father, perhaps more than you are aware, of the dark side of the sacerdotal state, and of the sufferings which are in store for the priest. . . . . I can perceive daily that I shall have to submit to the contempt or indifference of many persons, to whom the priest is a useless man. . . . I have read the Abbé Bautain's book, 'La Belle Saison à la

Campagne,' and all that he says about the life of a curé. Well, but if one is a true priest, the more one has of suffering, the more also of joy. Perhaps I shall be poor and in necessity: here, then, is another happiness, for what is a greater joy than to deprive one's self of everything in order to give the more to others ?"

And again:—" I must own that it is with a secret pleasure that I perceive myself to be not at all made to suit the world. To attach me here, I must have perfect creatures, whom I should, nevertheless, injure, by letting them come in contact with my imperfect and earthly nature. It is GOD alone, whom one can thus love without doing Him injury, because He is above us in all His perfections; He sheds upon us His graces, without our baseness and impurities having any power to sully His glory."

His correspondence during this last year at the Lycée is very remarkable. He had developed into a young man, and his mind expanded like a flower beneath the early sunshine. Literary studies increasingly captivated his fine understanding. He worked with indefatigable ardour, and frequently profited by his exceptional position to prolong his labours far into the night.

He was very fond of flowers, and, in one of his letters, mentions having visited, with a friend, some conservatories at Nancy. After describing their riches, he continues, "We chose two simple primroses, sweet and modest little flowers, and charming from their delicate perfume. On our way home, we met a poor old man, shivering with cold, and gave him all the money we had left. We were well rewarded. The poor man was so touched that his eyes filled with tears. As he held our flowers while we took out our purses, he admired and caressed them so much that they seemed to us more beautiful. I have my primrose now in my room, and take such pleasure every evening in looking at it, watering it, watching its developments, contemplating this charming little creature, which seems to smile at me and love me."

The beauties of nature and the love of God so filled Paul's heart, that amusements to which youths of his age were accustomed to enter into with eagerness, appeared to him poor and insipid.

"We all went to the circus," he writes one

day, "to see always the same things, to applaud without shame, and to fill ourselves with beer and lemonade. It must be confessed that this is not very interesting. There is something so sad in seeing these young men, full of strength, expose for a little money their health and life; or these poor girls who are made a prey to the gaze and coarse remarks of so many people, and whom one sees in the arena, rosy, smiling, and intoxicated with the applauses which are usually lavished upon the one who puts herself into the most unseemly attitudes, and yet whom I have seen, on entering, pale, weary, and with an expression of habitual sadness which has struck me."

On the Shrove Tuesday of 1864, when there were theatricals, songs, dances, and other noisy diversions which had little attraction for Paul, he spent the whole day with a gentleman who was ill and in great suffering, doing everything in his power to cheer and enliven him. "Thus," he writes, "Shrove Tuesday has been a happy day for me, and the clamours which I heard from time to time outside, made me enjoy my happiness so much the more.

"This morning a new joy. It is Ash Wednesday. Lent has begun: this beautiful time for repentance and for striving to purify one's self in the sight of GOD,—when one ponders these impressive words, 'Remember, O man, that thou art dust, and unto dust shalt thou return.' Ah! where is the time, when, at Angers, we took part in the solemnities of Lent? Here there is nothing of all these enjoyments; no singing, no psalms, no Retreat, no Benediction,—with the lights gilding the clouds of incense,—no Tenebræ; but always the same noisy, heedless barrack, marching to the sound of the drum. Well! it is the last year!"

The time arrived at last when Paul was to end his sojourn at the Lycée, which he left in July 1864. Though nearly nineteen years of age, his appearance was extremely youthful. His family desired a longer time of probation before allowing him to take any step towards the life to which he aspired, fearing lest his ardent spirit might not sufficiently realize its difficulties.

He submitted unhesitatingly to so reasonable a requirement, and it was arranged that he should spend this period in fulfilling the office of tutor to the young children of M. le Marquis du Dresnay, in Brittany, to whom he had been recommended by some mutual friends.

"And then," he writes, "this will be but for a year; two at most: and after that I shall be free to give up my life to Him who has ever been my life, my happiness, my hope, my joy."

CHAPTER II.

THE CHATEAU DU DRENEUC.

TOWARDS the end of September 1864, Paul Seigneret arrived at the Château du Dréneuc in the parish of Fégreac, two leagues from Redon.

He set himself to the work confided to him, with his accustomed energy, and regarded it as a fitting prelude to the priestly life to which he so earnestly looked forward.

Notwithstanding his youthful appearance, he speedily secured the respect and esteem of all the inmates of the château, by the delicacy and discretion with which he conducted himself in his various relations, and the fidelity with which he fulfilled his duties.

While his never-failing gentleness did not exclude the amount of firmness necessary to the well-being of his pupils, his kindness of heart put him at the service, or rather at the mercy, of all around him. His already insufficient hours of sleep were shortened that he might find time to give instruction to several of the servants of the household.

The poor soon found out his ready charity. "My money runs rather quickly through my hands," he writes, shortly after his arrival, "thanks to these poor dear people, whom I see in misery and want. It gives so much pleasure to them to receive a little money, and as much to me to give it; hence I generally return to the Château with some fresh happiness from my little expeditions."

Thus everybody became attached to "*Monsieur Paul.*" Madame la Marquise du Dresnay, who had constant opportunities of observing him, regarded as a special blessing from heaven the presence of one who, she said, was like "an angel in the house," and of whom she spoke with maternal affection as "Our little Saint Aloysius de Gonzaga."

But Paul had his trials. Besides that of continued separation from his family, he felt very sensibly the pressure of the new kind of life upon which he had entered, which involved the abandonment of the studies so dear to him, and which absorbed his time in functions requiring his intellect to stoop instead of rise. When he found that two years at least of this existence were in store for him, he writes, " A heavy cross has been laid upon me, because there I must crucify my aspirations, my tastes, my will. Let me give thanks to God : for what matters it, O my God, of what wood my cross is made ? *O mea bone Jesu ! Jesu dulcissime !*—Who hast suffered so much for me, what would I not suffer for the love of Thee ? Thus I desire to stretch myself all my length upon the cross Thou sendest me."

These were no vain words, without corresponding acts. Paul led a very mortified life. On one occasion, Madame du Dresnay thought it her duty to check, if possible, the excessive austerities of her " little anchorite," who, after reading the Lives of the Saints, and of the Curé d'Ars, was imposing privations upon himself which might seriously affect his health.

Finding that his uncle, the Abbé Seigneret,

had been informed of his practices, he writes, "I see forming at Angers a dark cloud of sermons and gentle reproaches, ready to burst upon me ... truly this is too much solicitude for *Messer Gaster* ... besides, I do nothing deserving either of attention or reproof, so there is no occasion to be uneasy on my account."

One morning the servant who arranged his room, found, on the bed, an object so perplexing that, before touching it, he went to mention his discovery to Madame du Dresnay.

On finding it to be a hair shirt, she ordered the room to be left as it was, until after the return of its occupant, who was thus spared the knowledge that his secret had been discovered.

This same hair shirt gave rise to one of the most charming letters he ever wrote. It is dated November the 5th, 1865, and is as follows:—

"MY VERY DEAR FATHER,

"A regret which troubles me, and also the kindness of your last letter, decide me to make a request, about which I have long hesitated. And first, may I tell you a story

THE CHATEAU DU DRENEUC.

which I read when a child, and which struck me very much?

"'There was once a prince, who, during his earliest years, was full of malice and of every fault, committing all the naughtinesses possible to a child. However, reflection came to him at last, and with it a desire to correct himself, and to compensate his parents for all the trouble he had caused them. In this praiseworthy state of mind, he went humbly to ask advice of his governess, who was a fairy. She gave him a ring, which pricked his finger every time he was about to do or to think anything wrong, and these warnings in time produced such an effect, that from being " Prince Scapegrace," he became " Prince Charming."'

"I also, without being a prince, am full of sin and imperfection. As a child, how often have I wished for this enchanted ring to help me to correct myself! As a young man, a bright thought, doubtless from my good angel, came to me, which realizes this fable of the ring.

"My dear father, I have long hesitated to unveil to you this secret, but your last letter has broken down the last obstacle to my desire to do so. Besides, when it is once confided to your fatherly heart, you will keep it there safely, and speak of it to none.

"There are people of the world who, at the very name of that of which I speak, would exclaim against it as a piece of antiquity only fit for the penitents of the middle ages; there are some also who would admire and wonder at it, when really it is the simplest thing imaginable! . . . .

"Last year, after earnest entreaties, my confessor consented to procure me a little instrument, which scarcely sees the day, except in monasteries—a hair shirt. This was my companion and monitor, which checked me when wrong actions, words, or thoughts, threatened to offend the Master of my heart. It was, in fact, one of my best friends. Alas! I most unwisely left it off during the vacation, under pretext of the heat, and hid it carefully away. In packing my trunk, the numberless preoccupations of departure made me forget it, but during the night, as by a beautiful moonlight, we were rolling on our way towards Paris, my unfortunate friend suddenly came to my mind. . . . . If you only knew how much I miss it, this little continual nothing, which unceasingly warned me to keep the thought of God in my heart! . . . .

"*You*, my dear father, will understand that my using it is not the effect of a foolish presumption which would lead me to try and ape the saint; but because I am a sinner, the prey of a thousand faults and defects, against which I strive as well as I can."

The world erroneously supposes the practice of corporal mortification to have the effect of narrowing the views and chilling the heart. To this prejudice, the life of Paul Seigneret is an emphatic contradiction. "If one is mortified," he used to say, "one only flies the better, and loves the more purely." His correspondence all through these two years is a striking testimony to the truth of these words; especially his home letters, which are more touchingly full of overflowing affection than any others.

In August, 1866, his father writes of him:—
"Paul has an innocence and simplicity of mind, adorned with thoughts and feelings, which fit him well for a convent. . . . I think he would do well to shut himself up in a cloister. The world, which pushes rudely

against everything it does not understand, would be too rough for him."

That Paul was of the same opinion with regard to his unfitness for ordinary life, the following account which he gives of himself will show.

The solitude of the Château du Dréneuc was occasionally enlivened by the presence of numerous and distinguished guests, and the young tutor had opportunities of mixing in that society which makes the charm of fashionable life. He fully appreciated this advantage, and admired, as much as any one, a great name worthily borne; but at the same time he felt that he was called to belong to a society more noble still. " For some time past," he writes gaily, "there have been visitors at the château. One day after dinner, as the company rose to return to the drawing-room, Madame de ——, finding herself without a cavalier, M. du Dresnay invited me to offer her my arm. In vain I stammered out some excuse about being too short; unhappily I was taller than the lady, and saw that I should have to be victimized. On this occasion, therefore, you might have beheld your son figuring as a gosling. Red to the ears, and unable to get out of the difficulty, I trembled lest I should tread on the foot, or incommode the shoulder of my lady. At last some one charitably came to the rescue, and, my punishment over, I did not dare to breathe a word before making good my retreat from the drawing-room. So you see what a figure I should make in the world!"

By degrees his own aspirations to the ecclesiastical state tended rather to the cloister than the seminary, as he considered himself to be personally unfitted for the active life of a priest, although constantly desiring to devote himself entirely to God in a life of mortification and prayer, and vowed a Novena of pilgrimages to the "Field of the Martyrs," near Angers, in the hope of obtaining enlightenment as to his vocation.

This field, which is about a mile and a half from Angers, was the scene of fearful massacres under the Reign of Terror, when the representatives of the people attempted to drown the "fanaticism" of La Vendée in blood. In the chapel which has been erected on the place of the executions, innumerable ex-votos testify to the favours there received.

A few days of vacation, which, shortly afterwards, Paul spent at Angers, gave him the opportunity of fulfilling his vow.

Every morning at daybreak he set out from "Le Petit Séminaire" of Mongazon, and at the close of the Novena felt a greater attraction than ever to the monastic life.

La Trappe was the chief object of his desires; but on its being represented that his constitution was utterly unequal to cope with the rigorous asceticism practised by the Order, he turned his thoughts to the Benedictine Abbey of Solesmes. A visit which he paid to this retreat of piety and learning increased his wish to be received among its inmates.

Upon learning the new form which his aspirations had taken, his father judged it advisable to prolong his time of probation; but from this moment the expectation of the day when he should be permitted to consecrate himself to God was ever present with him, filling his thoughts and sustaining his courage.

He writes on one occasion from a château in Poitou, in which, together with the family du Dresnay, he was staying:—"Only a few months more in which to share the life of the world, and to undergo the vain distractions, which are so much deducted from the love of

God. They have given me here a superb chamber; mahogany and marble, silk and velvet abound. All this luxury stifles and oppresses me. Only a few months more to share the table of the rich, and to sleep in a bed, the splendour of which dazzles me. I see in perspective my cell and little couch, my books and crucifix. *There* are no distractions; none of these kind but importunate attentions. *There* one is alone with God : God always, and everywhere."

On the approach of Christmas Day, he writes: —" On Sunday and Monday what delights await me! I shall then take leave of the château and my little pupils, to spend the time in the Church of Fégréac. As the knights of old watched by their arms all night, so shall I pass my Christmas eve in praying in the church, dim and silent, until the hour when this good and religious Breton population comes thronging into the illuminated aisles."

And afterwards he continues :—" This was indeed a night of joy. Choirs of children, alternating with the voices of the men, sang carols, of which the sweet and simple melody was exquisitely touching. One saw these men, these women, all this devout multitude, of which the church could scarcely contain the numbers, pressing without disorder towards the altar to receive Holy Communion.

"This lasted from eleven o'clock until three, and oh! how quickly have these happy moments flown, to which I had so long looked forward! They sparkle and vanish like the motes that dance in the sunbeam; but I carried with me, in my heart, the Source of all happiness and joy."

During the sojourn of the du Dresnay family at the Château of La Taillée, at some distance from Niort, Paul Seigneret frequently repaired thither on the Saturday evening, in order that he might pass the Sunday where he was unknown, and where his devotion could have free play. The room he occupied was near the Church of Nôtre Dame, but it was known that on these nights he never went to bed; and at daybreak, when the doors of the church were opened, he was already kneeling in the porch.

A letter to his father, dated June 29th, 1865, shows how these hours were spent. "So much happiness," he writes, " drives sleep away, and all night long, by the open window, I hear the wind sigh through the empty streets, and the night-birds cry from the spire of Nôtre Dame, which rises darkly into the sky. Every stroke of the bell thrills through me, as it tells me of the approach of the longed-for hour of Sunday morning. . . . .

"At three o'clock the dawn begins to brighten. Oh, beautiful clouds of gold! Oh, majestic globe of fire, emerging from the dimness of the horizon! how eloquent you are of Him who has made you so magnificent!

"By this time the inhabitants, their faces happy with a festal brightness, are busily occupied in adorning the way by which the Blessed Sacrament is to pass. They lay carpets along the streets, and scatter them with flowers, while the houses are gay with wreaths and garlands. Amid the odour of flowers and incense, the joyous harmony of the bells, and in the splendour of the morning sunshine, approaches this beautiful procession. There are young girls clad in white, and veiled, singing hymns to the Queen of Virgins, and children, with a thousand little banners floating in the air. The crosses and the standards are lowered and raised again, as they pass beneath the arches of green. Lastly, advances the God of Majesty and Love.

"At each of the 'reposoirs'* the people had erected in the streets, the band of the Lancers filled the air with jubilant strains of martial music, to do honour to the King of kings, after which, in silence, the Benediction was given to the kneeling multitudes.

"Oh, God! who art so full of love to us, grant that we may have but one aim—Thy glory; but one desire—Thy love, and eternal contemplation!"

A few weeks later on, a slight cloud unexpectedly arose, which somewhat overshadowed the happy *alone-ness* in which he had revelled on these festival days.

"About half-past eight in the evening," he writes, "I was retiring to take my dinner during a solitary walk, without fear of being seen. At these happy times, hunger as well as sleep seems to forsake me, and I find a small roll quite sufficient for a repast; but behold Monsieur de M——, an old officer, and a friend of the family, suddenly accosts me, and while I feel myself turning crimson from confusion, at not being able to hide my halfpenny loaf, he scolds me vigorously for not taking my

* Altars in the open air, where the Blessed Sacrament "rests" at intervals in the course of a procession.

meals at his house, and insists on my promising henceforward to do so. I am truly grateful for his kindness; but my days will have lost their charm, for I shall no longer be alone with God."

In the midst of the delight he took in the practices of religion, Paul felt the need of a more special direction than he had as yet enjoyed, with reference to the sacerdotal life. In reading "Népotien, or the Disciple of the Sanctuary," he discovered that many of his ideas respecting the priesthood were too vague and poetic, "à la Lamartine," and that he required a practical and definite training for the sacred office in more points than he had anticipated.

It was naturally at Solesmes, where he was already known, and to which he felt a strong attraction, that Paul wished to make trial of his vocation. Thither he went, therefore, in Holy Week, 1866, having, for three months previously, prepared himself for the time which he regarded as one of the greatest epochs in his life, and for the general confession with which he intended to commence his Retreat.

He reproached himself severely for the

smallest deficiencies in fervour and courage, accusing himself of weakness and cowardice, which, while looking forward to make the greatest sacrifices, finds heaviness in the sacrifice of daily life," and of a "contradictory spirit, which consumes itself in desires, instead of profiting by the present." And yet, at the same time, in the depths of his heart, there was a spring of never-failing hope and joy.

He was received at Solesmes with the most paternal kindness, and after his Retreat returned to Dréneuc, radiant with happiness, and more than ever confirmed in his desire to give himself wholly to God.

This thought forms, as it were, the *refrain* of all his letters from this period, which, nevertheless, glow more than ever with the warm and tender affection which filled his heart towards every member of his beloved home-circle. "And for you, my poor little sister, my darling of eleven years old," he writes, "I feel especially,—you, who always fly to me so jealously, so lovingly. Alas! we shall be far from each other then; but yet I feel that when the first grief is over, I shall, instead of giving up all you beloved ones at home, only love you with a stronger and purer love than ever in the shade of the cloister."

Before quitting the Du Dresnay family, Paul accompanied them on a little expedition in Brittany, which interested him greatly. During his sojourn at Dréneuc, he had often admired the simple manners of the people, and, above all, their antique faith, "firmly rooted as the oaks which overspread this land of granite," this "classic home of honour and fidelity."

Mingled in a crowd of Breton peasants, he joined in a pilgrimage which is made annually, on the Feast of the Holy Angels, to a little chapel not far from Dréneuc, and writes of it as follows:—"This chapel, poor as it is, makes an impression upon one. It is four whitewashed walls, with a roof showing the bare rafters like a barn, and which has only of late years enjoyed the luxury of slates. But a great and generous association is attached to this little chapel, which was built under the Reign of Terror.

"When the '*Blues*' were masters of Fégréac, and at the very time when, in this market-place, in front of the church, they were shooting nobles and peasants, a priest named Orian, whose family is still held in great veneration in the country, devoted himself for his parishioners, and through the whole time of the Revolution, contrived, by his incessant activity, and the evident protection of God, to baffle the pursuit of the enemy, and to afford the inhabitants all the ordinances of religion.

"It was he who, with the assistance of his faithful flock, built this chapel, which was only distinguished from the cottages around it by the cross cut in the granite over the door.

"Here I was present at Holy Mass. It was a living picture: an exact representation of the scenes of seventy years ago. On one side were the women, reciting the rosary, on the other, the men, grave and muscular, in their dark costumes, bent towards the ground in an attitude of the greatest recollectedness.

"We were all kneeling on the bare earth. No sound was to be heard but the voice of the priest, and the ringing of the bell, which told that our LORD was present once more in this lowly chapel, amid the sons of the brave forefathers, full of faith and generous self-devotion, who are now, I trust, reaping the reward of all their sufferings.

"The ceremony terminated by the benediction of the seed-corn which was about to be sown.

"How can people desire that the Breton people, with such scenes and such remembrances, should unnationalize themselves in the flood of ordinary Frenchmen ?"

During some days that Paul spent at the Château du Tromeur, near the village of Plouvorn, in Finisterre, he was much impressed by the melancholy charm which reigns in this part of the country, and by its severe aspect of rocky sterility, which is partly attributable to the strong sea-winds to which this region is exposed.

From hence he writes, "I was present, on the Eve of Saint Anne, at the most picturesque scene that I ever beheld.

"When night came on, the bell of the chapel summoned the people to a sort of terrace, where it is customary to burn, annually, on this night, an enormous bonfire.

"About a hundred peasants, standing with their arms crossed, in the proud and grave attitude which is habitual with the Armoricans, assisted at this singular rejoicing, in profound silence, their faces illumined by the blazing pile. When the crackling of the flames had subsided, and a red heap of glowing embers was all that remained of the fire, a tall young man advanced from the circle of spectators, and in a powerful voice slowly intoned a Breton 'Sône,' or plaint, of an indescribable melancholy. As he continued singing the fire died out, and the moon rose in splendour on this dream-like scene.

"In this song I seemed to hear the breathing forth of the spirit of sombre reverie which dwells in this strong old Brittany; a thoughtful sadness, which reveals the aspirations after higher regions than those of earth .... for do we not all, oh God, languish and sigh and wait, with a solemn and mysterious waiting? And this expectancy seemed to express itself in the plaintive melody of this song."

On returning from this journey, Paul passed a few more days at the Château du Dréneuc. When the time came for his departure, it was without emotion that he left a place where he had spent so many peaceful days.

Madame du Dresnay wrote of him, "He has passed like an angel among us: every one of his steps has been a good action, and every word he has spoken has always been to us a source of either edification or pleasure," adding, "I do not believe that the dear youth has committed a single sin during the whole time that he has been with us, unless, indeed, that of going away."

During his journey from Angers to Niort, he went from the little town of Airvault, in Poitou, on a pilgrimage to St. Loup, the birthplace of the young martyr Théophane Venard, Priest of the Foreign Mission, who, in 1860, suffered in China for the Faith, and whose last letter to his parents, which was written immediately before his martyrdom, is affixed to one of the pillars in the church.

About this time a curious incident took place in the history of Paul's vocation.

His longing for the religious life at Solesmes had continued to increase, and his happiness in the anticipation of it was so great that he was suddenly seized with the idea that he should find himself too happy there, and that he ought to sacrifice this happiness to God by seeking admission into the far sterner rule of La Trappe.

Before venturing, however, to name this new thought to his parents, he wrote for advice on the subject to the Rev. Father Dom Couturier, who had been his confessor during his retreat at Solesmes.

The answer was, that his excessive ardour deceived him, and that the step he contemplated as a means of perfection would, to such a temperament as his, be not only a terrible trial, but a real danger.

It was also urged that his health was not at all equal to the extreme asceticism of La Trappe. His chest was weak, and there were indications of an affection of the heart.

He strove, with no small energy and determination, to gain his point, and in drawing a comparison between the two kinds of life which lay before him, he said, " In the one I should be as happy as a bird of paradise; in the other it would be given me to follow truly, in pain and sacrifice, the royal road of the Cross which Jesus trod for me."

It was at last agreed that a sort of compromise should be made between his ardent eagerness and the indulgent wisdom of his guides, who consented that he should make the attempt, and if it should fail, as they anticipated it would, he was assured of finding the same welcome as ever at Solesmes.

When Paul presented himself at the Monastery of La Trappe, at Bellefontaine in Anjou, it was with considerable difficulty that he obtained admittance at all, even on trial, on account of his delicate appearance. In fact, after three weeks his strength was exhausted, and he was obliged to avow his inability and acknowledge his mistake.

It now became necessary for him to spend some time at home with his family in order to recover.

CHAPTER III.

THE ABBEY OF SOLESMES.

IT was in November, 1866, that Paul Seigneret returned to his parents at Epinal, where he remained until Easter in the following year, his health requiring great and continued care.

This delay was felt by his friends at Solesmes to be in all respects advisable, as it gave time to moderate the ardour, which, notwithstanding its evident sincerity, inspired some apprehension.

With his habitual activity, Paul profited by this time of leisure to resume his habits of study, which, for two years, had been interrupted. In January, 1867, he had read through the twenty volumes of Thiers' "Histoire du Consulat et de l'Empire;" and for the three months he was yet to pass at Epinal, he had traced for himself a programme which comprehended, besides Latin authors, Homer, several tragedies of Sophocles and Æschylus, and a review of the principles of philosophy studied at the Lycée—and all this that he might not arrive " all new " at Solesmes.

At the same time he allowed himself the free enjoyment of all the happiness of home-life, which his loving heart so keenly appreciated. The thought of the approaching separation came often across him "like the thrust of a javelin," but he calmly faced the sacrifice which, by anticipation, he realised.

It was about this period, that a sudden and unexpected form of self-devotion presented itself so forcibly before Paul's mind, as to threaten an entire change in his plans.

In April, 1867, rumours of impending war were producing a vast amount of patriotic agitation throughout France. His lively imagination already pictured to itself an invasion of his country, and his duty seemed to him equally simple and imperious to enrol himself, if need be, among her defenders.

He wrote to the Reverend Father, Prior of Solesmes, "If I am accused of folly or bravado because, with my feeble arm and woman's face, I dream of the hard life of a soldier, I would say that it seems to me the most sacred of duties, as soon as the frontiers are threatened, to fly, weak or strong, to their defence, and to employ at least the little strength I have received from God in protesting by my presence and my blood against the odious violation of the rights of my country.

"I say all this," he adds, "and yet I am coming to you, the counsels of my father agreeing with those of the Most Reverend Father Abbot; but, so long as I am not bound to the monastery by the ties of religion, if France, overwhelmed, should require the devotion of even her feeblest children, and if I might be of service to my parents, would you refuse me the exercise of my duties as citizen and son?"

This warlike fashion of beginning his noviciate, while it may have called forth a smile from the Fathers of Solesmes, did not augur ill for the future of the postulant to whom self-sacrifice was so easy, and, as it were, a matter of course.

On the 16th of April, 1867, Paul Seigneret bade adieu to his home, and entered the Abbey of Solesmes, where he found the reality of the religious life far to surpass his most sanguine expectations; and on the 19th of May he was received into the number of the postulants.

In a letter written at this time to his parents he says, "How can I thank you sufficiently for the touching kindness you have shown in sending me at this solemn time all that I most desired at your hands—namely, your entire approbation and your blessing? I have read this precious letter again and again, and have laid it where I lay all the letters I receive from you, at the foot of the crucifix you gave me."

The young novice brought to the practice of the religious life a disposition and good will that were truly admirable. The Reverend Father Dom Couturier writes of him, "The more painful was the obedience required, the more eagerly he embraced it, receiving everything with a contentment and willingness that made him the delight of his superiors and his brethren. He always sought those services which were least agreeable, and loved to take upon himself the burdens of others: constantly forgetful of himself, and thoughtful for every one beside.

The noviciate at Solesmes not only developed the excellent qualities of his disposition, but had also a happy influence on the mind of Paul Seigneret, which, though rich and cultivated in regard to secular knowledge, was as yet a stranger to the sciences which strengthen the inner life of a religious or a priest. His sojourn at Solesmes taught him to mistrust many of his previous ideas, which he modified, with perfect candour and loyalty, as soon as he had once become convinced that they were erroneous.

He threw himself with ardour into the course of study marked out for him. The Psalms, the Holy Gospels, and the Epistles of St. Paul were his favourite study, and next to these, Ecclesiastical History.

The daily chanting of the Divine Office in choir was also a constant delight.

When he had been rather more than two years at Solesmes his former aspirations for the priesthood returned with greater strength than before. It was with regret that he had ever laid them aside, under the idea that his insignificant appearance would unfit him from doing the good he desired, and that it was unsuitable to the dignity of the Office; but now that this obstacle no longer existed, he felt himself more strongly attracted than ever to the active ministry of the sacerdotal life.

It was not without a long and painful struggle that he came to the resolution to leave a place where he had found so much solid happiness, and where he had received spiritual benefits so many and so great.

He turned his thoughts towards St. Sulpice, having a secret attraction for Paris, where he saw a prospect of abundant work.

The idea was suggested to him of returning for a while to secular life; but he utterly repelled it, and desired to enter as soon as possible the house belonging to St. Sulpice at Issy.

In acceding to his desire for the active rather than the contemplative life, his superiors at the Abbey did not then see so clearly as afterwards the Will of God in regard to Paul, and they wondered at the energy with which he pursued his present aim.

"Nothing," writes the Reverend Father Dom Couturier, "could hold him back, neither the tears of the Brethren, whom he loved as if they had been members of his own family, nor the paternal affection of the Most Reverend Father Abbot. He passed through all obstacles, in spite of the many tears they cost him, leaving us astonished at a strength of resolution, the meaning of which we could not comprehend."

Paul left Solesmes on the 30th of June, 1868, and on reaching Paris, felt amazed himself at the thought of what he had dared to do, wondering how he had torn himself away from the place which had become so dear to him.

He arrived at Issy in his monastic habit, when the greater part of the seminarists were taking their departure for the vacation, and remained, therefore, almost alone, peacefully working in preparation for the time when they should re-assemble. After a few weeks, however, he was attacked by fever, which necessitated a period of repose at home. He, therefore, awaited at Epinal the close of the vacation in October, 1868.

CHAPTER IV.

SAINT SULPICE.

THE Seminary of Issy was a place eminently fitted to soften the regret of the young novice for his beloved Abbey of Solesmes.

This venerable habitation, with its modest cells, its various oratories, its fine old trees, has a peculiar charm, well-known to those who have passed there the preparatory years of their sacerdotal life. An atmosphere of fervent piety and fraternal charity pervades this place, where many generations of holy priests have been trained for their sacred labours, under the shadow of the venerated Sanctuary of Our Lady of Loretto, lately destroyed by the savage fury of the Commune, but which the sons of St. Sulpice are raising in renewed beauty from its ruins.

From increased mistrust of himself, Paul Seigneret was at first somewhat anxious and thoughtful about his future.

"If this new attempt should fail," he writes, "what would become of me, with the ever-increasing desire and longing I have to give my life for GOD ? I would go to the Foreign Missions, and should still be too happy; but I do not conceal from you that I should then sacrifice many of my dreams. With my temperament and inclinations, I fear I should find myself completely out of place among the Chinese: *and yet my life must be for God.*"

These apprehensions troubled him for a time, but after two months of the peaceful, laborious, and fortifying life at the seminary, his courage and confidence returned. He felt at rest in this atmosphere of piety and study, and speedily became an object of interest to those around him. The more intimately he was known, the more evident was the reality of his vocation to the priesthood. Duty, and the Will of GOD, were always the first thought and care of Paul Seigneret. No seminarist was more faithful to the smallest details of the rules, or more simple and humble in his observance of them. He was one of those who, in a community, require to be closely looked after, in order that they should not overstep the limits of their strength. He would obey simply and at once a distinct counsel or command, but would eagerly return to the common rule as soon as he thought he had sufficiently accomplished that which had been ordered. Being less known on his entrance into the seminary, and less betrayed at first by failure of strength, he contrived to pass the winter without a fire, and to fast through the whole of Lent.

The love of ecclesiastical study which he had learned at Solesmes continued in full vigour at Issy. He felt that, in these days more than ever, there is need for the priest to honour his sacred office by sound and cultivated learning.

The numerous MSS., to which he consigned the result of his studies, testify to an accuracy of mind and an activity of habit truly astonishing. Saturday, the 22nd of May, was fixed upon as the day on which he was to receive the tonsure. It was a day of great happiness to Paul; but almost immediately afterwards he was obliged, by order of the physicians, to leave the seminary without delay, his laborious studies, together with the keen emotions relative to this event, having been too much for him. The state of his health betrayed itself by frequent faintings, and with sorrow and regret he found himself compelled to depart.

At the same time, he troubled himself little about this over-fatigue, thinking it would soon pass away, and set out with further projects of study for the time he should have to remain at home.

In fact, after a few days of repose, he was able to resume, in moderation, the labours he felt to be so necessary a preparation for his future career.

"I wish you could see," he writes, "the loving care and kindness with which I am surrounded. The thought of the affection I have quitted, and that to which I have returned, is sadness by the side of joy; everything turning itself to love, for the love of God, Who is so beautiful in the reflections of His goodness. The more I see of men and of life, the more I comprehend the priceless happiness GOD has granted me in calling me to His service. GOD Himself, the Infinite, gives Himself to me, in order that I may give Him to others."

About this time, a sort of large register, in two folio volumes, was given to Paul, in which he could note down any passages selected from his course of reading. "They will last me my life!" he exclaimed, on receiving them. The folios were very large, and his life, alas! was to be very short, and yet he filled them almost entirely, besides adding a third to the other two. In looking over these books, in which he had amassed his treasures, one asks, with wonder, how, with his ordinary studies, which he never neglected, he could, in less than two years, accomplish this labour. Everything is distributed in order, with a table of contents, not completed, and written in a clear and firm hand. Plato, S. Augustine, and Bossuet, are the names which recur the most frequently. But texts from the Bible, the Book he best loved, and upon which he had meditated most, fill the greatest number of the long columns, on one of the last pages of which it was touching to find this short quotation from S. Ignatius Martyr, "*To be in love with Death.*"

In October, Paul Seigneret returned to the Seminary of S. Sulpice, in Paris. Although his health had benefited by the time he had spent at home, a dull and unceasing pain at the heart continued, of which he did not, however, think seriously. "I have full confidence in the future," he said, "because, without it, my life would be inexplicable and absurd." At the same time, a presentiment, not without sadness, would, at times, force itself upon him, which, nevertheless, lost itself in an act of acquiescence to the Will of GOD.

He writes:—" I must, before all things, make the most of the present, without reckoning upon an uncertain future, and take for my own the old device, '*Fais ce que tu dois, advienne que pourra*'—Do what you ought, happen what may."

At Paris, as at Issy, the same forgetfulness of self, and thoughtful charity for others, gave to his society a peculiar charm. To serve the Church, to save souls, to love GOD without measure, were the aims which daily and increasingly filled the heart of the young seminarist, giving a character of great simplicity to all his words and actions. He embraced, with fervour, the practices of the seminary, loved the devotions which are there held in particular honour, most especially those to our LORD, in the Holy Sacrament, and to our Blessed Lady, and followed assiduously the course of study prescribed. Moreover, those who knew him most intimately were happy in remarking the firm and resolute constancy with which he pursued the path he had chosen, and that his enthusiasm was no exaggeration of the true and profound conviction of his heart. His faith in the power of gentleness over the minds of men led him to adopt as his rule of conduct the words addressed by the Sovereign Pontiff to the Abbé Henri Perreyve:—" Strike errors courageously, but have the heart of a mother towards the erring."

Weeks and months of his seminary life passed rapidly away, and were happily and fruitfully employed; but, before the month of May, his health again gave way, and the pain at the heart became, at times, violent. He resisted as long as possible, but was obliged to yield at last, and, with a sorrowful heart, and tears in his eyes, own that he must again leave S. Sulpice. He set out for Sous-le-Saulnier, where his father, having been made Inspector of the Academy of the Jura, had gone to reside.

The physicians who were consulted on Paul's case considered it a grave one, and insisted on the necessity of a year's repose at home, together with the abandonment, for that period, of all serious and fatiguing study.

He made every effort to obtain a softening of the latter part of this sentence, about which also he wrote to beg for his uncle's intercession. Finding all his entreaties and representations to be, however, in vain, he resolved to obey the hard injunction, lest he should be opposing the Will of GOD in refusing to make this sacrifice.

In one of his private note-books he wrote, about this time, "Is there, then, for me no future in which to give myself, even for a little time, those who are so dear to GOD? The salvation of one single soul would far more than recompense me for the efforts of my whole life. . . . There are but two things in this world worth doing—to love GOD, and to make Him to be loved by others. If he denies me the second, I shall, at least, thank Him eternally for having shown me the sweetness of the first. Help me, O my GOD, to give up all my desires to Thee; only suffer me to pray that I may rather die than live a useless life."

He found great consolation, also, in contemplating the divine and imperishable work of the Catholic priesthood, so necessary to the world, and, in the hand of GOD, so independent of this or that individual. With his lofty thoughts and noble desires, he knew how to offer to GOD the little daily sacrifices which are impossible to those whose virtue has no depth or solidity. Suffering as he was, he marked out for himself a life of prayer and meditation as complete as it could have been in his beloved cell at S. Sulpice.

In a letter to his director, dated June 13th, 1870, he says:—"In the morning I am usually at the church from five o'clock until seven, for my best nights allow me about four hours of sleep, and the doctor himself has agreed that, during this fine weather, I may suffer less out of bed. Besides, in the old choir of the church, whither the joys of so many past generations seem to crowd upon me together with my own, I feel no fatigue, dividing my time between the Holy Mass, and prayer, or meditating on the designs of God for our souls, of which the inexhaustible thoughts make one thrill with more happiness than any of the splendours of this world.

"After this, my day's occupation consists of an hour's reading of the Holy Scriptures, a sermon of Bourdaloue, the study of Church History, reciting the office of the Holy Virgin, and glancing through the daily journals.

"From five to six in the evening I spend in the church, and, before bed-time, after thinking over my day, I read, according to an old habit of mine, a chapter of the 'Imitation,' a book which I never open without fresh delight."

While the days were passing thus peacefully and profitably at home, and in frequent correspondence with many at S. Sulpice with whom he had formed a warm friendship. Events of the gravest nature once more arose to give another current to his thoughts, and to call forth his love of self-devotion in another form. The fatal war of 1870 had broken out. Next to God and His Church, the name of his country was dear to the noble heart of Paul Seigneret. He followed with an indescribable anxiety the rapid succession of disasters which befell the fortunes of France.

At the commencement of the struggle he wrote, " The obscure self-devotion of the priest can alone, at such a time as this, prevent one's regretting the inability to make the brilliant sacrifice of the soldier. Life is so small a thing that it is a happiness to find a worthy occasion for which to offer it."

To escape from the ardent longings which disturbed his mind, he took refuge in study; but soon the very thought of repose, whilst so many others were toiling and dying in the war appeared intolerable, and he made repeated requests to be attached to one of the ambulances of the army.

His brother Charles was at Paris, and to him Paul wrote a letter, eloquent in its ardent entreaties, to this effect. Every one, however, except himself, felt this desire of his to be a generous impossibility, and even he was compelled to own his unfitness for the work, when, after taking a long walk in the hope of proving the sufficiency of his strength, he was punished by a month of fever and spitting of blood.

Scarcely was he recovered, when the unprecedented misfortunes of France brought back his eager illusions, as he said the hour was come which justified extreme resolutions, if even he were to "fall in the first ditch." One fear alone restrained him—that of doing anything incompatible with his priestly vocation.

He wrote, therefore, to his reverend director at S. Sulpice, a touching letter, in which he lays before him all his anguish and perplexities, and which concludes in the following words:—

"I am writing to you, my Father, in the silence of night, on the Eve of the Presentation. . . . *Will God, this year, grant me the favour of offering my life a sacrifice to*

Him? For it is to die for God, to fall beneath His justice, which weighs upon France. It would be so beautiful, that I cannot believe such happiness to be in store for me."

As it was impossible to yield to the longings which were, however, so soon and so fully to be granted, Paul Seigneret consoled himself by the thought that his turn would come soon, when, if not allowed the "easy duty of laying down his life for agonizing France," he should help to form a Christian generation, capable of repairing the public misfortunes, and of arresting the interior evils of the land. "In any case," he writes, "I hope to find some means of *dying* usefully, if to *live* usefully is to be denied me."

During the latter weeks of this cruel war, he had the consolation of being able to devote himself to the care of the wounded in the "ambulances" established at Sous-le-Saulnier. It is easy to imagine the happiness which he thus experienced, and the tender charity with which he visited and tended the poor sufferers, trying at the same time to leave in the minds of those with whom he came in contact "good remembrances, which should combat the prejudices and calumnies which are spread against the priesthood, to the injury of the divine religion of our LORD."

On the 30th January, 1871, came the "ominous tidings of the armistice, as a sign of the exhaustion of France, and the prelude to a ruinous peace . . . . . . peace, at the price of noble Strasbourg and of unfortunate Metz; peace, with two of our provinces and our treasure carried away! We must, then, say with Jeremiah, weeping over the ruins of Jerusalem, '*Et manum suam misit hostis ad omnia desiduabilia ejus.*'"

At last these days of poignant emotion and deep sadness passed by, and the state of feebleness and exhaustion which followed his too arduous exertions, convinced Paul of the unreasonableness of his late entreaties, causing him sincere sorrow and self-reproach, on account of the uneasiness he had given his parents.

The announcement of the re-opening of the Seminary of S. Sulpice on the approaching 15th of March brought a seasonable diversion to the regrets of his affectionate heart. He received the news with indescribable emotion. Believing his days to be numbered, he desired not to lose one of them. His malady being temporarily subdued, he set out, and arrived at Paris on the day indicated. After a difficult journey, a sleepless night, and almost a whole day without food, he reached S. Sulpice pale, worn out with fatigue, but radiant with joy. For the rest, it was a happy moment to all. We were met together again after a long separation and heavy trials, to find intact this beloved house of S. Sulpice, which had been in danger of destruction from the Prussian bombs. There was so much for each to ask and relate; and all were eager to see Issy again, and to kneel once more in the cherished sanctuary of Our Lady of Loretto, which had been spared by the projectiles of the foreigner, but which was to be burnt by the Commune.

In short, every one rejoiced at the thought of resuming this life of labour, of brotherly love, of peace in GOD, which make up the charm of S. Sulpice.

Alas! all this was again to be broken in upon by a storm of fire and blood.

CHAPTER V.

THE PRISON.

ABOUT eighty Seminarists from Paris and the provinces had responded to the summons of their superiors. The exercises commenced by a few days of retreat, which were not terminated when the hateful and humiliating insurrection of the 18th of March broke out. More sorrow was caused by this outbreak of the Commune, at first, than alarm. Paris at this time presented a singular appearance. The regular Government, discomfited and in flight, had left the field open to the insurgents, who had seized the reins of power, though it was not thought possible that they could long maintain possession of them. The situation could only be expressed by one word—uncertainty. As to the rest, with the exception of the sanguinary episode of the Place Vendôme, on the 22nd of March, a certain material order prevailed in the streets, especially in the quarters on the left bank of the river, where all was tranquil, while the storm was growling on Montmartre and Belleville.

The line of conduct which this state of things seemed to indicate as advisable, namely, that of waiting until events should declare themselves more decidedly, was adopted at the Seminary of S. Sulpice, though all who preferred were perfectly free to retire.

Very few availed themselves of this permission. It cost too much to abandon, sooner than was absolutely needful, a course of life which had been so gladly resumed.

The letters of Paul Seigneret during these few weeks show him unmindful of the danger, but preoccupied with the deepest regret for the anxiety which he had occasioned his parents by his agitation during the war. The terms in which he accuses himself would appear excessive if we did not know to what a high degree he carried his veneration for his father and mother, and how insupportable was the thought of having caused them pain.

He was, also, too well aware of the real state of his health, not to be at times somewhat anxious about his future, and resolved, if the active labours of the priesthood should be denied him, to obtain permission to end his days in a cloister.

In a letter written about this time, he

says:—" We are in a singular position here. Immersed in our peaceful studies, in the midst of Paris upside-down. We are left perfectly quiet, and hear nothing of the life outside, beyond the sound of passing clamours, the entry and exit of the National Guard, and the thunder of the cannon, which they fire from time to time, in token of their independence! Ah, when will the follies of men have an end? All this can scarcely result in anything short of further bloodshed." "That which we now see is more lamentable than all our former disasters. Paris is nothing but a camp: from day to day one hears French guns firing against Frenchmen, and know not what the morrow may bring."

On the 1st of April, Paul addressed to his parents the last letter which he wrote from the seminary, and in freedom. In it he says:— "But what have we seriously to fear? Bodily injuries? No one anticipates it. Incorporation into the National Guard? In spite of the notice placarded everywhere, declaring every available citizen to be a 'garde national,' they are more occupied in taking arms away from those whom they mistrust than in creating new soldiers. To be driven from the

Seminary? If so, we should doubtless meet at Issy or at Orleans. You see, therefore, that there is every possible chance that we have nothing to fear.

"And yet, many families are uneasy, and twenty of our seminarists have left Paris. I have, therefore, been asking myself whether, to prevent your being anxious on my account, I ought not to try and guess what your wishes might be . . . . but here are sixty of us remaining quietly together with our directors, and I think that you may approve of my staying among this little community. Besides, do not fear lest I should again give myself up to these illusions of self-sacrifice, to which you saw me so long a prey. No, I stay because here I am already, and because we really see no serious danger.

"Adieu, my very dear parents. I grieve to be away from you in the midst of the bitter sadness which must at this time weigh upon every French heart. The storm darkens on both sides, and threatens to be terrible."

The very day after this letter was written, Palm Sunday, April the 2nd, the Civil War broke out, not to be quenched until it had made heaps of blackened ruins, and shed rivers of blood.

This was the signal for the outbreak against the clergy, who were honoured by the most furious hatred of the Commune. The arrest of Monseigneur Darboy, the archbishop, on Tuesday evening, the 4th of April, that of the Jesuit Fathers, and the visits to various religious communities, gave the alarm. On Wednesday, the 5th, at noon, the pupils from Issy arrived at Paris, announcing that the "état-majeur," or "staff-officer," of the insurgents had installed himself at the Seminary, and was keeping the directors prisoners in the house, though the seminarists had been allowed to go free.

From this moment the peril was certain. On the advice of the directors, most of the students quitted Paris that same evening. A few, amongst whom was Paul Seigneret, believing little in the reality of the danger, or facing it, preferred to wait. Paul, however, being advised to go, resolved, notwithstanding his repugnance, to do so on the following day, in order that his parents might be spared any additional anxiety on his behalf.

Some of the seminarists who had left S.

Sulpice that evening, found that a new decree had been issued, forbidding anyone to leave Paris without a paper of permission, and were therefore obliged to return. This incident made Paul happy in the thought, that, at any rate, it was not through his fault, if his parents should suffer on his account.

On the morning of Holy Thursday, at the solemn services of the day, Paul received the Blessed Sacrament, and for the last time served at the altar in this church of S. Sulpice, in the beautiful ceremonies of which he had taken so much delight, and whither he would return no more until crowned with the glory of martyrdom.

Towards one o'clock, he repaired, with one of his fellow-students, to the Prefecture of Police, to obtain a passport; having been assured at the "Mairie" of the Sixth Arrondissement, that one would be granted, without difficulty, to any pupil of S. Sulpice not residing in Paris.

Arrived at the Prefecture, they took their place in the crowd of persons who were waiting their turn to be served with the papers of permission, when a national guard politely offered to procure for them what they wanted;

and, without the least suspicion of harm, they followed where he led them, into a room where a commander of the guard, seated at table with a woman, was finishing his breakfast. Empty bottles and glasses, and the odour of tobacco-smoke, gave to this place the appearance of the lowest tavern. The commandant allowed the two young men to make their request, and then, suddenly, as if seized with a fit of senseless rage, he cried out, "Cowardly rascals that you are! Lazy scoundrels! who think of nothing but running away, when all good citizens fly to the combat! Wait. I will give you a 'passport!'—you shall have a jail-warrant, and you shall be shot! I, too, have a relation who is a priest: I only wish I had him here! he would not have very long to live.—*Never*," he added, after pouring forth every sort of insult, "never shall we pay back to you all the mischief you have done us."

Paul and his companion received in silence the explosion of fury which the sight of their cassocks had produced, but at these last words Paul said, gently, "Is it, then, to *youths* that you use such language as this?"

After a few minutes the two prisoners had

the sorrow of seeing, first two, and then three more of their fellow-students, drawn by the same perfidious invitation into the same snare with themselves.

There they remained several hours, and the whole procedure which was gone through with regard to them, and which sent both to prison and one to death, consisted in making out warrants for their incarceration at the depôt of the Prefecture of Police.

These first hours of captivity were the most painful of any.

"What moments were those," wrote, later, one of the prisoners, "which we passed in that hateful office! Those jail-warrants spread out before our eyes, a prison in prospect, the future hidden by a dark veil, the aspect of these armed men who came and went around us, always with blasphemies in their mouths, and, above all, the bitter thought of our friends at home, and the anguish they would suffer on our account;—was not all this enough to press like a heavy weight upon our hearts?"

They were taken to the depôt, where the cells being all full, they had the joy of remaining together, and also of seeing themselves received, in the chamber where they were shut up, by six of the Jesuit fathers, who, with several of their novices and servants, had been there three days.

Here began for them a new community life, shaded by the uncertainty of the future, and painful from the numerous privations which the body had to endure, but fortified by faith and adorned with brotherly charity, and by the friendship of their companions in captivity.

Paul Seigneret was here, as everywhere else, simple, good, self-forgetting, and of an equable cheerfulness, full of the elevated and serious thoughts which were habitual to him. The day after his arrest he wrote to his director a few lines, not of resignation, but of joy:—"To be in prison, from hatred to my priestly habit, and on Good Friday; what could be more happy!"

Wishing to inform his parents himself of what had happened, he wrote to them on Easter Day.

After relating the arrest of his companions and himself, he continues:—"We were twenty-six in all, Jesuits, priests, and we, small trash, the seminarists. Our life is a veritable retreat, being chiefly passed in various spiritual exercises, and in the most tranquil joy. I am well, and procure little things occasionally to supplement the meagre regimen of the prison. We all love and watch over each other like brothers. It is long since I have felt so thoroughly at peace, and this is an excellent condition for my health. Sleep alone is rebellious, on the hard couch which is provided, and amid sonorous sounds to which I have not yet become accustomed. My only sadness arises from the thought of you and of your anxiety; happily, at the moment of my arrest, I was making my last efforts to prevent your having any. Besides, we have, apparently, nothing to fear.

"Adieu, my very dear parents. '*Hæc dies quam fecit Dominus: Exultemus et lætemur in ea!*' May GOD give you this joy, which is above all the sadnesses of this world!"

The sleeplessness which he mentions was habitual with him. He had, as it were, a fire within, which was rapidly consuming his frame. His countenance, which seemed to reflect his soul, acquired an expression peculiarly interesting and sympathetic, which was observed by his fellow-students, and which, of late, at La Roquette, had become very remarkable.

The fraternal affection of the seven young captives greatly struck those who witnessed it, and one of the Jesuit Fathers told them that he recognized S. Sulpice by this sign.

Paul loved to make up for the studies of which he was deprived by serious and instructive conversation, eagerly availing himself of the resources offered by the society of the distinguished men who were their fellow-captives. Literature, philosophy, and especially the Holy Scriptures, were the favourite subjects of discussion.

His imagination preserved all its freshness and vivacity. "I remember," wrote one of his fellow-captives, "how much he felt the deprivation of the sunshine, and to what charming thoughts he gave expression when, one day at dawn, a bird found its way to the bars of our only window."

One thought, however, prevailed over all others in this prison, into which they had been thrown with expressions of so fierce a hatred, and this was, what would be the issue of their captivity? By their piety and mutual charity the prisoners softened the hardships of their gloomy chamber, and at times sounds of gaiety, which astonished the keepers, proceeded from the listeners grouped round one of the Fathers, who possessed in a remarkable manner the gift of telling *well* an inexhaustible number of delightful stories. Yet these were but occasional distractions, which did not prevent the constantly recurring thought that they were in prison without any idea as to when or how they would be released. Behind bolts and bars, through which the light of day can scarcely penetrate, shadows deepen, and all around has a threatening aspect. They felt that at any hour they might find themselves suddenly face to face with death.

The attitude of Paul Seigneret under this expectation was not that of resignation, but of eager welcome and desire. The more he perceived the chances for this life to lessen and withdraw, the more joyfully his ardent nature offered itself a loving sacrifice to God. The hope of dying for the Faith seemed to change his words into songs of joy.

Together with his longing to be chosen as a victim, Paul Seigneret experienced to the last a horror of the kind of death which was, nevertheless, to be his own. He did not at all fear to die; but the thought of being massacred caused him a repugnance and shrinking which he set himself with all his efforts to overcome. His imagination represented to him a scene of tumult and disorder, in which executioners, eager for blood, throw themselves upon their victims like beasts of prey, and he spoke to his companions of this fear as simply as of his hope of martyrdom. When at La Roquette, some days before the sanguinary drama of the Rue Haxo, where he was to behold and suffer the things he dreaded, he said again, in his touching, simple way, that it had cost him a great many prayers to accustom him to the thought of this kind of death.

Nearly a week passed away without bringing any change in the situation of the prisoners. Holy Week and Easter had, for the first time, been passed without the solemn and beautiful ceremonies of the Church, and in the miserable barrenness of a prison.

Some few incidents only had broken the monotony of their life. On the day of their incarceration, Holy Thursday, in the evening, the seminarists of S. Sulpice had had the consolation of receiving the Benediction of Monseigneur the Archbishop of Paris. At the

THE PRISON. 73

moment of his being transferred from the depôt of the Prefecture to Mazas, the venerable prelate learned that seven of the students of his seminary had just been arrested, and paid them the touching attention of sending them a message by one of the keepers that he blessed them as his children. And on Easter Day a parcel from the seminary, containing a letter and some newspapers, reached the prisoners. It was a great relief to have some news of what was going on in the world outside, and, above all, a renewal of communication with S. Sulpice.

Wednesday, April 12th, was a day of more lively emotions, for it was then that the little community lost its chiefs; the Jesuit Fathers being restored to liberty after a brief interrogatory, which seemed to be gone through merely as a form. This event naturally gave great hopes to the young seminarists; those who had restored the Jesuit Fathers to freedom would not surely care to keep in confinement simple students who were without any sort of notoriety. Their turn would come soon; and they began to form plans as to what they would do on regaining their liberty. A question also was proposed, which gave to

Paul Seigneret an occasion of showing forcibly how he comprehended the true attitude of an ecclesiastic in confronting the Commune.

It was feared that, if they were set free, it might be on condition of their serving in the National Guard for an odious cause; in this case what line ought to be taken? Would any evasive answer be allowable in order to elude the question?

Paul Seigneret declared emphatically against the employment of any expedients. They might suffice for laymen; but it was *their* duty to guard in its integrity the habit they had the honour to wear. The thought of changing, even for an instant, the cassock of the priest for the tunic of a soldier of the Commune was revolting, and an apostasy. He would not even allow that they could be silent if the question were proposed, adding, "I will let them know my mind, if they shoot me for it."

It was not the first time that he had spoken on this subject. At the seminary, the evening before his arrest, he had asked one of the directors, "Which is best?—to die, or to serve the Commune?"

"Better die a thousand times than arm

against one's country," said the father, smiling at his ardour.

"That is well," he replied. "I thought you would say this. Now I know what I have to do." He had also said to several of his fellow-students, "Let us swear rather to die than to suffer ourselves to be enrolled in the National Guard."

But the looked-for day of interrogatory and liberation did not come. A caprice of the persecutors had now commenced a regular procedure; another caprice interrupted it; and the prison closed anew upon those who had not been fortunate enough to profit by the opening of its doors.

On Thursday, April the 13th, the seminarists were told that they were to quit the Prefecture of Police. One of the keepers, who could not help taking some interest in the fate of prisoners so different from those to which he was accustomed, said to them sorrowfully, "I believe they are going to transfer you to Mazas." In any case it was clear that no good was intended. To be ready for whatever might happen, the captives knelt at the feet of a priest, who remained with them, and received absolution.

Scarcely were they out of their cell than they found themselves in the midst of a great number of ecclesiastics, who were about to be transferred to Mazas with themselves. Their youthful appearance attracted much attention, and Mgr. Surat, Grand-vicaire of Paris, said to them, " I can understand how it is that priests and old men are here; but you, gentlemen, simple seminarists ! . . . However, it is a glory for you to share in the persecution of your ecclesiastical superiors."

The transfer to Mazas was made in cellular conveyances, of which all the hostages have preserved a painful remembrance, and of which one of them has written, " My greatest humiliation during the whole of this captivity was to see myself in this vehicle. To be shut up, under lock and key, in one of these cases, where one has no air, and in which the least movement strikes you against one of the four planks which enclose you, is to be shut up alive in a coffin."

A few days before the same treatment had been inflicted on Mgr. the Archbishop of Paris, his miserable persecutors having taken care not to spare the venerable prelate this needless indignity.

For the seminarists of S. Sulpice, the entrance into the cells of this van was the end of their imprisonment in common, during which they had been able to help and fortify each other. Henceforth their life was to be more painful and isolated.

When the heavy carriages had entered the prison of Mazas, each prisoner, as he descended, was shut up separately, until it should be decided in which cell he was to spend his solitary days.

Although the prisoners could not *see* each other, yet any sound was distinctly *heard* in the adjoining cells; and one of the companions of Paul Seigneret recognized his sweet voice singing verses of the *Te Deum*, and soon after, as if in a sort of singular and joyful defiance of the Commune, humming the *Marseillaise*.

Number nineteen of the Third Division fell to Paul. There we shall see him for six weeks making the solitude of his imprisonment yield abundant consolations.

"Let the world close upon us," were his words; "and with Jesus Christ we shall always have the sovereign joy."

In about a week's time he found that the next cell was occupied by one of his best friends, who had also shown him many kindnesses during their imprisonment at the Prefecture of Police.

Three little knocks at the wall served them for "Good morning" and "Good night," and even this was something to soften the solitude. In a letter written to his Director at S. Sulpice about this time, he says, "Time flies like a dream. I have been occupying myself delightfully of late with my New Testament. Those who are anxious about us little imagine us to be so happy as we are. Our only real privation is that of the Holy Mass, and this we feel greatly." He then warmly thanks the Father for a Bible he had just received from him. The Holy Scriptures had been his delight at Solesmes and S. Sulpice, and upon receiving this precious copy in his prison, he wrote joyfully, "And now the Commune may leave me to moulder here as long as it likes!"

From that time the days at Mazas seemed to pass too quickly, and he lengthened them by rising daily at four o'clock, and not retiring to rest until ten. Thus, at the end of his captivity, his notes and comments on his "beloved Bible" filled a thick roll of paper. These have never been found and, doubtless, perished in the pillage of the dead, which was made after every execution.

With his time and thoughts thus occupied, the desire of sacrifice grew stronger than ever, and he one day wrote, "I hope to be the last to go out of Mazas, and, if victims are wanted, I hope to be the first."

Not long after the incarceration of the seminarists at Mazas there appeared to be some hope of obtaining their liberation, the detention of these young men being altogether inexplicable.

When Paul Seigneret heard of the efforts which were being made with this intention by the Rev. Father Director of S. Sulpice, he wrote to him as follows:—

"I know all that you are doing for our deliverance, and am deeply touched by it: only, I beg you to remark that by adoption and affection I belong to the diocese of Paris, and that I cannot think of quitting the prison so long as our Archbishop remains confined in it.

"Also, that if any victims are required to appease the Divine justice, it would be far better that I should suffer, rather than any one of these venerable priests, who may yet gain so many souls to God. I beg you to reflect well upon this, as I have considered the matter carefully before writing."

In one of the daily journals which reached Paul, and which contained sanguinary threatenings against the hostages, he wrote in pencil, between two of the most violent paragraphs, before passing it to his friend in the neighbouring cell, " Te Deum, my dearest brother !"

The vicinity of this friend was a great solace to Paul. By means of little raps on the partition, they gave each other signals for the times of their devotional exercises. Every evening in particular, as at S. Sulpice during the Month of Mary, the two united in spirit in placing themselves for life and death under the protection of their Mother in Heaven.

They were able also to see each other for an instant daily, at the moment in which the one succeeded the other for the solitary walk granted to the prisoners; when from afar off they could exchange a smile and a sign of affection.

In solitary confinement these little incidents possess a great value, and were a source of keen enjoyment to the affectionate heart of Paul.

M. Hogan, a British subject, and one of the Rev. Directors of S. Sulpice, twice found means to penetrate into the cells of the prisoners and to visit each one of them. It was with tears in his eyes, and with the greatest warmth of feeling, that Paul Seigneret received the thrice-welcome visits of this excellent and devoted priest. He was unwilling to spend a moment in speaking of himself or of his health, but was overflowing with gratitude for the sympathy which had been shown him; and spoke of France, of Paris, of those dearest to him, of his young friends, and especially of those who were confined in the same prison, without his being able to see them.

The consolation of friendly visits was however soon interdicted. Citizen Garreau, recently installed at Mazas as director of the prison, on the 5th of May forbade all visits to any of the ecclesiastics detained there.

M. l'Abbé Amable, of the clergy of the Quinze-Vingts, living in the neighbourhood of Mazas, had undertaken to convey to the seminarists, by means of a charitable woman, various things of which they were in need.

These services, rendered by persons who had no connection with them beyond the ties of common charity, deeply touched the grateful heart of Paul, who wrote, "The more our captivity is prolonged, the more we feel the numberless proofs of friendship which it brings us. We shall not leave this place without an increased love of mankind."

The hope that had been entertained of procuring the liberation of the young prisoners had vanished. One only, M. Raynal, thanks to special influences, had been set free on the 13th of May. The Seminary of S. Sulpice had just undergone the shock of a new tempest, and there remained in Paris only one of the Directors, M. Sire, able to correspond with the captives. To him Paul wrote on the 15th of May: "We ought to be grateful to the Commune to have sent out of Paris our dear M. Hogan, who did nothing but expose himself to danger for our sakes, besides imposing on himself excessive fatigue.

"Adieu, dear M. Sire. My heart sings 'Te Deum' all day long; so, you see, I am scarcely deserving of pity. Alas! while I live so tranquilly, how many are suffering in all sorts of ways!"

The French army entered Paris on Sunday, the 21st of May. The Commune, driven to extremity, was determined at least to secure its victims. On Monday evening, the 22nd, the "Committee of Public Safety" sent to Mazas an *Order for the immediate transfer to La Roquette, (the Prison of the Condemned)— the Archbishop, all the priests, President Bonjean*, and, in short, *all those who might have any importance as hostages.*

A list was made out, including the name of Paul Seigneret, as well as that of M. Gard, another seminarist of S. Sulpice. These two young men were not priests, nor could they be of any "*importance as hostages.*"

But, to the men who executed this order, to be clad in a cassock was to be a priest, and "all the priests" were condemned by their title alone, independent of their name. It is this fact which sheds a glory on the death of those victims who were sacrificed out of hatred to the Faith and the Priesthood.

Two railway luggage waggons conveyed to La Roquette the eighteen hostages inscribed on the first list: and there, after six weeks of separation, the two young seminarists met again. The one who escaped death has since mentioned the profound impression which the sight of Paul Seigneret made upon him, and his bearing on this melancholy journey.

Carefully neat in his personal arrangements,

6—2

his face wearing an appearance of health which it had not for a long time previously known, his eyes remarkably clear and bright, and with a happy smile upon his lips, he looked as if he were still at S. Sulpice, on a festival.

His friend writes : " I never before saw him look as he did then ; and it seemed as if something of his sweetness and strength communicated itself to me. By his side I could not feel weak, and would willingly have been shot at that moment."

The two friends embraced warmly, and conversed naturally upon their situation, but he spoke little during the rest of the way.

Scarcely were the waggons outside the walls of the prison, when a spectacle, altogether new to him, met his sight. A hideous mob, chiefly of women and children, crowded upon the waggons, endeavouring to climb into them, and vociferating, " Ha ! There they are ! Let them be shot ! Down with the cassocks ! Cut off their heads ! To death ! To death !"

This frightful escort attended the prisoners with furious yells, and whenever a sudden movement opened the leathern curtains, shewing for an instant the figure of a priest, the clamours and insults redoubled.

Seated at the bottom of the waggon, in a place from whence he could witness these scenes, Paul Seigneret never ceased watching them. What must have then passed in his mind, full as it was of goodness and gentleness, and which found it so difficult to believe in evil? One thought, doubtless, was above any other, that his dream was about to be realised. The hope was visible in his serene and peaceful countenance, which, like those of the early martyrs, gazed calmly on the tigers and leopards that were about to devour them.

At last, about eight o'clock in the evening, the waggons reached La Roquette, and the portals of the Prison of the Condemned closed upon the captives.

Earnest endeavours were made to obtain their liberation; and one of the men employed at Mazas, in the absence of the Director, obtained from another functionary of the name of Cantrel, an order for the re-transfer to Mazas of the "two seminarists who, *by mistake*, had been included among the condemned."

The order was rejected, because the names of the two were not indicated.

Once more the "employé" made a journey, which the increasing disturbances rendered dangerous; but by the time he had obtained another order, the progress of the struggle had made the passage impossible.

The desire of Paul's heart was to be granted. "*Et mori lucrum.*"

CHAPTER VI.

DEATH.

THE first moments passed at La Roquette were full of anxiety. Gathered together in a low room, dark with the shades of approaching night, the prisoners waited more than an hour, ignorant whether the succeeding one might not be their last.

There, seated on a miserable bench, in the midst of his priests, was Mgr. the Archbishop of Paris, ill, and with his features altered by suffering, but resigned, calm, and courageous in this extremity.

One of the seminarists, on seeing him, could not repress a cry of sorrow, "What! Monseigneur here!"

"There are no *Seigneurs* here!" insolently shouted a half-intoxicated guard of about eighteen years old; "here are none but *citizens!*"

At last the captives were conducted in the darkness to the first storey of the fourth section of the prison. When each one had entered at hazard into the cell, which he found open, the door was shut and bolted upon him.

A bed, consisting of a straw mattress and a poor covering, composed the whole of the furniture. Certainly it was only for a short time.

Paul Seigneret found himself separated from his companions. It was in the cell marked No. 18 that the last four days of his life in this world passed away, in a peace which nothing could disturb; with death no longer in perspective, but close at hand. " Pater, venit hora."

As one window served to light two cells, separated only by a partition, the little space between this and the bars of the window allowed of communication with the inmate of the cell adjoining. Paul had for his next neighbour the saintly Abbé Planchat.*

* The assassination of this venerable priest is one of the most odious crimes of the Commune. From the day of his ordination he had quitted the higher ranks of society, to which he belonged, to devote himself entirely to the working classes, whose needs and sorrows allowed him no repose. He founded and maintained a number of good works for the benefit of apprentices, of orphans, and multitudes of poor, for

From the Tuesday evening the two captives, kneeling each in a corner of his cell, performed their religious exercises together. One of the hostages used to hear them reciting the prayers for the agonizing, and concluding the various devotions of the day by reciting the Rosary every evening. These two, who together so prepared for death, shared it together.

It is not certainly known whether, before his death, Paul Seigneret had the consolation which was granted to some of the other prisoners of receiving a last Communion. It is more than probable, and it will not be out of place to mention here the account of his own happiness in this respect which was given by M. Gard, the seminarist of S. Sulpice who escaped death.

On Tuesday, the 23rd, towards nine in the morning, the Rev. Father Du Coudray, who was his neighbour in the next cell, called him to the window, and confided to him that he had the honour of bearing upon him the Most

---

whom he was never weary of obtaining succour and relief. It was after twenty years devoted thus to the good of the people that the Commune caused him to be arrested, imprisoned, and massacred in the Rue Haxo.

Holy Sacrament, promising to give him Holy Communion on the following morning.

Deeply moved by this announcement, the young man fell on his knees before the wooden partition, which had thus become to him as the door of the Tabernacle, and adored his Saviour, saying, "*Terribilis est locus iste.*— Surely the Lord is in this place, and I knew it not!"

Being kept awake the whole night by the frightful noises of the sanguinary struggle that was going on in the streets, and the light of the fires that were consuming Paris, he thought with joy and consolation of this first Communion in prison, which might at the same time be his viaticum.

At six o'clock Father Du Coudray rapped at the partition, and the young seminarist received Our Lord from the hand of the priest who was that same evening to become a martyr.

If, as very possibly was the case, M. l'Abbé Planchat had obtained from any priest who possessed the Holy Eucharist a particle of the Consecrated Host, the same happiness would be accorded to Paul as that which was enjoyed by his friend.

However this may be, God clothed him with

fortitude, and shewed in this timid and gentle youth that love is stronger than death.

A common "recreation" daily re-united the hostages from the different sections of the prison, and in each section the doors of the cells were left open for a time. Thus, the prisoners were able to visit and converse with each other, which was an immense relief in these days of unspeakable anxiety, during which, while the struggle was thundering without, and slowly approaching with deliverance, the executioners within were decimating their victims.

The impression of all who saw Paul Seigneret through this terrible time was the same, and they have used the same expression of "Angelic," in speaking of his countenance and bearing.

Besides the society of his fellow-student M. Gard, he particularly sought that of a venerable missionary, M. Perny, who, after having passed his life in evangelizing barbarisms, had fallen into the hands of the more barbarous Commune.

In writing afterwards of the various traits of virtue in the victims of the 26th of May, M. Perny adds: "But what shall I say of this

Angel of *S. Sulpice*, Paul Seigneret? What simplicity! What modesty and purity of soul! He used to come and sit upon my couch and question me about the martyrdom of our Chinese neophytes. He was too humble to tell me that his happiness was at its height to find himself *here*, but his very dreams must have been of martyrdom."

A distinguished member of the University, M. Chevreaux, who shared at La Roquette the captivity of the Ecclesiastical hostages, was so struck with Paul's sweetness and serenity, that he refused to believe that the choice of the assassins could fall upon one so young and inoffensive, and his murder excited in his mind the liveliest indignation.

Another hostage, M. Evrard, who was also a layman, and sergeant-major of the 106th Battalion, writes of him: "That one of our companions, whose courage and resignation I most admired, was M. Seigneret. . . . He was of a fine figure, above the middle height, with beautiful chestnut hair, and regular features, of which the expression was not only engaging, but had in it something angelic. He had no hope of escape, and appeared detached from life, which at his age has so many attractions.

I admired in him the strength of faith, in a pure and virtuous heart. His only regret was the grief which his death would cause to his family. . . . His surprise was visible when I said that I would sell my life dearly to those miserable assassins."

One other testimony we must add, to complete the rest—that of his fellow-seminarist, M. Gard.

He writes: "I passed eight days with him at the Prefecture of Police: it was by his side that I made the painful journey from Mazas to La Roquette. In this prison of the condemned we passed together four of the most trying days. I saw him at the time when he was summoned to the massacre. On the Monday, at the Rue Haxo, I beheld his body stretched on the blood-stained ground, with fifty others; and on the Tuesday evening lying peacefully in its leaden coffin in the Church of S. Sulpice. And yet none of these memories—none of the impressions connected with him—have anything about them that is painful or sad, but are full of a kind of serious joy, which the thought of his invariable gentleness, serenity, and courage, always inspires."

On Wednesday evening, the 24th of May,

took place the barbarous execution of Mgr. the Archbishop of Paris, and of five of the principal hostages. Next morning, Paul Seigneret told M. Gard that from the window of his cell he had seen them pass by to execution, and that one of the assassins perceiving him, levelled his fusil at Mgr. the Archbishop, and looked up sneeringly to the window, as if to announce, by this expressive gesture, what they were about to do, and what *he* might expect in his turn.

On the morning of the 25th the banker, M. Jecker, was marched out, and doubtless shot in some corner of the prison. On this occasion, Paul again expressed the horror he felt at the thought of being shot in some lonely place, or of being given up to the hands of a furious mob to be massacred, but that he begged of God not to let this thought trouble him.

The same day, during the time of recreation, the two seminarists spent part of the time in walking with one of the Directors of S. Sulpice, also a prisoner. The conversation was grave: they spoke of death, of martyrdom, of Eternity. Paul remarked that he looked forward to being one of the first who should be summoned, and said what a happiness it would be to go to God. Then the three embraced and separated.

It was for the last time.

The following letter, which was the last from Paul Seigneret to his parents, was also written on this day, the 25th, on the leaf of a pocket-book, which was unexpectedly found at Versailles among numerous articles, which served as proofs against the assassins of the Rue Haxo.

"MY VERY DEAR PARENTS,

"I cannot send you a letter, but perhaps this pocket-book may come into your hands, as well as the few little matters I have with me. I thank you, my beloved father and mother, for the unbounded kindness you have always shown me. I die grieving at the thought of the sorrow which awaits you, and of the little which I have ever done for your happiness, but thankful if I can efface with my blood whatever in me may have been displeasing to you.

"I bid adieu to my dear uncle, to Alexander, to Charles, and to my dear little sister. Their happiness has always been a thousand times dearer to me than my own. I hope that God will give them all graces and all joys, and as bright a future as I could desire for myself.

"Say to all whom I love, that the thought of them has never left me a single day, and that it will follow me beyond the limits of this world.

"I quit you for a better life, in which, as you are aware, I have long since placed all my hope and all my happiness. May you, then, in your sadness, at least rejoice a little in my joy! I shall die saying the *Te Deum*. Soon we shall be re-united to love each other for ever.

"Adieu, all you whom I love so much! You have bestowed upon me a thousand-fold more than I have ever repaid. Let us hope that on high I shall love you as I desire.

"Once more I embrace you, full of gratitude. Be assured that our separation will be only material, and also, I trust, for a very little time.*

"Your Son,
    "Paul Seigneret."

---

* A few months after this letter was written, on the 10th of December, 1871, his beloved brother Charles died of a malady brought on by the toils and privations he endured in the Siege of Paris, and during his care of the wounded. Also, fifteen days later, the father died of grief.

The day after this letter was written, Friday the 26th of May, about half-past five in the evening, a new summons was made at La Roquette, at which all the prisoners were required to be present.

Brigadier Ramain, who accomplished his task with a cruel coolness, arrived with a list, and assembled all the prisoners of this Fourth Section, which had already furnished the first victims.

"Gentlemen," he said loudly, "pay attention; answer to your names. *Fifteen are required!*"

Fifteen! and about thirty were present. A sort of shudder ran through the company.

When the name of Paul Seigneret was called, he went simply, like the others summoned before him, and placed himself in the company of the condemned. He embraced M. Evrard, saying softly, "For a little while!" He passed before his fellow-student, M. Gard, who contented himself with grasping his hand as he passed, not for an instant doubting that his own name would follow, and promising himself to go to death by the side of his friend.

But the roll was ended, the required number being complete, and the victims, without weakness or ostentation, descended at once.

Paul Seigneret, in passing the cell of M. Petit, the Archbishop's secretary, saluted him with a gesture of adieu and a peaceful smile, as if nothing extraordinary was happening, At the prison gate, the fifteen were joined by thirty-five gendarmes. Then commenced the painful march from La Roquette to the extremity of Belleville, of which, even after the judgment of the Council of War, so few details are known. We only know that these calm and courageous victims, through all the length of their long "Via Dolorosa," were mobbed and insulted in every possible way, by multitudes of men, women, and children, who were more like wild beasts in their senseless ferocity, than human beings.

The place chosen for the shameful crime about to be committed, was No. 85 of the Rue Haxo, Cité Vincennes, the last refuge of the expiring Commune, and still a lonely and desolate place, as if a curse were upon it.

There horrible scenes were enacted, the hostages being given up to a blood-thirsty populace, who were literally mad with rage.

If we are to believe certain details, which are said to have been furnished by ocular witnesses, Paul Seigneret's death must have been a veritable martyrdom in suffering, as well as by the sacrifice of his life.

We are told that, at the entry of the avenue which leads from the Rue Haxo to the Cité Vincennes, he was brutally struck, at the moment when he was assisting a venerable priest to rise, who had fallen beneath the blows of the rabble, and that the executioners seemed to be animated by a special ferocity against this young victim, whom they overwhelmed with blows, and dragged along the ground to the end of the enclosure in which the massacre took place.

The same witnesses say also that in the midst of his sufferings, he was heard to speak some words of remembrance of his beloved family, and of pardon for those who were murdering him, until, being utterly exhausted by fatigue and ill-treatment, he became insensible, and fell to the ground. There, supposing that he was already dead, the assassins left him, until they had accomplished the execution of the other victims, when one of these monsters, observing that he was still alive, discharged his rifle at him, the last that was heard in the Cité Vincennes on that frightful evening.

How far these details are strictly accurate,

we are unable to say: but, we know, beyond all doubt, that his death was caused by a rifle-shot in the breast.

Thus the desire of his generous heart was accomplished, and that was granted to him which he had scarcely believed to be possible.

On Monday, the 29th of May, the day after the last struggle of the contending Commune, M. Sire, Director of S. Sulpice, and M. Gard, went to seek his remains.

It was only at the prison that they learned that the last massacre of the hostages had taken place on the heights of Belleville, which had thus become, as formerly those of Montmartre, the arena of martyrs. On reaching the Cité Vincennes, they had before them a fearful spectacle. Twenty bleeding corpses had already been drawn out of the trench in which the assassins had heaped their victims, and the rest were in course of being also removed from thence.

Amongst the bodies which were stretched upon the ground, the seekers had no difficulty in recognising that of Paul Seigneret.

He lay with his eyes closed; his face perfectly intact; white as alabaster, and without any stains or contractions. There were no traces of decomposition, and his countenance had that peculiar expression of serenity which had become so observable during the closing days of his life. His cassock, which was soaked in blood from the wound in the breast, was also pierced lower down by several bullets. He had upon him his Rosary, the Little Office of the Holy Virgin, and the New Testament. His body was borne to the Church of S. Sulpice, where it remained that night, and was, on the following day, enclosed in a triple coffin.

On Wednesday, May the 31st, a solemn Requiem Mass was sung, at which were once more brought together the priests of S. Sulpice and their disciples, the witnesses or victims of the mortal struggles of the past terrible weeks.

The fellow-students of Paul Seigneret, his brethren of Mazas and La Roquette, served at the Altar, where one of the Directors of the Seminary offered the Holy Sacrifice.

He, GOD'S chosen one, was also there, reposing in his glorious death: present upon earth in his sanctified remains, and present, doubtless, in spirit, and in remembrance of his fathers and brethren, before the Throne of GOD.

The Office being ended, the body was temporarily placed in the vaults beneath the

Church of S. Sulpice, but the same thought had occurred to all, that the place for the young martyr was at Issy, in the crypt of the Chapel of Our Lady of Loretto, which forms, as it were, the heart of S. Sulpice.

A year, however, passed away, before it was possible to put this design into execution. In the first place, it was necessary to raise up the walls of this beloved Sanctuary, from their ruins.

On Thursday, the 27th of June, 1872, a few days before the commencement of the vacation, the translation of the remains to the Seminary of Issy took place.

None who were present at this solemnity will ever forget it.

In the two Communities, who were assembled in the entrance-court to receive the body of their young martyr, there was not one present in whom the name of Paul Seigneret did not awaken sweet and holy recollections. The priest who presided at the ceremony was the uncle of Paul, and the same to whom, from his childhood, he had been accustomed freely to open his heart, and to whom he bore a most tender and reverent affection.

The Ordinary Prayers were said, according

to the rules of the Liturgy, and a Mass of Requiem was sung in the Chapel. At the same time, the office was less one of mourning than of triumph, and those who were assembled to pray around this coffin, upon which lay the white surplice of the departed Levite, and which was adorned with lilies and white roses, felt more of joy than of regret.

The ceremony took a still more touching character, when, after the Mass, the coffin was borne from the Seminary Chapel to the vault prepared to receive it in the crypt of Our Lady of Loretto.

It was remarked that a lively affection for him whose memory they were honouring must have prompted the preparations for this festival, (for such it was). The walks of the garden and park were adorned with arches of verdure, and decorated as if for a triumphal march. At various distances the paths were overhung with garlands of foliage, enwreathed with red and white flowers, the symbols of Virginity and Martyrdom.

Beneath these advanced the two long files of Priests and surpliced Seminarists, singing the "*Benedictus Dominus Deus Israel*," and followed by the rest of the procession.

When the coffin had been placed in the Chapel of the Sacred Heart, the *Te Deum* was intoned, as if by a sudden inspiration, every voice responding to this note of triumph. It was not named in the programme of the ceremony, but was a spontaneous expression of the feeling of all present.

The body of Paul Seigneret reposes under a slab of white marble, engraved with emblems often found on the tombs of the martyrs in the Catacombs, and with the following inscription:

Hic Quiescit
Paulus-Maria-Joseph-Claudius-Seigneret
Clericus
Seminarii Sancti-Sulpitii Alumnus
Qui Puer Ingeniosus et Sortitus Animam Bonam
Vitam Brevem
Sed Caritate in Deum et Homines Eximiam
Constantique Crucis Christi Desiderio Flagrantem
Sanguinis Effusione
Gaudio Exultans Complevit
Parisiis Die XXVI Maii An D¹. MDCCCLXXI Ætatis XXVI
In Odium Religionis Trucidatus
Desiderium Cordis Ejus Tribuisti ei
Domine. (Ps. xx. 2.)*

---

* Here rests Paul-Mary-Joseph-Claud Seigneret: Tonsured Clerk, and Student of the Seminary of Saint

Thus we have arrived at the close of this short life, which, although for the most part so bare of extraordinary incidents, was so full of merit in the sight of God. We may imitate the virtues of a martyr's life, though few dare hope to win the glory of his death; but the prayers of those who, through suffering have won their crown, gain strength for us, the feebler pilgrims, who far down the mountain side, are toiling upwards, often in dimness never in despair, towards our Home.

PARIS, May, 1873.

Sulpice: a youth admirably endowed with excellent gifts. His life, which, though short, was filled with love towards God and men, and consumed with desire for the Cross of Christ, he joyfully offered up by the shedding of his blood, at Paris, May 26th, 1871, in the 26th year of his age, being put to death out of hatred to the Faith.

"Thou hast granted him, O Lord, the desire of his heart." (Ps. xx. 2.)

THE END.

, h. WASHBOURNE, PRINTER, 18 PATERNOSTER ROW, LONDON.

www.ingramcontent.com/pod-product-compliance
Lightning Source LLC
Chambersburg PA
CBHW022146160426
43197CB00009B/1442